"In *The Psychology of Software Teams*, Cat Hicks has delivered an indispensable and long-overdue message that demystifies software team development. With touching compassion for software developers as people with individual needs and essential social connections, she brings research and insight to explode the tired debates about "developer productivity" and provide real answers and practical approaches for improvement.

The Psychology of Software Teams is essential reading for anyone engaged in building, supporting, or growing software teams."

Eli Israel, *Managing Partner, Gartner Consulting*

"If you lead engineers and believe culture is 'soft,' this book will disabuse you of that notion quickly. Psychological safety, learning, and collaboration aren't perks, they are infrastructure. Ignore them and your systems will fail, slowly or catastrophically."

Scott Hanselman, *VP of Developer Community, Microsoft*

"This book presents an empathic, evidence-based analysis of developer productivity and provides practical guidance based on the author's own research for avoiding or fixing common traps. The result is the most important new perspective on software development in years."

Greg Wilson, *third-bit.com*

"*The Psychology of Software Teams* by Cat Hicks is a vital companion for any leader building a humane, high-performing organization. She skillfully dismantles the 'Brains-in-Jars' myth, proving that innovation is not a solitary act but the result of social learning. By introducing cognitive scaffolding and fostering thriving ecosystems, Hicks provides the missing link between organizational design and the individual human experience. This book aligns perfectly with the principles of fast flow of value; it is not just about speed, but about empowering people to excel without burnout. Essential reading for forward-thinking leaders 'moving beyond the machine'."

Matthew Skelton, *Holistic Innovation matthewskelton.com.*
Co-author of Team Topologies *and* Internal Tech Conferences

The Psychology of Software Teams

To build the future, we need new ways of supporting software teams. This book will give you a secret weapon: the psychology that creates resilience for developers, sustainable practices for software teams, and innovation for organizations. You'll learn from rigorous empirical evidence gathered from top engineering organizations and thousands of developers around the world, revealing powerful principles software teams can use to guard against failure and drive cultures of collaboration and problem-solving.

Making incredible software doesn't have to be a death march—this book presents a humane alternative for software teams looking to use the transformative power of behavioral science to understand what drives technology businesses forward. *The Psychology of Software Teams* provides a model for developers and leaders who want to bring the human back to tech and take a science-based approach to unlocking the "black box" of software engineering.

This book is for the developers and builders of the future. Bringing science and heart together, *The Psychology of Software Teams* will teach you how to untangle your thinking from pervasive myths about software work and harness the superpowers of psychology to create more joyful, innovative, and thriving environments for software.

Cat Hicks is a psychological scientist who creates open science to drive change for people doing technical work. She holds a PhD in Quantitative Experimental Psychology from UC San Diego and is the founder and principal scientist of Catharsis, a scientific consultancy that helps organizations transform with human-centered evidence strategies. drcathicks.com

The Psychology of Software Teams

Cat Hicks

CRC Press
Taylor & Francis Group
Boca Raton London New York

CRC Press is an imprint of the
Taylor & Francis Group, an **informa** business

Designed cover image: Ashley Juavinett

First edition published 2027
by CRC Press
2385 NW Executive Center Drive, Suite 320, Boca Raton FL 33431

and by CRC Press
4 Park Square, Milton Park, Abingdon, Oxon, OX14 4RN

CRC Press is an imprint of Taylor & Francis Group, LLC

Library of Congress Cataloging-in-Publication Data
Names: Hicks, Cat author
Title: The psychology of software teams / Cat Hicks.
Description: First edition. | Boca Raton, FL : CRC Press, 2027. | Includes bibliographical references and index
Identifiers: LCCN 2026006872 (print) | LCCN 2026006873 (ebook) | ISBN 9781032963396 hbk | ISBN 9781032963389 pbk | ISBN 9781003589112 ebk
Subjects: LCSH: Computer software developers—Psychology | Computer software—Development—Management | Software engineering—Management | Teams in the workplace—Management | Organizational behavior
Classification: LCC QA76.76.D47 H525 2027 (print) | LCC QA76.76.D47 (ebook)
LC record available at https://lccn.loc.gov/2026006872
LC ebook record available at https://lccn.loc.gov/2026006873

ISBN: 978-1-032-96339-6 (hbk)
ISBN: 978-1-032-96338-9 (pbk)
ISBN: 978-1-003-58911-2 (ebk)

DOI: 10.1201/9781003589112

Typeset in Minion
by Apex CoVantage, LLC

To everyone who chooses building over breaking.

Contents

Acknowledgments

MY DEEP THANKS TO THE MANY PEOPLE WHO PROVIDED ME WITH generous and important feedback, collaborated with me in science, and shared my vision of a human-centered open science for software teams, especially: Cate Huston, Titus Winters, Fred Hebert, Ana Hevesi, Danilo Campos, Hazel Weakly, Carol Lee, John Flournoy, Kristen Foster-Marks, Greg Ceccarelli, Greg Wilson, Marian Petre, Matthew Skelton. Thank you to Alex, who has always been my personal example of an engineer who can care equally about psychological and physical safety. You thought I belonged in tech far earlier than I ever could, and every single time I struggled with this project I thought, "You owe Alex this book." I hope the citations stack is heavy enough for your purposes. Thank you to my incredible partner in life and creativity and my inspiration for courage in the service of others, Ashley. These two little Vulcans are making it.

A massive thank-you to my wonderful editor, Randi Slack, for the support and expertise you brought every step of the way, which steered this book to greater impact and clarity. When you sign up to do a book, you don't always know what's going to happen to you in the life *around* the book, but I found the right collaborator for one of my toughest years. I will forever remember not just this creative partnership, but every time you said, "I want this book to sound like you." Sincere appreciation to the entire production team at CRC Press, and every person in this creative getting-things-done-chain for this book. Thank you also to every person whose problem-solving gave me and many others more tools to write, organize research, analyze data, and create all the output of science, including but not limited to every developer who worked on Scrivener, Zotero, Google Scholar, PsyArXiv, and the R ecosystem we have used across all our papers, including especially brms, ggplot, and tidyverse.

And of course, thank you to the amazing Cat crew across the internet. To all of you who across the years have shared my work, followed my long threads, tolerated (or escalated!) my jokes, shared your stories and thoughts, especially those who radiated compassion and understanding when I was struggling with the overwhelming bigness of technology. You reached across the boundaries of time and space to provide a community I could never have designed or imagined. Your engagement with my work is the reason that "psychologist for the humans of tech" turned from a wild idea I kept having into a reality.

Credit: Figures 2.1 (the Brains-in-Jars), 3.1 (the crow), and the book cover were illustrated by Ashley Juavinett. Figure 6.1 is reproduced with permission from IJzerman, H. *et al.* Use caution when applying behavioural science to policy. *Nature Human Behaviour* 4, 1092–1094 (2020). Springer Nature.

CHAPTER 1

The Brains and Hearts That Build the World

EVERY DAY, WE'RE SURROUNDED BY MAGIC WE HARDLY NOTICE. We set alarms, play music, cook dinner, send messages, and run our transportation with it. Our governments depend on it as we attempt to face the biggest human challenges we have: food, healthcare, education, poverty, and climate change. We trust it to manage our money and our groceries. We use it to store our memories. As we start billions of individual human days, most of us go through those days without ever questioning the background technology that runs through so many lives. We take for granted the stability of our paychecks and businesses, structures as big as nationwide utilities or as small as our phones, and capabilities as diverse as talking to family on the other side of the planet or coordinating thousands of people for a concert or running surgery operating rooms. But those actions and many others are enabled by an invisible network of human problem-solving. This magic is real. It's software.

Software is so pervasive it's almost impossible to remember to see it. Right now, you're likely trusting software with your money, your life records, and the functioning of every industry you come into contact with, not to mention using it to do your job. For a sizable percentage of human activity on this planet, we invoke software to talk to each other, capture memories, keep ourselves and loved ones safe, and use information. Software is invisible everywhere.

DOI: 10.1201/9781003589112-1

One of the reasons it's difficult to really learn to think about software is that software is not really just one *thing*. Unlike laptops and smartphones, software is less a single entity than it is a strange universe of ecosystems, where many dynamic layers of cause and consequence meet, move, and transform in unexpected ways. Staggeringly large codebases can be behind simple interfaces. Small butterfly effects can cause global outages. At the same time, with software, simple, small, and elegant solutions from individual people can scale to shape the fabric of reality. Software is a universe in which one good decision can improve the lives of millions, and learning to wield its powers can change a single person's life forever.

Yet the invisibility of software has a cost. Even inside of the businesses that employ the most developers to make the most famous software in the world, building software is still treated like a dark art. Despite all the power, prestige, and paychecks in modern software development, there's a critical oversight in what we think about when we think about the thing that runs our world:

Software is built by people.

THE PEOPLE WHO RUN THE WORLD . . . BUT DON'T GET TO FEEL LIKE PEOPLE

Developers[i] are the explorers of this strange universe of software that we depend on. Developers' problem-solving, creativity, and collaboration play a foundational role in modern technology. And because technology changes constantly, how well these developers can keep solving problems, creating, and collaborating is at the heart of maintaining any technology organization's performance. Developers' problem-solving matters everywhere.

Recently, I met someone at a friend's weekend brunch who said, "Oh, I'm just a software engineer," when we were introducing ourselves.

As a psychologist for software teams, I've done too many research interviews to let moments like this pass me by. "But tell me, what do you work on?"

"It's software that's used on ships, I won't bore you," he said. And he shrugged, with the resignation of someone who is frequently asked to fix other people's computers but infrequently asked what he thinks about it.

A thing that researchers learn in qualitative interviews is to always ask a second question. I asked one of my favorites: "Tell me more about what that's like. How do people learn to do what you do?"

He thought for a moment, and then in a true engineer fashion, he answered with far more precision than expected. There were specific, proprietary codebases involved in how these ships were run to which only certain people were allowed access to. There were a limited number of jobs in which you could gain that access. The pathway to that job required years of training, and the job wasn't a glamorous software engineering role at a famous tech company, so only certain kinds of people would tolerate the training. At the end of all that, he counted the number of people who could do what he did on two hands and still had enough fingers left free to hold his coffee.

"Got it," I said, and asked another question: "How many people are currently on ships that do something with your code?"

The number of people his work affected, on any given day? Between 50,000 and 100,000. His code helped ships communicate and coordinate their navigation in situations of close proximity, something which becomes pretty important when two very large ships bring all of those people into a port, in this case, the port of the city where we both lived.

This is a common story. Software allows the work of startlingly few minds to work at a startlingly vast scale. Being able to programmatically engage with the world explodes the reach of a mind working in software, allowing just one mind to use technology in a way that creates an incredible number of actions and solutions. For example, how ships will talk to each other every single time they interact, on a scale that would be impossible for a human to manually handle.

But despite the scale of software, the people doing that work are missing support. Sometimes this is as simple as not having enough staff for a team or a problem, or keeping up with technology's rapid shift with new expertise in these fields. But often, the story is more complicated than headcount or technical specialties: it's about how software development work is seen, how the developers are treated, and whether their psychological needs are designed for and valued. I told this engineer that his situation reminded me of stories from developers I'd met who worked in healthcare, in governments, or as part of scientific organizations. Many of these developers were on tiny teams responsible for surprisingly key capacities, and they often put in heroic effort to solve unanticipated software problems. But few of their leaders seemed to even notice when they were successful. Because of the invisibility of software in these contexts, many developers who work outside of the most glamorous feature development jobs find themselves embedded in the heart of what their organization does but rarely remembered.

My new friend nodded enthusiastically. It can be hard to get developers to open up, but once you show you care, they have a lot to say. By this point we were jamming, both our coffees going cold on the table beside us. He told me about learning the idiosyncrasies of the systems he worked on and the predictable mistakes that he'd seen every new colleague make when they started working on these ships' systems. Because of the confidential nature of their technologies, they learned on the job. Each person in his role tasked with another set of ships had to teach themselves to navigate a brand-new codebase and make their own specific adaptations.

It was clear he loved his work, but he also worried about how hard it was for the newcomers. He wondered why it wasn't obvious to anyone above him that despite all their technological advances, keeping their ships running was getting riskier and more dangerous for those new coders, not better. So I knew I could ask my final question: "If I could give you a free day a week to spend on something that would move the needle, what would you do? What would you change?"

Without hesitation, he told me he'd spend it teaching. Maybe he'd make a small course, a better type of onboarding for people in his role, so they wouldn't make so many of those predictable mistakes. Maybe he's also do some measurement. He'd go around to the handful of people in his position and get them to tell him the most common mistakes they saw, so they could design against it. He told me he was certain he could turn that one day a week into hundreds of saved hours for the next person trying to learn what he'd had to learn from hard reality, not to mention improve how he slept at night. And he was certain he could do it.

"The entire system would get safer," he told me frankly, "If they'd just let the engineers all talk to each other, once in a while."

I pointed out that he worked on problems of communication. If the ships were allowed to talk to each other, surely the engineers should be! We laughed, but I could tell it wasn't the end of the story, so I reached over the table to refresh his coffee, and waited. The most important skill of research isn't actually what questions you ask. It's how you listen.

And finally, he asked me a challenging question of his own: "How do we convince our bosses to let us do more of these things that actually help us?"

This book is my attempt to answer that question.

SOFTWARE TEAMS STRUGGLING TO BE UNDERSTOOD

Designing for human needs simply hasn't been at the forefront of how we put software teams together or how we run technology organizations. It's showing up in developers' stories and data. Across decades of research on software teams, one thing is startlingly clear: developers do not feel understood. A study looking across teams at Microsoft found that developers and their managers often significantly diverge even in their definitions of productivity.[1] In the Developer Success Lab, the open science research lab that I founded to create empirical evidence for how developers work, learn, and thrive, we surveyed over 1200 developers across 12+ industries and many countries, using psychological measures that we had intentionally designed to explore whether software developers felt like their technical work was both visible to and valued at their organizations, across peers and leadership.[2] In my research, 88% of engineering *managers* readily agreed that making technical work visible and valued was an important part of their job. But how many developers reported getting *visibility and value* for their technical work? Only 24%. In other words, even when you're one of the most highly valued knowledge workers in the world, you've only got about a one in four chance of feeling like your work is understood by the people making decisions about your career.

Despite the pervasiveness of software, people studying developers have been documenting an emerging struggle for software team effectiveness for a long time. Across the board, software teams battle competing priorities, bad planning, and frequent failures. Software projects fail frequently, and they fail hard, costing businesses enormous amounts of money. And money doesn't seem to be making it better: businesses might be pumping as much as they can into engineering investments or funding enormous projects, but the annual cost of poor-quality software is estimated in the trillions.

Beyond this enormous financial and business impact, there is a significant and mounting cost to the well-being of the software teams that keep our world running. Solving problems in software means blurring the lines between the inside and outside of businesses, as technologies rely on key open-source projects or increasingly complex services, with knowledge about these dependencies spread unevenly throughout the developers at any particular business. These practices have successfully increased software delivery velocity, but they have also scaled the impact of software systems' failure. When GitHub goes down, technology teams all over the world can no longer push, pull, comment on, and deploy code.

Battling mounting complexity, developers lament feeling misunderstood, and software leaders struggle to communicate about their teams. As software engineering as a field is subject to increasingly disruptive technologies, software researchers have been sounding the alarm that developers' ability to access psychological factors vital to their work, such as creative collaboration, has long been understudied and underappreciated.[3,4] Increasingly high stakes demands for developers to master new workflows and skills during development with new technologies such as generative AI make understanding developers' needs even more central for many organizations. In my research project that looked at visibility and value, we also found that only 14% of developers surveyed thought their work was being evaluated by their organization in a way that they agreed with, and that helped their teams. In qualitative interviews, one experienced engineering manager expressed the cost of this bluntly: "It doesn't matter how well you manage your team if you're not aligned or bringing visibility into the place that your team or department has within the organization."

If you run a technology organization, you might be wincing in recognition right now. I think this visibility and value gap is why when I introduce myself as a psychologist for software teams, the most frequent questions that I get sound a lot like that developer I spoke to at my friend's brunch:

> How can I convince my leadership that our developers need . . . [insert objectively obvious thing that all humans need, like time to learn new skills, or a reasonable work schedule, or time for their families]?
>
> How can I convince our leadership that developers . . . are people?

Both the science and the real-world evidence about software teams show again and again that meeting the needs of developers as people is a vital ingredient for technological innovation and a thriving future for technology. However, in order to access that developer science, we need to overcome the myths about software developers and their work that hold us back.

MODELS AND MISCONCEPTIONS

How did we get here? How is it possible that software is so valuable, and software developers are so needed, and yet the work of doing software is in such a constant state of crisis? How are developers simultaneously one of the most valuable workforces in a modern organization, yet always questioning whether their leaders understand that they are people?

I think this is because we're using the wrong model to understand developers and, more broadly, to understand technological problem-solving. This is a critical mistake that I call seeing developers as Brains-in-Jars, and it's a misconception about what really drives innovation and quality in software work. Brains-in-Jars thinking happens when we strip away the humanity of developers and treat software engineering organizations like a simplistic, inhuman machine. Instead of seeing the foundational psychology of software teams as an ecosystem we need to care for, we see technical work as a magical output that we can squeeze out of isolated individuals. Understanding developers and investing in their needs has long taken a backseat to harnessing the market force of technology.

But this model doesn't match the reality of complex knowledge work. As soon as you enter the strange universe of software, simplistic models fall apart. Technical decisions can be right one day and wrong the next. Modern codebases extend across countries and teams, and are often too large for any single developer or team to be familiar with. The interactions and outcomes that developers try to make happen (or solve when they don't) all day long are increasingly work that's *sociotechnical* rather than just technical: successful software systems require the people, the hardware, the code, and the diverse processes between them to all function. This work extends far past programming to include interactions between both digital designs and physical realities, all of which may rapidly change.

Instead of facing this, it feels easier to believe in the simplistic Brains-in-Jars myth. But Brains-in-Jars encodes a tremendous number of misconceptions about developers' productivity and problem-solving. We assume that hard work should feel like grinding, and that being able to work with software is an innate, immutable trait. We think of developers as fungible, independent pieces on an assembly line that can be easily and interchangeably swapped. This leads us to create poor cultures that discourage learning, and punish creativity. We mismeasure programming work with abstract metrics of output and constantly miss key intervention points that could've saved our developers from getting trapped in mountains of short-term decisions that were unsustainable. And we lose tremendous value inside of our organizations when we don't realize that developers are building in teams and across collaborative relationships and fail to protect that unique expertise.

Without a human-centered understanding of developers, organizations and leaders treat software engineering like a black box. If they tackle it at all, it's with a hodge-podge of approaches, attempting to drive effectiveness with a combination of oversimplified manufacturing analogies and gut instinct. With this limited view, organizational policies can seem to make sense on paper but sabotage the very activities that best support high-quality, innovative software: cutting developers' learning time, breaking up high-performing teams, and failing to reward senior contributors for mentorship.

Facing this mess, software teams are often left to scramble on their own. One staff engineer in my research put it this way: "Every software team does things their own way . . . and that means none of us know how another team really works. I feel like I have to reinvent the wheel every time I join a new team. We call it autonomy, but it's really confusion." My research grounded in empirical psychological science has revealed that many developers are struggling with high rates of anxiety, including doubting their ability to succeed in the future. In a study we conducted with over 3,000 developers, at least 43% reported significant worry about maintaining their success and even their very identity as a developer when thinking about the new skills required for AI-assisted coding, a phenomenon I named *AI Skill Threat.*[5] Tellingly, developers aren't just worried about how the skills of software development will change but also whether or not their leadership and communities will be accurate and fair in what they expect from an AI-assisted future. This collision of social and individual pressures, supercharged by rapid shifts in technology, is hitting like a match to a powder keg when software teams already feel misunderstood and unseen as people in their organizations.

Further recognizing this need, multiple movements within software engineering have risen up, all in their own way attempting to right this fundamental oversight: Agile methodologies, DevOps, platform engineering, and the new and emerging field of "DevEx" or Developer Experience are all movements that have attempted to center software work on principles of collaboration and frame successful software work as sociotechnical rather than purely technical. Despite their differences, these movements have all resonated with software practitioners by taking the perspective of developers themselves. Each of these software transformation movements has had a particular way it tried to force businesses to reckon with the fact that developers need more support for the human side of software work. The Agile Manifesto said, "Individuals and interactions over processes and tools." DevOps made the argument that cohesive processes in software development needed to be invested in, measured, and improved. And these movements have made significant strides for the voice of software teams at the business table: DevOps has been widely adopted as a practice by large technology companies with a focus on engineering excellence, even if maintaining an entire DevOps investment is still beyond the reach of a lot of smaller organizations. In more recent years, developer experience has emerged as organizations realize developers themselves are a core market for tools and products.

These movements have increased software teams' velocity, improved planning practices, and begun to shine a light on the massive costs of bad tooling on developers' output. But they still haven't solved the crisis of software work. Whether organizations are calling their engineering enablement investments Agile, DevOps, Platform Engineering or DevEx, every engineering organization I've ever met with is struggling with implementing these ideals in the real world.

The thing is, moving from big ideals to real-world change requires answering some challenging psychology questions for our specific situations and organizations. Why do some teams consistently produce great problem-solving and what blocks it? How can we design for problems that we haven't encountered yet, and frictions we have yet to imagine? What helps individual developers stay motivated and learn? How can we repair the intergroup conflicts that seem so pervasive in our workplaces? And how do we measure the impact of our changes, and pick the most powerful ones to invest in, when we all have limited time, attention, and resources?

Instead of reinventing the wheel, we can bring the rich methods of psychological science to software teams and find real answers. We need evidence and a sound framework to create high-quality innovation and problem-solving that's grounded in how human beings really work. When you have that, you have the key you need to understand how to improve your software organization.

THE PSYCHOLOGY OF SOFTWARE TEAMS

This book is my attempt to give you the greatest secret weapon I've found for leaders, managers, and developers themselves trying to navigate and build in the ever-changing world of software: using psychology to unlock what creates a successful software team. Software teams aren't alone in wanting to know the answers to those challenging real-world questions. For years, social and behavioral scientists have studied how to encourage adaptive and resilient human behavior in the toughest environments. Healthcare, education, and public policy have all benefited from the science of human behavior and psychology. But software teams haven't.

As a psychologist for the humans of tech, I've spent years bringing together research teams of PhD social scientists to work *with* software teams. I've examined hundreds of software team problems from two lenses, as a rigorous scientist creating new empirical data to answer tough questions, and as a research leader with an open science consultancy that helps software teams develop their own evidence strategies. Across both my public-facing open science and my partnerships with real working teams, I've had one goal: create a shared science for software teams that helps real developers in the real world. In the lab and in the field, I've developed and tested software-team-specific measures for constructs like the visibility of software work, developer learning culture, and how software teams can face and make good decisions around technological shifts like AI. In this book, you'll learn from real world data from thousands of developers working across industries and dozens of empirical research projects. I've also paired the quantitative with the qualitative, diving deep into the voice of developers with focus groups and research interviews, learning from developers' unique stories and incredible insight. The truth is, I love working with software teams because I know what it's like to fight for the value of your work. Every research study I've led on software teams has been hard-won as I've raised funding for these projects and partnerships, or built the research teams from the ground-up that could enable the evidence to exist.

By applying the lens of rigorous psychological science to the stories of thousands of developers, we've found strong and reliable signals for what drives developers' long-term and sustainable performance. The psychology of thriving software teams doesn't have to stay invisible and unheard. Psychology gives us an incredible toolkit for understanding developers' experiences and building teams that are creative, high performing, and good for the people on them.

For the first half of the book, Chapters 2–4, we'll dive into the basics of understanding our minds and countering some of the biggest stereotypes about software development thinking and problem-solving. This is a practical survey of key insights I've found most useful to software teams, not a comprehensive summary of every possible psychological theory. We'll learn about thinking traps that lock organizations into the Brains-in-Jars model, core features of our social learning, metacognition, and problem-solving, how the Performance Paradox can undermine our motivation, and how cultures of learning and belonging can restore us.

For the second half of the book, Chapters 5–7, we'll move from the basics to the complex environments we encounter in social interaction. We'll tackle how groups fall into conflict and form coalitions. We'll see how healthy measurement practices change the information flow available to teams and learn about how investing in systematic evidence strategies can unite teams around positive change. And finally, drawing from intervention science, we'll explore moving our organizations and ecosystems away from Brains-in-Jars models and toward psychologically resilient, thriving models.

BRINGING DEVELOPERS THEIR OWN SCIENCE

When I told a close friend that I was starting a research lab to study software developers, she said with full and total sincerity: "But Cat . . . I thought you studied people!"

We laughed at the mental slip, but it showed me how hard it is for so many people to remember the people making software. Despite the fact that the most valuable knowledge work in the world comes from our human minds, psychology has also become the invisible everywhere of knowledge work. I find that many leaders are wondering how to scale up what seem to be rare, incredible developers and teams. Instead of leaning on a few rockstars, leaders know they want a resilient, healthy engineering organization. Developers want to work on good teams, not just pursue paths of individual stardom. But across technology communities, we're struggling to close the gap between the individual and the organization, and find generalizable patterns rather than chasing one-off success stories. Because we haven't closed the visibility and value gap for software work, and because we haven't invested in the psychology of software teams, the hard-won insight that's brewing inside of the most innovative software teams often isn't used to drive leadership decisions.

At a recent tech conference, I'd given a keynote and then fielded a long Q&A with a highly technical audience of CTOs, engineering directors, and engineering managers. One VP of Engineering had stayed for the entire time, asking several excellent technical questions about the complex statistical modeling I'd done.

But once everyone else had left, he and I had found ourselves alone in the hallway, and he turned to me, leaned in close, and said quietly: "Ok. Can I tell you what I'm really worried about? I know that once everyone starts doing better, the work will follow, and the quality will go up. How do I know what to do to help my developers *as people*?"

Leaders trapped in the Brains-in-Jars model of software development don't just cut developers off from their human needs. They also cut themselves off from the rich world of psychological science and its insights and from truly living up to their own potential to become human-centered leaders. In my research I've found that this often isn't a failure of empathy or compassion. Engineering leaders already know that developers' problem-solving matters—after all, they've lived it. Rather, the failure is in the structural environments and cultures that surround technology work and convince us that we need to devalue our human needs in order to continue to belong and be taken seriously. But psychological science is a superpower for the leaders who have the courage to transcend this climate, and psychology needs to become a shared conversation instead of a whispered secret. Our software teams may operate in many different contexts, but there are clear principles we can follow that cultivate sustainable, resilient productivity instead of chaotic burnout cycles.

Perhaps most important of all, when an organization really takes the psychology of software teams seriously, developers feel it immediately. A supported software team can become capable of triumphing over incredible friction, while an unsupported software team might flounder despite the biggest resources. It's not just software that can feel magical when it works—when we use accurate psychology to design for productive human problem-solving, even small investments can yield enormous, cascading impact. I firmly believe that building within, rather than against, our own human cognition, collaboration, and creativity is what will unlock the greatest innovation for our shared world.

If the number one question developers ask is how they can get their human needs met, the number one reaction I get from developers when I share my research is this: *I recognize this. I can't believe someone has finally put words to this thing I've always experienced, but never named.* Developers are hungry for a new conversation about software development, one that feels relevant and real to their own experiences, draws from real empirical evidence, and helps them develop a strategy for a lifelong career full of technological innovation and joy. Leaders who can provide this vision will be able to build authentic, trustful relationships with their technology teams and lead their organizations to breakthroughs.

The aim of this book is to treat developers as whole people. Brains, hearts, and everything else.

NOTE

i. Throughout this book when the word "developers" is used, I'd like you to take a moment to broaden who comes to mind. Technical problem-solving happens across many roles, and the developer of the future will look different from the roles we imagine today. In this book I'll often default for simplicity's sake to describing software teams and software developers but take "developer" to be taken as broadly as possible. I welcome and encourage you to apply these insights to any other folks building in our complex technical worlds.

CHAPTER 2

Breaking Up with Brains-in-Jars

LISTENING TO DEVELOPERS

I first started listening to software developers over small cafe tables in San Francisco. For a year on most weekday mornings I woke up earlier than I wanted to, before the commute traffic started, and walked several long blocks to a cafe selling the tiniest and most expensive coffees I'd ever seen. I waited with a laptop and my phone ready to record audio, nervously tweaking an interview script, telling myself I knew what I was doing. Every time the cafe door jingled, I'd look up in the warm lights to see if the person who walked in was scanning the tables to find me.

One developer laughed as she sat down, saying, "I was asking myself, what does a psychologist for software teams look like?"

"Let me know when you find out," I said, because it was a job I was still inventing.

I didn't know what I was doing. Oh, I knew how to do research. I'd done a PhD in psychology—specializing in the science of how people learn, perform, and then tell other people about their learning and performance. Then I'd landed a tech job that my mom had excitedly described as "the best thing that ever could've happened to you." But my work had taken an unlikely turn after I did the unthinkable: I quit that job. I left security and stability behind to study software developers, working with a friend to co-found a small startup. We were building the prototype of a software tool to help developers take better documentation of their thinking while

 DOI: 10.1201/9781003589112-2

they wrote code, a fascinating problem for us. Founding a software startup involved many challenges I'd never imagined facing as an empirical scientist: developing pitches that won over VCs, communicating a vision that could resonate with users, and staking my own survival on the power of our idea. But I'd become irrevocably hooked on a new, unexplored scientific question, and I needed to follow it (I'll admit it took me a while to call my mom). The shining question that had captivated me was this: what drives developers' innovation and problem-solving?

I'd spent years studying the science of how people learned, and when I got to tech, it had seemed obvious to me that psychological processes like social learning and collaborative problem-solving were at the center of how developers built technology. Likewise, it seemed obvious to me that technical breakthroughs across software communities were most likely to emerge when those communities were psychologically healthiest—able to build with cumulative cultures, responsive to challenging ideas and supportive of new contributors, and full of pathways for individuals to succeed. But as I started conducting qualitative interviews with programmers working across diverse contexts, I learned they lived in a world that saw their minds—and psychological needs—very differently.

"There's the work you do, the work that truly contains your thinking, and the work you get to show and talk about," a developer told me frankly. He worked on a large, distributed team, and we were discussing everything that went into ramping up into a new codebase, as far as he could talk about it (I had already learned that developers navigated a thousand invisible decisions in even opening up about their work to others). He seemed eager, urgent even, to talk to someone about the effort of coding.

He described navigating a new codebase as taking hours of learning, and that he loved making mental maps of the new world of other people's code. "It feels most real to me, the things like this, the navigating through all of this software, the searching through code to find the tiny little connection point that's going to make it all pay off. But it's not the work you get to show."

In interview after interview, I found this theme repeated: every single person I interviewed described effortful learning as absolutely integral to solving problems and pushing software forward, yet nearly all of them also described a deep tension between how they saw their work, and how they felt their organizations saw it. It was clear to me that developers weren't getting the time and space they needed to learn.

Our startup was a glorious two-and-a-half year adventure of exploration (and indeed, successfully pitching VCs!), but ultimately the changing macro-climate around developer tools and fundraising caused us to close that iteration of our idea. But I was hooked on the problem of developers, and the years of stories I'd been collecting as I sat next to them at work were about to change my path forever. Scientists are driven by one unquenchable question, and I found myself asking it again and again: "Why?"

Why did developers think so much of their development work was necessary but had to remain unseen? Why did they consistently tell me about hiding learning from their teammates and managers? Why did even developers who acknowledged that their cognition was deeply valued by their organizations, and that they loved working in software, consistently say they didn't feel seen *as people*? Across the interviews, developers revealed their conviction that their organizations and teammates wouldn't understand if they needed time to learn. Believing this, they described systematically disinvesting from revealing their moments of learning to other developers. This created a bizarre mirage at the organization in general, where people constantly assumed that they must be the only one who wasn't a perfect, omniscient super-programmer.

I named this damaging cycle *learning debt*: when developers clearly needed to push the frontiers of what they knew to solve new technical problems, but the shared organizational norms about how developers should perform explicitly discouraged them from doing it in public, cutting teams off from the benefits of shared advancement. And I was captivated by this invisible, unspoken tension that you would only know about once you asked the developers themselves. I would go on to lead teams of interdisciplinary social scientists in studying many such elements of developers' experiences, testing empirical theories to better understand developer problem-solving with thousands of participants, and applying careful statistical modeling and psychological theories to help us better understand what developers experience. Alongside my scientific work, I continued to listen to developers, traveling around the world to visit engineering teams and have hundreds of in-depth conversations with practitioners. I came to believe that *learning debt* was not just an interesting problem for a few organizations but a specific example of a much larger cultural and psychological problem facing software development.

Something critically important is revealed by the tension software developers felt between how software development demanded they use their minds and whether technology environments saw and valued their psychological experience. This tension is like the black hole at the center of our storytelling about software teams, an invisible force warping our ability to lead these teams through collaboration and community at work. It's not enough to talk about individual software developer production. To build the technological future we want, we need to understand what nourishes the collaborative and emergent properties of collective software developer productivity. When we don't create the right psychological environments for software work, developers disinvest from the very processes that create technological outcomes in our organizations. This isn't just because toxic environments are distracting or causing people to burn out. It's because *good psychology* is *how* good software work happens.

One developer described the current state of software development with a particularly expressive analogy: "It's like coding in the dark. Every once in a while someone comes in to turn on the lights and stare at you, like [code] review, but then you feel like you have to defend something . . . mostly I feel like I'm just sitting here with all the lights off."

I couldn't get that image out of my mind. I named that very first research study I shared in public about software developers *It's Like Coding in the Dark.*[1] By the end of those interviews, I was hooked on the stories of software developers and the stories that developers were telling themselves about what it meant to be a developer. It became my conviction that psychology had something to offer software teams, validating the important experiences of practitioners while also challenging us to build something better. Unraveling this requires unpacking misconceptions we have about how software engineering works, the stereotypes we have about how technological work gets done in the world, and our deeply held conceptions about what leads to innovation and world-changing impact with software problem-solving. For the rest of this chapter, we're going to take a bird's-eye view of these pervasive misconceptions and how they keep us from joyful software engineering environments.

BRAINS-IN-JARS

Picture going to a party and introducing yourself to a new acquaintance. In that moment, you have a wide range of choices you could make, choices that often align with different identities that both matter to you and are cognitively and emotionally salient in your current environment. For instance, I love being a psychologist, but if we were meeting at my local music store, I might tell you that I play harp and I'm always scouring music stores for rare folk harp sheet music. If we met at a dog park, I might tell you that I'm a dog person (an identity I incorporated later than many people, after falling in love with a dog that we were fostering). And each identity carries along other sets of beliefs about who we want to be and how we want others to see us. Take a moment to imagine a highly successful software developer. What comes to mind? What behaviors, activities, and interests do you believe make that person successful? Before you finish this chapter, it might be useful to take a piece of paper and write down a few features of a "successful software engineer"—or if you own this copy of the book, feel free to record those characteristics right here. I'll wait!

A Highly Successful Software Developer, in your own words
A highly successful software developer is . . ..

When we think about a professional field like software development, we activate a mental model around what we believe drives success. This is called a *model* because it's composed of interacting parts. Our assumptions about what creates success in software are not formed by one single belief but rather suites of related beliefs. Mental models are impacted by our experiences, our perceptions of ourselves, our stereotypes, our cognitive biases, as well as cues from our social landscape and how our cognition is impacted by those around us.

Over years of working as a psychological scientist with software teams, I've seen hundreds of software organizations struggle with a self-perpetuating, limiting model about how developers think and problem-solve that creates traps for both engineering leaders and individual contributors. Despite our best intentions, this model can drive leaders to disempower software teams, developers to perpetuate unhealthy cycles on their teams, and organizations to cut developers off from the very things that they need in order to innovate. I call it the Brains-in-Jars Model of software development.

Picture that classic sci-fi trope setting, an evil scientist's laboratory. In a room that always seems to be dimly aglow with blue-tinged lighting (in actual labs, harsh overhead lighting is the norm), detached pink blobs float in glass jars filled with a transparent, viscous jelly. Perhaps the camera pans outward from a close-up on the one jar to reveal many, many jars in neat rows in a staggeringly long vista. Brains! In! Jars!

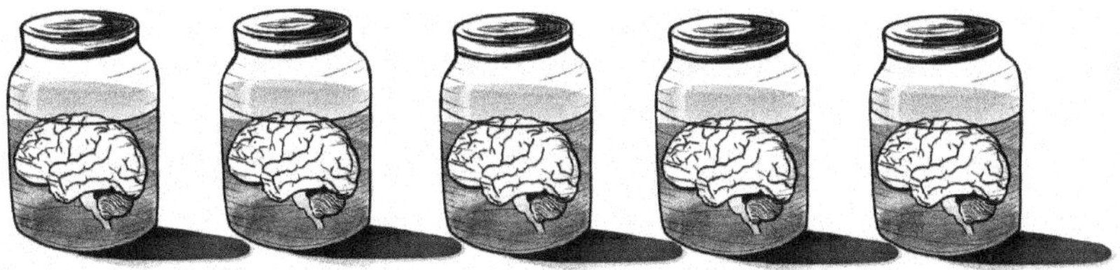

In a Brains-in-Jars model, developers are isolated, fungible individual brains and nothing but brains. We assume that innovation in software comes primarily from individual cognitive ability. We also assume that all of the "soft stuff" (psychological safety, collaboration, and core psychological needs like our need to trust that other people think we belong, or believe that we have agency over our actions) are just "nice-to-haves," and not necessarily related to the rigorous and exceptional "technical work." In Brains-in-Jars orgs, leadership primarily imagines their engineering organization as a place where software gets written in discrete pieces by human beings with interchangeable skills. The most valuable thing about a developer is their sheer output, and that output is frequently measured in overly narrow, simplistic (but easy to access!) individualized and granular metrics like lines of code, or quantities of commits, or speed over time. The Brains-in-Jars engineering organization is less a collection of human beings working together than it is a spreadsheet. Interactions, social learning, and shared problem-solving are invisible in this model.

As silly as this image is, once I started using it to describe the environments of those truly unhappy software teams, it really stuck. Developers in my research worked in many contexts, from small startups, large corporations, government offices, sprawling banking systems, to local hospitals. Their tools and resources vary, the sector constraints and priorities are different, and the specialties of software differ. But the Brains-in-Jars idea provided clarity, threading through the complexity. Whether or not an organization kept echoing destructive but common misconceptions about developers' minds, and therefore, misconceptions about what their work should look like, limited their engineering workforces and limited the possibilities that leaders saw for their people. In short, the Brains-in-Jars model perpetuates bad psychology about developers.

This way of seeing software developers isn't reducible to a single belief. Instead, Brains-in-Jars thinking represents a complex suite of beliefs, assumptions, and stereotypes about software developers and software work that create reinforcing cycles. By limiting what we share and value in software, they change what types of work become visible inside of software organizations. And because the way we think about technical work and technical people bleeds over into many contexts, the Brains-in-Jars model can also be seen outside of big tech companies where it influences boundary-crossing technological ecosystems. The open-source maintainer who is pressured to handle an endless queue of requests is being treated like a brain in a jar, and so is the engineering student who is being told that they'll only make it in engineering if they grind all night, or the infrastructure engineer told to hold an entire organization's internal developer experience together until after the next feature launch, or the next one, waiting for a moment the organization will invest in empowering their engineers that never seems to come. As one startup founder told me in a rueful tone of voice, "We keep saying we'll get to culture . . . eventually!"

Teams and organizations vary in how much they express these patterns, or when these patterns emerge—it's rare that any organization will be so dominated by the Brains-in-Jars model that they'll never recognize the complexity of software work or developers have at least some human needs (after all, famously, many tech company campuses provide free lunch!). However, when we have persistent stereotypes about technical work and the people who do it, these are easily activated by contexts that bring those beliefs to the forefront during our organizational decision-making.[2,3] When that happens, we're capable of tricking ourselves into staying locked in damaging, short-term cycles, like learning debt. The reason getting handed a pizza party after a death march software project feels so demeaning is because when your psychological needs are constantly being dismissed, no amount of swag or snacks will fix it.

The good news is that psychology has real answers. By learning to recognize and replace Brains-in-Jars thinking with empirically backed models grounded in real human evidence at scale, we can find our way to the alternatives that we recognize when we feel our best and when developers are most successful. Through my empirical research and the research from other scientists, I've come to believe that the Brains-in-Jars model in software is characterized by three pervasive misconceptions about how people work and solve problems, what matters to people inside of their teams and organizations, what technical brilliance looks like, and who gets to do it. These misconceptions about software developers are thinking traps, rooted deep in the suite of beliefs, feelings, cognitive biases, and social conventions that color our everyday decisions in the Brains-in-Jars model. Defaulting to these thinking traps may help us achieve certain strategic goals of short-term productivity and survival, and that's why they feel good to us and can take on a life of their own inside of technical groups. But over the long run, these short-term strategies fail in the face of emergent complexity, change, and pressure. They fail to match the real ways that software developers think and problem-solve, and so the Brains-in-Jars model keeps us banging our heads against the wall, wondering why we're working so hard just to stay in the same place.

You can think of these three "villains" as red flags that signal a need to dive deeper into whether your technical environment is falling into the Brains-in-Jars model: (1) It's gripped by Brittle Productivity, (2) it leans on Lone Genius stereotypes, and (3) it's marked by a Chilly Climate. Throughout this book, we'll explore why these thinking traps lead software teams astray and create dangerous fragilities inside of technical organizations. Resilient, sustainable organizations learn to overcome these thinking traps. But it's not enough to say things are wrong. We also have to know how to change them. Let's start by taking a deeper look at each one.

Trap 1: Brittle Productivity

Take a moment to imagine the story of a software team success, the kind of success many technology leaders aspire to drive: delivering a critical product feature that needs to launch during a pivotal window, taking advantage of a rapidly emerging change in what technology can do that changes the market for an existing product.

Let's say that the software team tasked with leading the feature development is motivated, engaged, and high performing—after all, that's why they were assigned to lead out this exciting feature development. Unfortunately, because this is cutting-edge work, unexpected setbacks and friction begin to take a toll. After all, it's the rule rather than the exception that software projects change their timelines and budgets.[4–6] Perhaps a senior technical contributor works closely with the engineering manager to advocate for increased support for the team, but not all of it can be granted, and so the team starts to put in long hours. Weeks turn into months of stress for the team. The manager and technical lead find themselves spending much of their time reminding the team about how much the organization is counting on them, and how important it is to pull together and make this happen. Delivering the product feature feels mission-critical, and this software team cares deeply about their work and their organization. They rally together and motivate each other with reminders that they're the best of the best, that this is an opportunity to prove once again that they're high performing, "10x" engineers, and that failure is not an option. They deliver a successful product launch that's a hit with customers and the industry at large. The software team is generously financially rewarded.

Perhaps this sounds familiar. If it does, I encourage you to take a moment to imagine (or remember) being in this position. How did it feel? Now, I'm going to ask a complicated question: was this a success? Or was it a failure? From the point of view of psychology, the answer might not be inside of this story, but in what happens next.

Many stories about software development end with the successful product launch, the end of the initiative, or the software project surmounted. But if we want to understand developers as people, we need to ask what happens to *them*. If we time travel to a year in the future, would we find that this software team has maintained its impressive productivity, or would we find that these high performers have an elevated risk of quitting the company?

The answer might surprise you, but it wouldn't surprise a psychologist. Psychologists studying people who work with high levels of passion in their workplaces have documented the toll that unregulated super-commitment takes *after* achievement, even when you win. Even when organizations attain short-term success, when that success relies on people working past their own psychological needs regularly, they're more likely to quit, and business outcomes suffer.[7,8] This problem is exacerbated when employees feel especially out of control of whether or not they need to work hard. For instance, when their professional identities and social standing at the company are at risk, as may be the case when a software team is told they're the only ones who can solve a particular problem. On surveys at large tech companies that do their own research on software developers' experiences, developers frequently report significant gaps between how they want to spend their time and how they feel they have to spend their time, and that gap is associated with a decrease in satisfaction and productivity.[9] These factors drive up the risk of teams suffering burnout, and we have empirical evidence from software developers that their burnout is associated with future attrition.[10]

This is a story about an organization becoming increasingly brittle: everything looks productive on the surface, but because we've missed the mounting toll on the team, it could break at any moment, leaving our organization significantly more fragile than before. And like black ice on the road, this particular dynamic is a particularly dangerous feature of Brains-in-Jars thinking precisely because we're so prone to missing it. We fixate on the short-term success, and it distracts us from the compounding stress fractures under the surface. There may be more overtly toxic or harmful situations that leaders and organizations need to deal with (for instance, dealing with a bad actor who harasses others), but they're also more obviously harmful. Brittle Productivity is particularly revelatory for explaining the unpredictable rewards that keep us trapped in Brains-in-Jars thinking. By thinking about moving from productivity at any cost to considering the potential costs of different *kinds* of productivity, we can begin to develop our intuition for what keeps highly complex knowledge work sustainable over time.

The Brittle Productivity trap happens when an organization has a shared notion of developer productivity that fixates on performance over effort and relies on teams grinding over investing in sustainable, supportive work practices. And it's a trap because it looks like it can measurably produce outcomes that we want (like a product launch in a timely fashion, or exceptional technical problem-solving from developers who fear what will happen if they don't bring their all). Cramming for a test is a Brittle Productivity behavior, and so is pulling an all-nighter to finish a term paper—both strategies that classic learning science research has discovered we gravitate toward but are highly ineffective for real learning.[11,12]

Across many different research areas, psychological scientists who study achievement have aligned theories and evidence that uncover the same, overarching pattern: fixating on performance as the only form of success leads people to learn inefficient and destructive patterns, and ultimately stops the very strategies that made them productive and high performing in the first place. In education, scientists have realized that fixating on performance outcomes often leads people to double-down on psychological strategies of avoiding challenge.[13] Measuring how strongly people endorse a "performance" mindset across thousands of people and many research studies, psychologists discovered that when we constantly monitor and worry about whether we're being seen as high performers, we also begin to systematically avoid moments when we might fail, risking breaking others' beliefs that we're competent, that we belong, and that our work is a valuable contribution. The problem is, those frightening moments of looking like a low performer are actually key to learning, creativity, and innovation. Paradoxically, the more emphasis we put on performance, the harder it begins for us to see the value in the effort that leads to it. In other words, the things that actually make us perform better in the long run can feel very counterintuitive in the short term.

Human beings simply are not production engines. Without a psychologically supportive environment that allows space for failure, we will eventually burn out, and we can burn out hard. While we're capable of short-term pushes that look highly productive, if we overly fixate on performing productivity, we wind up in a very fragile place. But because the short-term benefits of grinding are immediately obvious, and the long-term costs of these cycles can go unnoticed and undocumented (or be borne mostly by individuals), we often fail to recognize that we're locked in the Brittle Productivity trap. A software developer who came up to me after I gave a talk about productivity at a tech conference described his own experience of the aftermath of a Brittle Productivity project in poignant terms: "I started to feel hollow inside, and no reward at work seemed to matter anymore. Even a nice word from my manager and my teammates, who I really liked, didn't seem to penetrate. Recognition only made me feel worse, because I knew I would just be asked to overdeliver again."

Our beliefs about how productivity works, and what signals of productivity other people are looking for and will value, steer us every day.[14] Across decades of studying how people achieve, psychologists have consistently found that our beliefs about how performance operates in a specific environment have a measurable impact on whether people can sustain achievement over time.[15] For example, a software developer who believes that making mistakes, iterating, and trying again is not just ok but actually a normal and productive part of their day is more likely to persist in their problem-solving. The emerging science of our beliefs about achievement and success has also discovered that what people believe drives success in a specific field can have an enormous impact on their strategies for working in that field (we'll take a deeper dive into this in Chapter 4).[16]

One of the reasons I believe software teams can default to Brittle Productivity is because we aren't necessarily great at noticing, monitoring, and making accurate inferences about what creates our success in the first place. Across many areas of behavioral science, researchers have demonstrated that groups of people tend to favor individual explanations over structural explanations about human behavior, even when structural changes might lead to the outcomes that we want.[17] In an engineering organization, the individualistic bias can lead us to emphasize individual actions at any cost and fail to value structural solutions and the contributions of large, environmental factors when we're thinking about individual developers' work.

Trap 2: The Lone Genius

Picture three scenarios:

- You're in a team retrospective, and a manager tells the team: "To be honest, I think you're spending too much time together. I want this team to focus on lean, mean production. I want to see you earn that social time with your real work."
- You're at a tech conference, and you overhear a founder boast that their startup is only interested in "10x developers, the people who are the real builders."
- You're discussing how to design a hiring process for a technical role, and an technical lead says: "Sometimes it's actually a red flag if someone likes people. I think, sure, that candidate has amazing collaboration skills, but can they really hack it on this project? We need the kind of people who are hardcore coders."

These aren't imaginary. Each of these is a real moment I experienced while doing research with software teams and writing this book. While each statement was filtered through the particular perspectives and social contexts of those different individuals, I was struck by just how much they collectively illustrate a specific set of beliefs: the best technical work is driven by rare outliers whose needs should be supported even when it comes at the expense of others, technical thinkers are inherently antisocial, tech excellence is the exclusive provenance of a gifted few, and we can identify it with harsh skepticism and scrutiny. I call this the Lone Genius trap. The pervasive industry story that there's a "10x developer" (typically defined as someone capable of performing isolated, individual development tasks much faster than others) is a legendary example of the Lone Genius trap, or the idea that there's a mysterious "programming brain" that we can detect, hire for, and privilege.

The problem is, our best evidence about what drives innovation in software work—and predicts high achievement in general—simply doesn't support this myth. As we'll explore more deeply throughout the whole book, software development requires excelling at collaboration and shared innovation and draws on diverse cognitive abilities. In fact, when we put the work into actually measuring it, the *collective* benefits of strong, psychologically supportive cultures usually predict long-term innovation and high-quality work *better* than focusing on individual attributes.[18] In my own large-scale quantitative studies with thousands of developers, supportive psychological cultures are among the strongest predictors of effective teams that we've found. Below, I've visualized real data from nearly two thousand individual developers on neutral-to-highly effective teams, a subset of participants from a study where we found that developers' access to a strong learning culture was associated with significantly higher team effectiveness.[19] Rather than summary judgments from managers or leaders, we chose to focus on developers' own direct ratings of their team's effectiveness over a recent period of time, and signals for learning culture like developers sharing learning moments with peers, and engaging in shared (not isolated or hidden) learning goals. Our study revealed a strong relationship between better learning culture and team effectiveness, including when we carefully controlled across 12+ industries, types of engineering roles, organizational sizes, and developer demographics in our complex statistical models. But the story gets even more interesting when you look at the distribution of the data. While effectiveness increases in general for every increase in learning culture, teams are far more likely to land in the *highest* effectiveness bucket if they also achieve a truly committed learning culture. This points to a very different story than Lone Genius effects, where rare individuals scattered around our organizations at random are what supercharge our teams.

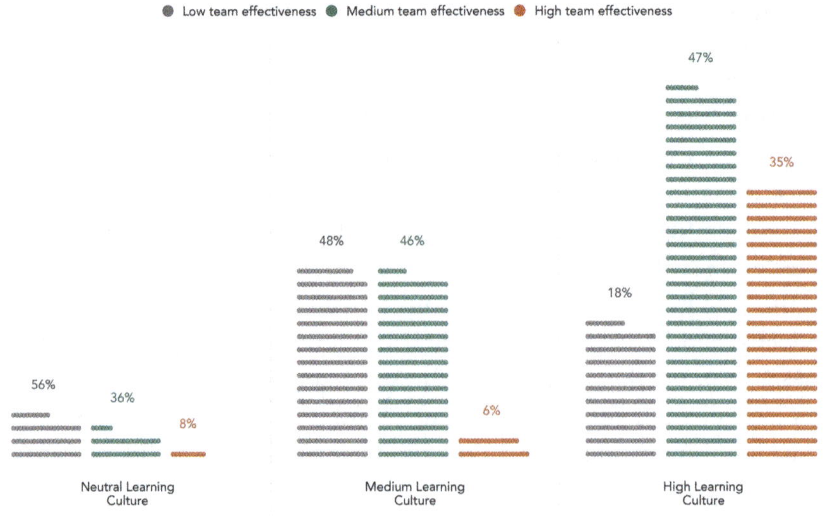

Learning Culture Shapes Team Effectiveness.

This evidence doesn't tell us learning culture is the *only* thing that matters to teams. Team effectiveness is something I like to call a "suitcase" concept, meaning it contains *many* complex factors, and many things in the world can change it. For any given team, lots of factors in their particular context will impact their effectiveness, from developers' life experiences to shifting organizational factors to macroeconomics. But even with all that complexity, dialing in on measuring just one core psychological feature like learning culture provided us with a remarkably strong signal for where we would find more effective engineering teams. I believe, along with many other software practitioners and researchers, that we can pick up on this strong signal because access to good psychological environments is a fundamental force shaping the software outcomes we get out of our teams. Putting this to the empirical causal test more directly, many of the most well-studied interventions that have been successful at measurably changing how much people achieve or how long they persist in challenging tasks come from changing the larger environment around people, giving them better psychological support to face challenges.[17,20] A comprehensive meta-analysis looking at over 22,000 people and 5,000 groups documented that environmental factors show larger effects than individual traits and that psychological environments are often better predictors for task performance than individual differences.[21]

Troublingly, we also have strong evidence that fixating too much on stories about Lone Geniuses hurts our motivation and resilience. Organizations that reinforce the message that software success comes from individual genius alone may unwittingly sabotage developers' ability to sustain achievement in challenging work. Damaging effects emerge at scale when knowledge workers endorse "brilliance beliefs," the stereotype that the highest forms of success are only achieved by those who have some quality of innate brilliance. When we believe that brilliance in a professional field is fixed (people can't learn or develop it) and rare (few people can or should be allowed to have it), we end up with tremendous uncertainty about whether we can belong in a team, are less likely to invest in the daily persistence that leads to outcomes, and feel deep fear about whether we'll ever be seen as one of those brilliant people.[16,22] The story that software development is the domain of rockstar coders and genius programmers might feel celebratory, but these stories at scale flood our minds with magical thinking, undermining the value of effort, experimentation and persistence. Scientists studying brilliance beliefs have documented that people with high brilliance beliefs often engage in *prove-you're-really-smart-enough* confrontations, trying to validate their status rather than truly problem-solve together, and warping an organizational culture toward contest over collaboration.[23] The more we feel a content culture around us, the more we internalize the belief that innate brilliance is required to succeed in software, that brilliance at software must go along with being ruthless and competitive, and that success is an individualistic, zero-sum game (in Chapter 4, we'll look at what one of my studies on this found for how this dynamic undermines software teams' ability to face change).

As we'll explore in Chapter 3, individual performance defaults paradoxically *decrease* long-term productivity and creative problem-solving, because people mire themselves in "performing" productivity rather than actually achieving it together. And the Lone Genius trap doesn't just hurt existing teams. It also hurts healthy software development career pathways. Learners and early-career developers are harmed by stereotypes that make them believe programming rests on innate abilities that only a few possess, and the more people believe this, the less likely many people are to want to learn to code, a pattern of discouragement that researchers have observed happening around the world.[24] This pattern even distorts our view of the real evidence about achievement: One reason that Lone Genius explanations are sticky and persistent is because of a cognitive bias we have to attribute outcomes solely to individual merit, even when the true explanation is often environmental.[25] Ignoring how much environments help people unlock their highest potential leads us to disinvest from the real work of forming collaborating, cohesive teams, and discount the harmful impact of individuals who damage team morale. One example of how insidious the Lone Genius trap can be is that it even seeps into moments we think we're providing positive feedback or encouragement. The manager who tells a junior developer "you can be a rockstar," or "you're a technical genius" might assume they're providing an encouraging compliment. But because this type of feedback implicitly conveys the idea that success comes from a fixed trait, "genius" praise can actually further cement developers' beliefs that software triumphs don't come from effort.[26] The developer who believes they're a technical genius might feel uplifted for a time but will tend to give themselves less room for effort and learning and is at higher risk for crashing into distressing negative beliefs.

Even though the Lone Genius thinking trap is powerful, it rarely stands up against lived experience when we get the chance to contrast what it truly takes to perform a job with stereotypes about it. While high-achieving performers always exist in any field, there aren't enough of them to build an organizational strategy around, they're less predictive than environmental factors, and fixating on them has a lot of downsides compared to improving environments. Turning into isolated and uncaring Lone Geniuses doesn't even align with most developers' values or goals: I've found that the vast majority of software developers in my research (over 90%!) agree that "helping others" is an important part of their job, and many of them have seen just how much the glorification of individual productivity instead of team effectiveness undermines real technical problem-solving.

Trap 3: The Chilly Climate

The third trap that marks Brains-In-Jars thinking gives us some important clues for why ignoring developers' psychological needs pushes our technology organizations further away from the outcomes we want. But that's not the only reason this trap is the final villain in the Brains-in-Jars model. This is also the one that makes the most software developers wince most visibly every time I talk about it. As a scientist who does both qualitative and quantitative work, I've learned that the most important insights come not just from tallying up numbers and finding statistical associations but also from carefully observing what people react to the most, even while they find it difficult to talk about.

Software environments are often marked by a shared set of norms that scientists call a Chilly Climate. Originally surfaced by psychologists studying the ways that women in engineering have to face down cumulative messages that their abilities will be doubted because of their identities, the Chilly Climate is a set of stereotypes that engineering ability and success are associated with coldness, isolation, and even antisocial behaviors. When I interviewed developers about their difficulty finding time to learn, many described fears not only about whether they would find time to learn but also that the mere act of helping others could also be seen as a mark against their technical prowess. Strikingly, this feeling was something that I often saw developers internalize, questioning their own immediate experience of the value of these activities. This association is so strong that even "ambient cues" in technical environments (subtle but pervasive signals that give us information about who is expected to belong to a group, like objects we associate with technical skill and computer science, like a video game, compared to unassociated objects like a nature poster) can have a profound impact on how people evaluate an environment.[1,3,27]

How can this happen? Social learning and collaboration are integral to software development, and psychologists studying how innovation works on the scale of entire cultures have documented how technological innovation depends on this collaboration.[28] How is it that so many software engineering organizations struggle with a culture that diminishes collaboration and cooperation? Here, too, psychology can help us understand why this paradoxical trap catches us. In the Brains-in-Jars model, because we see software work as so individualistic, we frequently undervalue the impactful work of collaboration, dialogue, mentorship, and everything that's deemed more "social" than technical. As we'll explore in more depth in Chapter 5, our minds are powerful pattern makers, and we can be heavily influenced by the shared social beliefs of the groups around us.[29,30] The more that an organization's shared norms around what "being technical" looks like are associated with a chilly, aloof, individualistic stereotype, the more difficult it becomes for any developer in that organization to break from the mold, and the steeper they expect the cost to be if they do.

When we associate software triumphs with being sterile, separate, and devoid of human context, we also tend to believe that it's ok (or even necessary for results) to treat people inside of software development with coldness. In fact, people who succeed in work despite running against the default stereotype—such as a developer being warm, supportive, and outgoing—can even face skepticism at their accomplishments or harsh backlash for their success because they provoke *stereotype incongruence.* It feels mentally uncomfortable to us when we see someone fail to match the stereotypes we have in mind, and we can react to this discomfort by thinking someone is less competent than they are.[31] Technical organizations haven't created their stereotypes in a vacuum: many societies, but particularly the Western cultures that have shaped software, have a long history of pre-existing stereotypes that associate "brilliance" only with majoritized racial and gender identities and discard the idea that brilliance can be shown through collaboration and interpersonal work, despite the fact that this work is needed to drive outcomes[32]. In other words, a culture that devalues collaboration can directly keep us from seeing its effects. Another stereotype that props up the Chilly Climate is the idea that negative interpersonal traits like cynicism must mean someone is more intelligent—a wide-sweeping series of studies that included over 200,000 people from 30 countries found that while a popular lay belief is that cynicism reflects mental acuity, cynical people perform no better or even *worse* on competency tests.[33]

The Chilly Climate trap can add discouragement everywhere that software developers learn, grow, and make decisions. In a series of important studies, Sapna Cheryan and colleagues documented that students considering whether to take on the work of learning computer science navigate through thinking about whether they might feel lonely and isolated not only inside of computer science but also among people outside of computer science, a form of "double isolation" that added a negative penalty, especially for minoritized people considering entering the field.[34,35] Across open source software, which can be integral to many of the technologies that software developers work with no matter their role, research has documented a continuing struggle for newcomers to gain entry into these worlds, particularly when new developers don't match existing stereotypes about who "must be technical." Across many technical worlds, Chilly Climates result in long-standing disparities in technical skill development that create shortages, imbalances of opportunity, and forestall innovation.[36–40] Chilly Climates aren't just happening in niche corners of technical fields. Even at some of the most prestigious engineering organizations, like Google, software researchers have documented that developers who are more likely to be seen as different from the software developer default stereotype by their age, gender, or race can experience systematically higher amounts of pushback as they attempt to make technical contributions to their teams.[41] The Chilly Climate trap does damage not just to the well-being of individual software developers but across our organizations, and encountering it can be systematically more punishing for minoritized developers.

The issue isn't just that Chilly Climates are punishing for developers to deal with. It's also that *warm* environments are tremendous incubators for breakthroughs and problem-solving. Software developers meeting to do pair programming, or mentoring, or brainstorming together, or investing in shared documentation, are all serving a vital function for the team: such activities could be increasing a shared sense of belonging, be providing a safe space for junior members to learn from senior members, be serving other important psychological needs like social support, or be driving up group creativity. But because developers' social-psychological needs are less tangible to us than tech requirements, they're that much easier for technical leaders and technical people to dismiss. However, evidence from organizational science tells us that even if we don't realize it explicitly, people want to feel that they belong in their organizations, pay attention to whether they are treated in ways that are consistent with their core needs, and constantly monitor whether they are being seen as whole human beings. When we believe that our belonging and humanity are threatened at work, our safety to innovate, connect, and sustain motivation suffers dramatically. At its furthest extreme, when developers experience feeling treated like objects at a large enough scale and for a long enough time, they may even begin to internalize the feeling that they are seen as "less than human," an experience that psychologists have named dehumanization, and one that can lead to dire negative outcomes for our overall well-being.[42,43]

FROM PROBLEMS TO SOLUTIONS

At this point, we've walked through a laundry list of factors that hold us back from thriving in software. Perhaps you recognize Brains-in-Jars thinking in your own life and across your own career: moments when you felt forced to grind past what was reasonable, moments when you worried about whether you belonged or saw someone else face skepticism about their "brilliance," or moments when you felt exhausted by a Chilly Climate. This can be difficult to confront, and these memories and experiences can be painful to process. Before we move on, I want to offer a hopeful counterpoint.

While Brains-in-Jars thinking creates challenges for software teams, I also believe software development already holds the keys to a more supportive, psychologically restorative, and innovative future. Culture is a dynamic thing that we build together, and within our organizations and across our teams, change is the rule. Psychological mindsets are multilayered, and we can hold many different beliefs at the same time. This means that you don't need to endorse every aspect of the Brains-in-Jars model to still buy into other parts of those beliefs. Within any one person, different ways of seeing the world can be *activated* by different situations, made more or less likely by the environment around us, our own personal belief systems, what we think others want from us, and commitments we've made, such as personal value systems.[2]

Identifying the villains of Brains-in-Jars isn't about pointing the finger at individual people, because all of us fall into misconceptions, have cognitive biases, and make mistakes when we think about others. Instead of individual blame, my focus as a psychologist for software teams has been on identifying pervasive patterns in the systems that we are both part of and creating with our own actions, and helping teams learn to shift those patterns toward more adaptive strategies and away from maladaptive ones. The dynamic nature of our beliefs can be scary, but it's the very thing that allows us to learn, grow, and change.

It also means that when you invest in learning more adaptive strategies that work with rather than against your mind, it can protect you even when you have to navigate inside a Brains-in-Jars organization. Across my research, I've seen that developers who report being on teams that highly value open and safe learning, and feel a strong sense that they belong and are welcomed in software and by their teams see a cascade of benefits. These developers report feeling less threat, fear, and anxiety at work. They're also both more productive as individuals and more likely to be on highly effective teams. In the following chapters, we'll dive into the scientific reasons that strong cultural alternatives to Brains-in-Jars models work so well. These thriving developers show us it's possible to get there.

Think back to those brains in jars. Early scientists often made the mistake of assuming that everything important to our thinking could be reduced down to simplistic models of brain regions or isolated cells. But as we invented new and more accurate ways to see *real* activity across the body, we've learned that so much of what human beings feel and experience happens as part of a dynamic system. The central nervous system isn't the full picture; like developers iterating on problems, our distributed nervous system implements change, signals back to the brain, and cross-talks with other complex systems across our entire bodies. Those brains in jars may have seemed tangible and irrefutable, but they were actually dead samples, detached from the living, breathing, thinking reality of what brains evolved to do. Likewise, when we look at how real software developers solve collaborative and distributed problems, we find that they do it with a sophisticated suite of activities and skillsets that provide a far richer picture than tired stereotypes. The Brains-in-Jars model is a dangerous choice for technical teams precisely because it can produce a just-good-enough outcome for a while. But the end result is an organization that throws away real value and understanding. Fixing this is worth it to get to joyful collaborations that drive innovation, a long-term healthy workforce that our networks, nations, and neighborhoods are relying on, and more meaning and well-being for the millions of software developers who are building our world.

ABOUT THE EVIDENCE

To develop a counter-vision, we need evidence about what good psychology for developers looks like. However, the longer I listened to software teams and their fascinating stories about technological innovation that showed the connection between psychologically healthy environments and "good code," the more I became convinced that most organizations are plagued by a knowledge gap that keeps them from the very tools they need to break out of Brains-in-Jars thinking.

How we talk about software teams often fails to integrate good science. Even though there are plenty of individually helpful anecdotes, case studies, and in some cases large-scale empirical studies about software teams, I was frustrated that in most industry commentary on software teams and their outcomes, integrating core scientific findings about how to move human behavior seemed like an afterthought. One challenge we face is that it is difficult and expensive to do large-scale research. For example, construct development and validation (in other words, making sure our measures perform well and map onto what we think they're measuring) can be rare in software research.[44,45] On the other hand, psychology is rich in examples of what helps steer better outcomes in general and has created many constructs and measures but rarely studies software developers. Software development is ever-changing, and people who can harness its power face unique responsibilities, pressures, and experiences. Too few of those experiences have made their way into the scientific record. I knew that I needed to propose a way forward that was rooted in psychology but also tested and validated against the real concerns and specific, situated challenges of people working on software.

My aim is to provide you with a guide to some of the most interesting and important evidence from psychological sciences that I've used to help real software teams and developers. To do that, we're going to take a pluralistic and wide-ranging approach, examining evidence from a diverse range of methods, topics, and teams. Throughout each chapter you'll notice references, a scientific way of giving you a map to the original source that supports the argument I'm making. Many of these references are specific examples from rich areas of science, and their literature reviews are a great guide to how scientists think and study certain topics. As an experimental psychologist, that's my primary focus. But understanding people is a challenge taken up across many fields. Both the researchers and the practitioners whose insights inform this book might fall under many labels: behavioral science, software research, cognitive science, behavioral economics, human-computer interaction, design, systems thinking, and other fields make an appearance in these pages.

Many research methods can create evidence about human behavior. Each method has its advantages and disadvantages, and every individual study has limitations (we'll walk through more of this in Chapter 6). Surveys are a way to capture direct reports of experience but are subject to biases such as social desirability (for instance, people are reluctant to report things about themselves that are true but distasteful) and a wide range of perceptual biases (for instance, our memories are fallible over time). Laboratory experiments are fantastic for allowing scientists to directly manipulate the nuances of different variables, but lab experiments can sometimes be an artificial proxy that doesn't perfectly recreate complex real-world conditions. Observational studies take us closer to the real world of practitioners, but because of that, they introduce many factors that are out of researchers' control, including hidden confounds we may not notice or be able to control for. And using large-scale trace data available in the world (such as many software metrics) can bring us tremendous data but means we're frequently hunting through variables that weren't really designed to answer human questions. As we explore the science, we'll also try to keep in mind its limitations.

Science is as much a human endeavor as software development is, so we also need to consider the context of evidence. Because knowing how to change human behavior is so valuable, there's sometimes a rush to put novel, compelling, or flashy findings into practice that have yielded disappointing results, and many grandiose claims based on shaky or exaggerated evidence have fallen flat. Thankfully, this reckoning has also led to many positive structural changes in the way we evaluate behavioral science, and many areas of social science now promote a much stronger emphasis on replicating findings and improving methods. For example, more labs now collaborate on joint replication projects, and more scientific fields have a dialogue about the robustness of research findings. Like software development, social scientists achieve much closer results to each other when our questions are more precisely defined, suggesting that better clarity about what we mean and what we're measuring to ask helps us move forward. Method improvement is also an ongoing part of making our evidence stronger. For example, psychologists have often created brand-new measures to chase down their ideas instead of re-using, re-validating, and re-testing the same measures as a community, which can make it harder for us to synthesize across many small variations in *how* we study the same topics. Like all of science, psychology hasn't yet studied every topic that matters to people. There are also systematic gaps in our research evidence. One glaring example is that many areas of behavioral science have a history of relying too heavily on what we call "WEIRD" samples: recruiting participants and generalizing about all of human behavior from groups of people that are primarily Western, Educated, Industrialized, Rich, Democratic.[46–51]

I've aimed to provide context and synthesize where existing research can reasonably inform the choices we make toward others and our teams. One of the things that I've invested a great deal of effort into in my studies is broadly recruiting across demographic categories such as national origin, race and ethnicity, gender identities, and career experiences, allowing us to analyze our findings with large, international research samples so that you can have greater confidence in the strength of this evidence. However, there remains a great need to invest in more research that elevates the voices of all developers. We have also published many of our methods so that you can reuse the very same research measures that we've tested and learned from in my studies. Maybe you'll find something different than we did!

When selecting the science behind this book, I used several criteria to evaluate the strength of evidence: emphasizing methods and not just findings, considering whether there are multiple studies that support an overarching research story, and inviting you to compare and contrast the scientific record with your own experiences. Here are the guidelines I followed in reading (and re-reading!) the evidence:

1. Rather than just highlighting isolated effects and findings, provide context about how researchers gathered that evidence in the first place and examples of how we can push for deeper understanding. This means that for many of the studies cited in this book, I read not only the original paper but also a number of the related papers that cited the original work, as well as the references that the researchers were influenced by. The empirical examples in this book point to bodies of literature and theoretical perspectives that emerged over many years of scientific inquiry.

2. Rather than over-indexing on the findings of a single study, make sure that every major argument has been tested in multiple contexts and is supported by at least several different forms of evidence—for example, qualitative stories from the field and directly from software practitioners, but also large-scale quantitative studies. I've frequently

chosen well-cited papers (in other words, papers that have been influential enough for other scientists to name them as critical references), but because counting citations is an imperfect measure of impact (rather like counting lines of code), I've also tried to include small-but-mighty studies that highlighted an unusual insight or provided a significant provocation.

3. Rather than taking scientific findings as rigid laws that can only be passively consumed, dialogue with the evidence, and compare and contrast it with your own experience. Throughout, I hope that you'll take a scientist's skeptical-but-curious lens to how we operationalize and measure human experience. I've tried to prioritize researchers not only because their findings are interesting, but because they're careful and intentional about their strength of evidence and open to criticism of their theories.

Scientists and practitioners only get to the truth when we're in dialogue. Scientists don't always get every element of the story right; we're often focused on making sure we can measure a small number of things very rigorously but might lag behind the real world. Practitioners, on the other hand, are often focused on generalizing about large actionable patterns and use their lived experience to develop important intuitions about what matters but don't always have access to powerful evidence at scale. It's because I think we have so much to offer each other that it's become my mission to bridge the gap between developer science and software teams. But none of us can do it alone: I encourage you to continually support, partner with, and demand a science that recognizes, gives voice to, and protects your important lived experiences. After all, rigor is a form of care.

QUESTIONS TO ASK WHILE EVALUATING WHETHER YOU'RE STUCK IN BRAINS-IN-JARS

- What do I think truly explains success here? What feels like it "counts" as successful to others? How do we know that we are successful? Do managers and leaders define success differently than developers do?
- How is effort recognized in my organization? Are people rewarded for hard work on tough problems even if it didn't lead to the outcomes we want?

- Does my technical area have a career path that feels sustainable? Does everyone burn out of this specialization? Can I identify things that protect me when I need to do hard, unpredictable technical work?
- Do we take a long-term perspective on our work? Do we care about human outcomes like developers' well-being? Are we including human outcomes and experiences in our decision-making? If we think we are, how are we making sure this represents all developers? How are we making it safe for people to tell us about difficult experiences?

CHAPTER 3

More Bands and Fewer Rockstars

FROM SOLITARY TINKERER TO SOCIAL LEARNER

It's a lovely morning in the lab, and you are a New Caledonian crow. Bright eyed and inquisitive, your attention and cognition are laser-focused on your key objective: finding food. You explore your space and detect the faint but unmistakable smell of a small chunk of meat that appears in your enclosure every morning. Victory!

But something is different today. Unlike every morning before, there's a strange obstacle between you and your food. The food sits in a small bucket with a handle, but the bucket is trapped inside a tall plastic tube, too far down for you to reach. You consider your dilemma: food, obstacle . . . and then you see something else, a long, straight wire in your enclosure. You seize upon it—a potential tool! You're a clever crow, and you understand how to use novel objects in your environment, like sticks, for tasks such as dislodging objects. Holding the wire with your beak, you poke it into the tube. But the bucket stays firmly in place. You fail once, twice, three times.

Then something clicks. You need a different solution, shaped like your new problem. Your crow brain fires with resolve. You use your fabulous beak to push the wire against the ground, bending it into a gentle curve. Holding one end of the wire, you insert it into the opaque tube, secure the bucket handle in the wire's curve, and pull out your prize. Actual victory! Day's quest satisfied, you feast. And somewhere in your crow mind, you store away a memory of this curved wire solution.

DOI: 10.1201/9781003589112-3

This wonderful moment of tool invention isn't fictional. It was documented by a scientific team interested in how we make tools and come up with solutions—and here '*we*' means minds more diverse than just human beings, because the science of problem-solving can include animal cognition. In their report, Alex Weir, Jackie Chappell, and Alex Kacelnik detailed the remarkable success of a crow who was able to improvise a new tool to solve the problem that the researchers came up with: retrieving food in a small bucket inside of a tube which could only be fished out if the crow made a hook from a flexible wire.[1] Not to be outdone by crows, rooks can also shape hooks out of wire despite not using tools in the wild and learn to drop rocks down the tube of an apparatus to force a platform to collapse and reveal a worm (as of this writing, you can watch some great videos of bird solution-crafting in the supplements for these studies. And people say reading citations is boring!).[2]

Such demonstrations are delightful even if they only help us appreciate the minds with whom we share this planet. But science stories like this also contribute important insights about our own cognition. Unlike other animals, humans are remarkably adept at using novel tools, so much that our technologies traverse the globe. What helps us do this? Driven by this question, psychologists set out to test how well young human minds generate novel solutions and discovered something surprising. Despite humanity's collective prowess at tool innovation, children younger than about 5 to 7 years are pretty terrible at it! Facing the exact same tests, toddlers are consistently worse at solution-crafting with novel objects than crows.[3] But any parent can tell you that toddlers are remarkably competent at operating technology. Toddlers successfully interact with hundreds of objects they've never seen before, from plates to smartphones. And over our lifespans, we learn to create and manipulate technologies, innovating with incredible fluency. So how do we get there?

The answer lies in the fundamental architecture of our cognition and points us toward new answers about what drives technological success. Rather than prioritizing solo solutions, our cognition prioritizes being a phenomenal *imitator.* And we're also exceptional teachers. For example, when scientists model a solution rather than asking children to invent it, even very young children immediately grasp it. After that, young children are able to teach a modeled solution to other children with a high degree of fidelity.[4] Especially compared to when they're asked to generate novel solutions, the success rate that young children achieve with *taught* solutions is dramatic. As long as they have access to a good teacher, young children can even achieve adult levels of success at difficult tasks. With these building blocks, making learning and teaching swift and efficient is how shared culture helps individuals coordinate to scaffold many different innovations together, pass them on, and achieve transformative advancements in how individuals are able to live and create.[5] Our capacity for social learning scales individual problem-solving.

All of this might feel a little strange if you're used to assuming the most productive thing a developer's mind does is generate novel solutions alone. Our creative and generative capacities are indeed incredible, but this reframe—thinking of our mind as a social, imitative learner rather than a solitary tinkerer—is the first of several reframes to help you invest in the strategies that cultivate greater software success at scale. One simple trick I've found helpful for making this mental switch? Change a single word. Rather than getting stuck on the worn-out and contentious concept of "*developer productivity*," in this chapter we're going to focus on the factors that most reliably empower developer *problem-solving.*

For organizations, unlocking technical problem-solving isn't just theoretically interesting. It's a make-or-break challenge. Successfully turning individual solutions into technology advancements, and ensuring developers consistently engage in iterative problem-solving, is the foundation for software outcomes that create business value. Inaccurate models about developer problem-solving are dangerous. Imagine a senior developer who generates plenty of code but is routinely intolerable to teammates and hostile to collaboration. Evaluating productivity through the narrow lens of Brains-in-Jars thinking, a manager might believe their coding velocity and quantity is all that matters, and see all that activity as good problem-solving. But widen our view to include the long-term effects of this style of work, and we're likely to rapidly reveal that individual quantities of code fail to outweigh the costly devastation they're leaving in their wake that suppresses collective productivity. In fact, even with strong individual skills, people who can't participate in shared work usually hit roadblocks in what they can implement alone. We are rarely accurate observers of our own work. Perhaps they open the organization up to risk by piling up unmaintainable code, failing to update their knowledge, or never integrating creative feedback.

To target sustainable problem-solving, I often think: "more bands and fewer rockstars." It's easy to get caught up in the glamorous idea that all we need is charismatic rockstars, solo acts capable of dazzling on stage, even if offstage, they sever relationships and wreak havoc with erratic, dysfunctional behavior. But if you're a music manager focusing on the real business, what you might dream about is finding a really functional *band*. Bands also create dazzling performances, but the ones who stay together are also collections of people who remain capable of consistent creativity over time, complementing each other's diverse strengths. And when you're leading an entire organization, successfully delivering software might be more like operating on the level of a music festival, ensuring that many different creative acts come together at the right times to create experiences that users and customers value. Solitary rockstars who burn out in a blaze of glory make good stories but bad investments.

The "more bands and fewer rockstars" mindset helps us avoid getting stuck on a second big mistake: assuming we *have* to tolerate psychologically unhealthy behaviors if we want software success. Across technology, both our pre-existing stereotypes about programming ability and the ways that our post-hoc explanations for success are often biased make us prone to *attribution errors* about what will predict software success. Many early investigations into programming achievement focused on overly narrow individual attributes, a history that's still reflected in many of the processes we use for hiring or the technical stories that we applaud. But because of the immense power of social learning, the evidence consistently reveals that focusing on a healthier collaborative environment is our best shot at increasing the probability of a breakthrough. A mental model that tells us to only look at developers' short-term and isolated output misses the social thinking that software decision-making relies on or dismisses it as a lesser form of activity that takes away from "productivity."

Of course, individuals are capable of powerful breakthroughs. But technology problem-solving takes advantage of developers' remarkable capacity to imitate and flexibly apply the solutions that they see from others, and learning to see the power of social learning can help you create it. Cultural and social factors are often better predictors of real-world achievement than individual characteristics, even for types of problem-solving that we often believe must be driven by individual differences, like math and science.[6] Exposure to other people's thinking, their experimentation, and the ways that past minds solved past problems train our capacity for reasoning across a given domain.[7,8] Developers make sense of new technologies by paying attention to signals in the reactions of their communities.[9] Calling software development *social* doesn't mean I'm asking you to believe all developers like going to parties. It just means that solving software problems takes advantage of our remarkable ability to imitate, be influenced by, learn from, and build on others' solutions. Social learning is both an essential catalyst for individual problem-solving and the way we scale it to others.

As many developers have told me, it's not just about how much code you write, but making sure it's the right code. Enough space to build collective social knowledge and ramp-up into domain expertise is a critical piece of this process at the individual level. Getting it wrong could mean you hire and promote for the wrong skills, reward the wrong behaviors, and miss important work happening in your organization. But getting it right helps level up teams, technologies, organizations, and industries. In this chapter, we're going to myth-bust some common misconceptions about software problem-solving and unpack why the most effective tactics to improve it are improving problem-solving environments and learning strategies.

A BRIEF HISTORY OF FAILED ATTEMPTS TO PREDICT GOOD DEVELOPERS

It's 1968. Most households in America don't yet have a computer, universities like Yale are experiencing both public debates (by leadership) and secret meetings (by groups pushing for change) on the question of whether to open their doors to women, and it's the year in which an important Civil Rights Act passes.[10] This is not necessarily the year to which we might turn our gaze to find the most comprehensive and enlightened model of human intellectual ability. However, this was the year in which a surprisingly influential case study was published, "Exploratory experimental studies comparing online and offline programming performance," from Sackman, Ericson, and Grant.[11] This unassuming paper has an opening salvo whose more ominous notes are perhaps only detectable to those most fluent in academese: "the human costs of computer programming continue to rise and one day will probably greatly exceed hardware costs." In other words, we'd better start to understand how to sort out the most gifted developers from the rest of them, because they're turning out to be quite costly. Feel familiar?

With a small sample (two groups of six) described as experienced programmers, participants were asked to complete a series of problems considered representative of debugging from the era. Successful performance was judged by the time it took a programmer to work through a task. The unusual tasks (including solving algebraic problems) are clearly reflective of programming in this early era. But despite the chasm between programming then and now, there's a recognizable through line of attempting to detect who's capable of good problem-solving by observing how fast individuals worked an abstract, idealized problem. Technical interviews deployed by companies all over the world are still criticized by developers for using a similar approach.[12] The ominous opening line about the cost of the human is finished with a few familiar conclusions by the end of the paper: that there are consistent individual differences in programming ability and that technology businesses should detect and remove "low performers" from software development based on their work (what passes unacknowledged is that the people observed are almost certainly all men; participant characteristics don't get an acknowledgment in the paper, where people are described as "programmer trainees," but time is even referred to as "programmer man-hours").

This case study went on to be cited as settled science. One example, Fred Brooks' influential book of essays on software, *The Mythical Man Month*, repeats Sackman et al.'s claims about best and worst programmers and dresses this shaky claim up as business sense in a cost-for-productivity thought experiment: "the ratios between best and worst performances averaged about 10:1 on productivity measurements. . . . In short the $20,000/year programmer may well be 10 times as productive as the $10,000/year one." Note that the description of the evidence has moved from being about the simple time it took people to complete a lab simulation of a small programming task, to being treated as a comprehensive measure of productivity and a robust population estimate.[13] One of the first proposed estimates for persistent individual differences between developers—that a few rare developers produce 10x more or work 10x faster than others—was born.

Frankly, as a psychologist who's long been interested in how we measure (and mismeasure) human potential, when I read back through this chain of claims, I found it disturbing but not surprising. This story is straight out of the Lone Genius trap, where outcomes driven by many complex factors are narrowly attributed to immutable traits of individuals. For many domains, but especially technical and scientific work, we often internalize the limiting stereotype that true talent can only be available to a chosen few, which leads us to discount the possibility of individual growth. Our minds have a strong tendency to see behaviors in terms of fixed individual traits, even when environmental and situational factors are at play. On top of this, programming specifically is often relentlessly presented as an innate ability rather than a learned skill, a stereotype that many people internalize as early as 6 years old, right around when we begin to think of others' skills and ability at all. We tend to associate programming ability with abilities like math, where we *also* routinely overestimate the size and scope of individual differences while ignoring evidence that achievement in these areas is greatly shifted by culture and environment.[14–17]

Counterarguments that explore the powerful causal role of the environment and social learning in software outcomes have always existed alongside the 10x stories, like Gerald Weinberg's Psychology of Computer Programming, or arguments from software authors Tom DeMarco and Tim Lister who argued that environmental affordances could be large enough to explain observed variances between programmers.[18,19] But the individualistic myth is hard to shake and the assumptions behind it can warp organizational thinking because they continue to show up in how we try to detect technical aptitude. In the first years of software development, companies like IBM eagerly adopted programming aptitude tests despite its limited predictive validity for real work outcomes.[20] If you've ever had to jump through the hoops of a strange "cognitive assessment" for a software job, you may have encountered this legacy. I regularly see wild, poorly evidenced claims that organizations can predict how good someone will be at software with distal ability tests, or even that we can predict who can code with facial scans, eyetracking, or noisy and imprecise measures of brain activity, despite no proof of these measures' validity. These claims aren't remotely in keeping with the real science of assessment.

While people's individual abilities do vary, it's important to keep in mind just how incredibly difficult it is to accurately assess potential. How we define aptitude (a person's capacity for *future* performance) remains the subject of decades of heated debate, and purely cognitive measures often fail to capture the practical expertise and strategies that make people successful in the real world.[21] In fact, assessment scientists conclude that even large-scale assessments, with lots of effort and research behind them, should only be taken as measures of learning and interpreted in light of structural and environmental effects, not as direct measures of immutable individual traits.[22] We also know that differences in the skills people have for test taking, such as how they regulate effort or how well they understand the constraints of a test, can muddy assessment accuracy.[23] The amount of time someone takes to solve a problem isn't a direct measure of their problem-solving efficiency or solution quality, a critique long made by psychologists who study assessments and what they fail to predict.[24] Even the way we structure tests can distort our view of aptitude. Many technical evaluations are static rather than dynamic, giving test takers one shot to solve a problem, setting right or wrong answers, and providing no feedback. But dynamic tests, which provide feedback after incorrect attempts and allow people to iterate over time and correct their mistakes, give us a richer, more multidimensional picture of someone's abilities, which can be far more predictive of outcomes.[25] You may have felt this difference in your own career if you've ever failed a whiteboarding interview because of a frustrating misconception, or conversely, experienced getting to have an authentic back-and-forth with an interviewer that taught you both more about how the other person thinks and problem-solves.

Plus, simplistic laboratory tasks shouldn't be generalized to the many tasks of modern-day software engineering. This is because of a problem that scientists call *ecological validity*: how well the variables and structure of a study reflect what happens in the real world. In fact, even far more robustly tested assessments *often* fail to predict a large amount of the variance in how people problem-solve in the real world, meaning they're not capturing important drivers of real-world success. And small case studies simply don't include enough people to ask whether measures perform over representative samples (for a start, any assessment you want to apply to the entire population of software developers, or estimate you want to make about them, absolutely must be tested across many different demographic groups). Far too many historical assessments of ability have been loaded with cultural biases, meaning they can make unfair assumptions about the cultural background or knowledge of a test-taker and can systematically underestimate people's true abilities at scale.[26–28] One compelling example of this is that supposed cognitive deficits can be erased or even reversed when measures of them are redesigned to better reflect the problems that people practiced solving in their daily lives.[29] Careful meta-analytic work, along with experimental research, has shown that grades *and* tests can systematically underestimate the abilities of marginalized people who are forced to devote some of their cognitive energy to processing worrying about whether an evaluator will discriminate against them.[30] Even when we think we're looking at individual performance, we're always also measuring the social and structural effects around that individual.

With this complexity in mind, I was already skeptical of the idea that we should focus on detecting fixed individual differences if we want to design for successful software teams. But in a large-scale research project, I found myself in a position to put it to the empirical test, exploring just how complex the real picture is when we look at developer time on task. In a study we named "No silver bullets: why understanding cycle time is messy, not magic," led by my collaborator John Flournoy, we analyzed over 55,000 observations of cycle time across 216 companies, work done by 11,398 software developers for an entire year.[31] John is a social scientist and statistician who's driven statistical methodologies for thorny human questions, such as measuring well-being over time. All the companies in our study followed a ticket process to catalogue a "start" and "close" for tickets assigned to individual developers. This gave us a time measure poetically similar to the task-based "programmer hours" idea that Sackman et al. had tried to simulate in their lab task, but we were looking at thousands of developers in the real world. While carefully preserving the anonymity of individuals meant we didn't know developers' jobs or project contexts, the scale of this dataset meant we were able to examine cycle times while accounting at least in part for their collaborative networks (for instance, including when multiple developers interacted with the same ticket), along with variance between the companies, using Bayesian hierarchical modeling. What this meant was we could look not *just* at individual developers but also ask whether cycle times fell into larger patterns between organizations, as well as look at patterns that seem influenced more by *when* the developer was working than any attribute of an individual.

With this powerful dataset, we asked just how good an explanation individual differences was for variance in cycle times when compared to our other factors. We were also curious about how consistent individual cycle time was. Our results looked shockingly different from the blithe assumption that immutable individual differences would be reliably revealed by software time metrics. All those thousands of software development tasks did not resolve into neatly consistent patterns, with a few rare rockstars predictably outpacing everyone around them. Instead, software development cycle times were wildly variable and difficult to predict, differing both within individuals and between organizations. An individual developer's past ticket closing rate was not a good predictor for their future rate. While we found some signals for lowering cycle time, these matched the commonsense wisdom most software practitioners already know. For example, we found a positive association between more days that developers were able to actively commit code and shorter cycle times—likely signaling the days when they had more focus time, a situational factor rather than an individual characteristic.

Our evidence shows that even if the *only* thing you care about is predicting developer velocity, a great deal more context about the situational and environmental factors is necessary to accurately predict outcomes and compare velocity between types of engineering work. If the developers in an organization are being dragged down by a planning cycle, and it's showing up in their cycle times, fix the planning process. Our evidence also shows that if you focus on gathering data about developers' average task completion times without any care for the heterogeneous nature of their tasks, you'll be comparing a lot of apples to oranges and generating meaningless metrics. Demanding that people meet simplistic benchmarks, aggregated without a principled reason, can collapse meaningful differences into mush. Developers working on highly complex tickets may get blamed for not being as fast as developers who are given easy tasks, even if they're actually succeeding at their work. Likewise, teams who continually take on more difficult problems will be penalized when compared to teams that get the easy side of the technical problem. Squashing collective problem-solving down to fit an individualistic box distorts how we see it.

This may feel familiar because it matches what many software practitioners find themselves criticizing when they look at attempts to measure developer productivity: too little focus on the systemic levers that constrain or empower problem-solving, too much noise, and too little respect for how hard it is to predict unknown problem spaces. Why do we so easily fall into assuming software outcomes are driven only by individual developers, even though we also widely acknowledge that software outcomes are complex and hard to predict? I suspect that learning to recognize when you're falling into the *fundamental attribution error* can help. One of the most famous cognitive biases psychology has ever uncovered, the fundamental attribution error leads us to favor explanations centered on innate characteristics over situational ones. We frequently overly attribute outcomes to individual merit, forget the role of environmental factors when we look back at past success, and make inaccurate inferences about people's innate characteristics from the situations we see them in.[32,33] Simply observing a difference in how people perform on a task doesn't mean we have evidence for an immutable individual difference that should be seen as a trait. Psychological evidence at scale across millions of learners has shown us that performance encodes large social factors and, compellingly, that even long-lasting performance gaps can vanish when people are given more equitable education.[6]

As you reflect on your experiences with Brains-in-Jars organizations, you might catch the fundamental attribution error haunting the stories we default to about software triumphs. Rather than crediting the infrastructure team decisions that allowed a single software developer to rapidly brainstorm and test specific solutions with less friction, we credit the software developer. Rather than crediting the distributed open-source project work that allowed a product to flourish on the market, we credit a technical founder. The lesson here is not that individual aptitude and effort never play a role, they're just often a far smaller piece of the puzzle than we think. In the real world, individual performance is rarely the strongest predictor of group outcomes. In fact, the strongest predictors of developers' self-reported productivity tend to be social and communal factors, like peer support and work structures that allow for more self-directed problem-solving.[34] Focusing on improving the problem-solving environment *around* developers is the evidence-backed strategy.

FINDING ANCHORS WITH SOCIAL LEARNING

"You can spend days trying to find an anchor in the code," a software engineer told me in an interview. I was captivated by that imagery, which he used to describe ramping into a new codebase. Despite stereotypes about lonely coders sitting in the dark generating esoteric computations like wizards, rarely are technical contributors starting their days writing code from first principles. In most roles, software tasks start with staring into a vast ecosystem of other people's programming, architectural, sociocultural, and project choices, and deciding how to make the leap from mere observer to active contributor. Most people across our organization succeeding at this type of task, over and over again, is what keeps software working and injects new ideas into our work.

But even if it's typical, integrating into others' code is no trivial challenge. In fact it's not just code: to identify the right problems to solve, developers need to navigate the less-easy-to-name accoutrements that shaped other people's decisions about which code to create, like documentation and chat logs, decision records and software philosophies, social norms around review and quality and safety thresholds, code styles and political battles over code styles, and for many teams now, a rapidly emerging new infrastructure of automation across AI-augmented design and development. Picture joining an orchestra while it's already playing a symphony you've only heard once before, or leaping into a laboratory experiment in the middle of someone else's ongoing protocol. Given all of this, we should take a moment to step back from all of our fears about software complexity and marvel at how good developers are at social learning on a daily basis. It is, as many a senior engineer has ruefully told me, incredible that all this works as much as it does.

Like the physical infrastructures of water or electricity that allow us to share together in common utilities with significantly less effort, software ecosystems are vast networks of many people's solutions that supercharge individual problem-solving. Other knowledge workers have solved past problems, enabling us to focus on our own. These solutions are shared across both time and space, and developers continuously collaborate with new innovations to apply old insights to new problems. The flexibility and socially interwoven quality of software problem-solving gives truth to the old software joke about a critical skill being learning to be a "senior copy/paste engineer." Not having to start from scratch is one of humanity's greatest superpowers as a social species: we love to beg, borrow, and steal—and perhaps less appreciated but equally important, we love to give our solutions back to our communities when we discover them. The history of software has been shaped by the dynamic exchange of novel solutions. If open source software is coming to your mind, you're not wrong. Eric von Hippel, an economist specializing in the dynamics of innovation, calls the open disclosure and sharing of solutions *free revealing*: when user-innovators generously share knowledge so it feeds back into the system as a whole, producing large economic benefits.[35,36] Likewise, software researcher Mary Shaw described navigating "open resource coalitions" as a defining behavior in programming, including composing across software components, third-party resources, and layers of technologies.[37]

The point is, despite stereotypes about Lone Geniuses, solving software problems requires social cognition. Our minds' adaptive imitation and teaching strategies can be seen in the working practices of developers as they go beyond static textbook knowledge about code and learn from the specific decision paths chosen by other developers. And because technologies shift rapidly with consequences that cascade through dependencies, developers rely on each other to stay current, adapt, triage, and innovate in this ever-changing landscape. In one powerful demonstration of this, a group of researchers analyzed 21 million lines of code over 14 years of online programming contests and found that solutions propagate in the patterns social learning predicts: individuals' problem-solving was transformed by previous generations of tweaks and leaps.[38] "Finding anchors" was a developer's description of learning from others' problem-solving as he identified relationships between parts of the code that he understood. From initial anchors, he built certainty outward, like a rock climber testing potential holds on a route, reconstructing someone else's thinking. "I spend nearly as much time reading, doing these small pilot tests, and building an understanding as I ever do writing code," he told me, "But the time I spend understanding makes my code way more valuable."

This eloquently describes the journey of moving from an outsider still exploring to a confident domain expert able to generate novel solutions that drive complex outcomes. Crossing the explorer-expert bridge comes from building a working mental model, and being able to start our work on top of someone else's thinking gets us there faster. Crossing the explorer-expert bridge happens not just longitudinally in our careers as we move from novice to expert, but whenever we need to form new domain expertise.[39,40] Across hundreds of different contexts, developers have shared examples with me of this critical shift from exploring to appropriately identifying the next solution in the chain. Using social learning to bridge the explorer-expert chasm characterizes much of the deep work experienced by domain experts as they build their tacit knowledge, finding the specific and contextual ways that more global skills need to translate into workable solutions.[41,42]

Let's pull up from that moment of ramping into an unfamiliar codebase and think about tasks across a single day. Here the social learning in software development becomes even clearer. Imagine that we're able to quietly observe a software developer at a small startup beginning work on a new problem identified as part of feature work designated a priority by her cross-functional team. Her initial materials include input from product research, advice from her manager about a few possible solutions she might explore, assignment to a specific part of the problem, and an example use case, along with her own skillsets developed over the last several years of learning a new programming language. She's new to the startup, and therefore new to the codebase, and so devotes some time to understanding and testing how her area of work might relate to existing technologies. Since it's a startup, she also recognizes the constraints in what they can afford and looks for online examples from other people in startups discussing how to efficiently work in those technologies with a low budget. She realizes that the use case has been defined generally but that there are specific decisions which need clarification, so she reaches out to a colleague. While waiting to hear back on that, she starts to craft some initial code that she knows she'll need and identifies an unexpected gap in her knowledge about a framework used in the codebase. By the end of the day, she reaches out to a senior member of her team to update with her early idea for how to solve the problem and is excited to learn her team has a tool they use to implement a particular part of the solution, which will help her move more swiftly. They make plans to meet the next day, and conscious of the need to maintain her thinking, she documents a few notes about her in-progress work to look at the next morning.[43]

By getting concrete about the tasks across just one workday for one individual, we can check the attribution error that pushes us to hunt for one single magical immutable attribute inside an individual and appreciate the bigger picture. Software development requires completing many different types of tasks, where different cognitive strategies may help best. These tasks are scaffolded by *both* individual and social work practices. On even just the individual level, problem-solving is best described by a word that both psychologists and software engineers love: complex. We use many different elements of our minds, over time, to achieve our goals. For this, we recruit core cognitive building blocks such as the executive functions (put simply, this is the collection of cognitive processes that our minds use to direct our behavior. For instance, inhibition, working memory, attentional control, and cognitive flexibility). But our multisystem minds also bring these capacities together with higher-order thinking. This is where we get creativity, planning, causal reasoning, and social learning—all different types of thinking which can help developers to design and implement solutions.

Psychologists who study culture take a very long (across centuries!) and very broad (between and within species!) view of cognition and problem-solving. From this perspective, all of software development is just an example of our human proclivity to work with tools. Our ability to marshal and draw on multifaceted cognitive and social mechanisms plays a critical role in the development of tool innovation across human societies. One strong piece of evidence for this is that cross-cultural research has measured strong associations between children's development of these capacities, and their ability to produce solutions with tools, in many cultures around the world.[4] The diversity of our mind's strategies also makes us more resilient: a single person can foreground and background different strengths as they work, which gives us a tremendous ability to still succeed even if we struggle in one area. It also means we can't ever reduce software development down to just one "thing" in our brains. At certain points on a problem-solving journey, a developer might need to lean into creativity to follow an unexpected edge case. At other points, she may be better served by using strong inhibitory control to focus. As we solve tasks, we flexibly harness diverse and powerful forms of cognition. Achieving complex goals requires maintaining problem-solving over time and directing an adaptive orchestra of abilities.

COGNITIVE SCAFFOLDING WITH METACOGNITIVE STRATEGIES

Narrow cognitive functions and tiny velocity gains seem like poor intervention targets to change technology outcomes at scale. So what helps individuals navigate multidimensional developer problem-solving? Developing the metacognition, or thinking-about-thinking, that helps developers choose better *strategies*.

Take a moment to remember a class you took, if you went to high school or college (not everyone who becomes a developer did; an amazing thing about software is just how much people can break into it without a single degree in their pocket. Across my research, more than 60% of software developers report self-teaching skills needed for their job, and every developer I've interviewed agrees that life-long learning is a core part of being a developer). Do you remember how you studied for this class? Like many students, you may have devoted evenings leading up to a test to "cramming," staring deep into the pages of a textbook and reading passages over and over again, attempting to imprint the words on your brain.

But if you're like most students, odds are that this strategy didn't work as well as you thought it did. One of the problems with observing our own minds is we're often wrong about what kind of effort leads to the outcomes we want.[44] Students studying for a test often cram, but cramming leads to worse performance on tests compared to more spaced-out, small but frequent study sessions. But the vivid perception of effort often leads us into less efficient strategies. Cramming feels effortful, and so we tend to remember effort as performance and enthusiasm as success. Likewise, as you reflect back over your experience writing code, thinking through architecture decisions, or untangling a messy knot of technical decision-making, you might be able to remember days you spent mired in inefficient strategies. But you might also recall crossing that explorer-expert bridge as, like the developer in my study, you learned how to find your own "anchor points," methods, and habits for traversing and building your mental models of code and technical problems. These can be game-changing moments that change *how* we work, and the psychology of learning has a term for it: upgrading our metacognitive strategies.

Metacognitive strategies are a powerful intervention lever. Importantly, unlike many aspects of our individual cognition, one of the things that makes them a lever is the fact that they're *malleable.* Our thinking strategies shift how well we're actually able to benefit from the effort we pour into a task.[45] Including metacognition in how we see developer problem-solving can help us understand why experts in a domain can come out of the same amount of time as less skilled practitioners with more reflection, self-monitoring, and robust learning outcomes. Anders Ericsson, a psychologist who led widely influential research studying how expertise develops, argued that expert performance is best predicted as an outcome of acquiring complex skills over time. Even complex skills, which experts themselves struggle to articulate or explain, are often the result of acquired expertise and deliberate practice. If we want to understand how to foster expertise at the scale of organizations, Ericsson and other expertise scientists argue that we have to focus on the strategies experts use to *transcend* the limits of individual cognitive factors like working memory.[46,47] Expertise-forming strategies include structured exposure to worked examples in a domain and iterative practice that gives people concrete feedback on their understanding and work—exactly what developers get inside of a vibrant, social learning-friendly technology culture.

Metacognition even helps us untangle some of the mixed results we see during technology shifts, where some teams seem to struggle and some thrive. As software teams increasingly adopt AI and augmented development, shifting programming toward more management and abstract critical thinking, metacognition has been identified by software researchers as a key skill for developers to engage with these systems robustly, guarding against errors, and maintaining active problem-solving.[48,49] Developers' reflecting and self-monitoring about what tasks they automate and what they dive deep into are metacognitive skills, as is practicing strong self-regulation across complex collaborations. Despite how good all of this sounds, research from psychologists and cognitive scientists finds that predictable illusions can distract us from the types of effort that lead to better performance in the long run.[50] For instance, we often learn more efficiently and have stronger recall when we generate rather than simply passively consume content. This is called *the generation effect*. If you try to memorize a pre-determined list of words and compare two different techniques for studying, one where you're just staring at that list trying to review it, and the other where you quiz yourself using a list of words with some missing, forcing you to fill in the blank, you'll come out of that quiz strategy with a stronger memory for the new content.[51] But trying to generate answers also feels uncomfortable, like reaching for incomplete information, and often results in making more mistakes in the moment of learning, which can distract us from the actual long-term benefits we're gradually accruing. So when we're trying to learn we often default to passively consuming information, robbing ourselves of the learning-boosting impact of generation.

Thinking in terms of scaffolds, rather than replacement, can steer you toward learning. Shifting your metacognitive strategy toward active learning is a fantastic habit to improve problem-solving. I've often thought that the reason forums such as Stack Overflow had such a powerful impact on so many developers' careers was not just because developers could copy-paste others' code, but because articulating a specific problem, its blockers, and failed solutions to other developers was a good way to invoke the generation effect (not to mention a powerful way to practice social learning). Rubber ducking (fondly named for the practice some programmers maintain of discussing a problem with an inanimate object, such as a rubber duck) may provide a similar cognitive benefit. Retrieving previously learned information and trying to apply it to a new task is itself an active, learning-enhancing activity for our minds.[52] Practices that encourage developers to actively spend effort recalling their technological expertise and applying general strategies to a specific moment of problem-solving (say, in a paired programming session or a shared design session) help their minds to take advantage of retrieval-based learning.

Something that many developers already intuitively gravitate toward is also a metacognitive strategy: quickly getting our hands dirty in real, testable working examples in a problem space. People acquire skills better and more efficiently when they have real examples to learn from compared to problem-solving in isolation, which psychologists call the *worked example effect*. Worked examples help direct people's attention to the most critical aspects of a problem state, freeing up cognitive resources. One critical nuance, though, is that *experts* can fly through novel problem-space without the same cognitive overload as new learners (this is called expert reversal, when the opposite strategies help in unfamiliar domains compared to familiar domains). Bringing it back to programming automation, developers can benefit from a metacognitive strategy like distinguishing between novel tasks and domains where they're still learning (where you should find ways to use the generation effect and get worked examples), versus bringing more abstract automation to the work where they have significant expertise and familiarity.[53,54]

These metacognitive skills aren't just about individual choices. Whether developers are encouraged to engage in them can be environmentally supported or suppressed, something I've taken to calling *cognitive scaffolding* when I work with software teams who want to design for high-quality problem-solving habits. Saskia Giebl and co-authors explored the counterintuitive but powerful impact of using cognitive scaffolding to make sure people kept learning even when technology could generate the answers.[55] This study recruited 240 programming learners, all at a beginner level in coding. First, participants were taught basic programming concepts in Python. Next, participants were given a challenging task for a beginner, which required some of the same concepts they had just been taught—but with a catch. An extension of the concepts was needed to be successful (for instance, manipulating multiple variables, when they had been taught how to handle just one variable), which could be found with a web search. Half of the participants were randomly assigned to immediately access a web search, a more passive condition. The other half were instructed to attempt to solve the task first. For their outcome measure, rather than using the slippery assumption that "time on task" was all that mattered, the researchers used assessment principles to develop a multiple-choice concept test with many items that tapped into a principled measurement of common misconceptions and programming logic mistakes. The test was also graded by researchers who were blinded to the conditions that the participants were in. The pretest group—which had initially struggled at the problem with incomplete concept information—showed deeper understanding outcomes.

Even small metacognitive strategy shifts, like using pre-testing to actively engage with problems before you give yourself assistance, can deepen technical thinking. People often struggle to believe in the power of active learning and remain convinced that passively consuming a solution is a better use of their time than actively trying to generate one, even when shown the benefits of pretesting on their own memories and performance.[56] Metacognitive strategies like pretesting are so effective because they help us think more carefully about new information, prompting us to become more knowledgeable about our own misconceptions and knowledge gaps as we learn. And expert software practitioners—like experts across other knowledge work domains—seem to develop rich toolkits of metacognitive strategies to maximize their effort. Software researchers Marian Petre and Mary Shaw summarized over three decades of research on high-performing development teams and their strategies to promote creativity.[57] Experts continually use thoughtful contrasting to spark creativity, moving between solutions and approaches to challenge their thinking. These accounts show expert software practitioners tapping into metacognitive habits like generating, worked examples, and active learning.

Metacognition lights our way to another valuable reframe on developer problem-solving. Because of the industry-level stereotypes about developer learning and thinking, good developer problem-solving is constantly described as "frictionless." The more ease developers experience, we assume, the better developers are flowing through solution-crafting. Now of course, meaningless friction at work is undoubtedly a waste of time and energy, and can be profoundly demotivating. Increasing abstraction and automation has also had a profound effect on how easily developers can do certain tasks, which is beautifully distributed problem-solving. But if we don't have good metacognition, feeling friction can also be a false signal to our minds, pushing us to divest too soon from the work that pays off. Getting better at problem-solving *should* feel effortful: active learning is like resistance training, loading our mental barbells with more weight so we adapt. Ignoring this means that we can be swayed by false signals on an organizational level. If you've ever seen people resist an effortful but positive change, like improvements to safety and quality, you've likely felt the frustrating limitation of only measuring developer experience in terms of what feels easy. But if you've helped a junior colleague learn to explicitly orient and plan before coding, and design for testing multiple solutions, you're likely teaching metacognitive effort.

This long-term view of problem-solving is one of the reasons I encourage organizations to focus on richer outcomes than just people's perceptions of friction. We need signals for adaptive problem-solving cycles, such as whether software teams report feeling motivated, engaged, and like they can take action. Our cognitive architecture benefits deeply from engaging in *desirable difficulty*: the effortful strategies that lead to better long-term retention of information and performance.[50,58] Just as a certain amount of movement is essential for healthy muscles, fully taking advantage of our cognition requires using it. Many technical practices that strengthen developers' problem-solving are types of active learning—modeling solutions to others, defining goals, and self-regulating with clear feedback.[59] As we'll explore in Chapter 4, active learning also provides critical fuel for motivation when we see ourselves overcome challenges. Better performance at scale rarely comes from assuming people aren't trying to work hard, or that only lone geniuses are capable of success. In fact, if we're interested in the highest leverage solutions for our orgs, summaries across hundreds of studies have found that giving people better metacognitive strategies and supportive learning environments that supercharge their existing effort is one of the most reliable and largest effects for improving how quickly people gain expertise. Metacognitive skills, and access to efficient and accelerated learning, are both things we can actually intervene on and better predictors of expertise gains than conventional measures of general intelligence.[60–62]

THE FUTURE OF DEVELOPER PROBLEM-SOLVING: DIVERSE THINKING, GOOD SCAFFOLDS, AND SOCIAL LEARNING

An important takeaway for leaders, teams, and organizations from this journey into the myth, history, and emerging science of developer problem-solving is that we should expect solving complex problems in software to be inherently diverse and to benefit from diverse approaches. Thankfully, our minds have also come up with diverse ways to tackle shared problems. This complexity might make it very difficult to find a single magic measure that detects productivity, but it also creates far more resiliency for real knowledge work. Even though our biases often encourage us to reach for explanations that center immutable individual differences, the environment and the strategies people learn are often stronger predictors of outcomes. When developers sit down to write code, they pull on the skills and talents they've honed as individuals. But they also draw on the collective problem-solving around them.

Unfortunately, this expansive view of human problem-solving isn't always how organizations see technologists' efforts. When the tech industry talks about developers' cognition, instead of thinking big and social, Brains-in-Jars thinking tends to seize on simplistic and machine-like measures for developers' problem-solving, like fixating on how quickly developers can churn out tasks. As we saw with the No Silver Bullets study, picking a narrow slice of the software development process and using simplistic averages about time-on-task can create misleading results. Similarly, looking only for innate traits to explain software outcomes rather than the more powerfully predictive environmental explanations is Brains-in-Jars thinking, reducing our flexible minds to an overly narrow activity or task and ignoring the rest of developers' sociocognitive experience. I call this *cognitive cherrypicking*—and it's hard for us to resist it when our judgments are being clouded by the fundamental attribution error.

Here's another reframe for a model of developer problem-solving that focuses on growth and strategy: set your sights on building good *cognitive scaffolding*. To get to high-quality problem-solving, we need organizations to help software teams lean into good metacognitive strategies and social learning at the right time in their problem-solving. With these two orienting principles in hand, I've seen developer experience initiatives turn up an entire slew of small but lasting improvements to the organization's problem solving. For instance, when solving a software problem is asking a lot of your developers, do they have the scaffolding at hand that helps them dig in? Are teams engaging in reflection? Do software processes allow developers to access worked examples and monitor the quality of their output? Will their effort be rewarded? Are moments of mentorship seen and valued? Are diverse solutions spread across teams to maximize social learning? The most powerful and immediate changes you might be able to make for your teams could come from asking simple questions about the health of your organization's social learning and its cognitive scaffolding. It's more effective to think about *where* and *how* software developers are spending their valuable effort, than to fantasize about a world where they spend no effort at all.

Turn to what the developers in your own organization ask for to find opportunities for metacognitive support. For example, many of the biggest needs practitioners report suggest lots of low-hanging fruit for cognitive scaffolding.[63] Somewhat surprisingly, given its frequent appearance in best practices lists and the increasing centrality of clear context in AI-driven development, what makes for quality software documentation and good learning context around codebases is an understudied aspect of software engineering. Developers frequently report needing more correct documentation, without erroneous code examples, reported by 59% of practitioners in one particular study![64] An emphasis on designing context that allows for actively engaging with diverse examples mirrors the many findings from across learning sciences that show how much active learning, over passive consumption, supercharges people's thinking.[65] For an organization struggling with cognitive scaffolding around their codebases, securing better metacognition could come from investing in a thoughtful social learning culture that allows developers to make sure their ramping-up-into-the-problem time strengthens their expertise, and their ramping-down-from-the-problem-time feeds back into social learning for the whole organization.

On the organizational design level, successfully directing infrastructure problems to a team empowered to work on improving the structural constraints of other developers' problem-solving is an example of cognitive scaffolding *across* teams. Just as sharing in utilities makes cities collectively more efficient, thoughtful engineering leadership can create impact across an engineering organization by stewarding collective problem-solving benefits. In the era of AI-augmented software development and increasing layers of abstraction, investing more carefully in the metacognitive architecture, which makes individual workflows more robust and accurate may spell the difference between empowered, problem-solving developers and stuck ones, and can protect teams from dire mistakes based on unvetted solutions.[66] Judging the success of all of this by coding velocity seems borderline quaint in an era where code is generated in an instant. But encouraging developers to draw on rich metacognitive strategies, and share them across the organization, protects the developer problem-solving we depend on even when the tools change around us.

Cognitive cherrypicking understandably frustrates software practitioners, who want to shift their organizations' focus away from bad definitions of productivity and toward what solutions do in the world and the goals they're trying to achieve. But even more troublingly, sticky and unscientific Brains-in-Jars stereotypes about immutable individual ability can push your organization into making consequential decisions based on biased evidence about problem-solving. Challenging ourselves to fully imagine the behaviors needed for *software development*, not just idealized, isolated moments of *programming*, can help us retrain our intuitions about developer-problem-solving and help us recognize that many people can succeed by following different paths. A developer who spends a great deal of her time ideating on new and unimagined solutions may become more successful the more she cultivates well-honed creativity, whereas another developer who is focused on diagnosing security incidents may need to lean on their causal reasoning and communication skills. Many individual strengths are needed in our organizations.

Focusing on improving our problem-solving *environments* instead of fixating on individual traits also helps us buffer our software teams from the changes that affect every mind over time. Developers, like all human beings, experience impacts on their problem-solving from changes to non-cognitive factors like stress or health. In a large enough population of people (for instance, several thousand in an engineering organization), people will experience any number of stressors that deplete individual resources. To observe this, you don't need a study: simply miss a night of sleep, and see if you feel as quick on the draw the next morning. You may find yourself forgetting items or struggling to recall names. Thankfully with a good night's sleep, your cognitive abilities swiftly recover—and with the support of social learning, your problem-solving can be protected by other people's collaboration. A conclusion we can draw from this, which I find poetically mirrors advances in software itself, is that designing for flexibility and optionality has been a more successful strategy for our collective problem-solving than anything else. Strategically dialoguing with and remixing other people's solutions empowers developers to navigate the complex worlds of software.

Brains-in-Jars thinking pushes us toward emphasizing purely individualistic and narrow explanations for what makes software work. But these explanations consistently leave us in the dark, predicting only tiny amounts of the variance in real-world outcomes and distracting us from the investments we should be making in the diverse forms of support that can help developers grapple with technology problems. The most actionable and largest improvements we can bring to people's problem-solving come from how we design the larger environments and whether we've unlocked healthy social learning and metacognition for developers.

CHECK YOURSELF BEFORE YOU WRECK YOURSELF WHEN IT COMES TO CLAIMS ABOUT DEVELOPER PROBLEM-SOLVING

- Does this claim consider the vast range of tasks and activities needed for software development at scale?
- Is a theory about developer problem-solving broad enough and complex enough to be able to give us useful insights about thousands of people in an organization? Or many millions of people doing technical problem-solving?
- Recognize that all evidence is incomplete in some way. Does our evidence consider within-individual and over time variance? Are we using simplistic averages that could be misleading?
- Look for three Rs: is the evidence for this claim representative, replicated, real? One case study with five software developers from the same company, with the same backgrounds and identities, isn't robustly generalizable evidence.
- Do software stories about high performers feel accurate to my real experience? Do they help me predict real outcomes? Do we need new stories?

CHAPTER 4

The Performance Paradox

WHEN WINNING ISN'T ENOUGH

Shaun[i] is, in his own words, "book smart." Anything that came in front of him in a classroom was a thing at which he could, and did, excel. He blasted through math and science in his small California high school and quickly maxed out on the number of honors classes the school could provide.

That's when he found programming.

Shaun's high school afforded him the opportunity to take computer science, which was a stroke of luck, unlocking a lifelong passion for coding. Actually, "luck" is a big word that covers a lot of things. As we just learned, achievement psychology would attribute Shaun's programming skill development to multivariate factors, many of them situational. Environmental factors such as access and opportunity likely interacted positively with individual sociocognitive factors such as Shaun's early motivation and interest. As an example of those systemic factors, whether or not people even know about programming at a young age is often gated by early opportunities; many high schools around the world still can't offer a full computer science curriculum, and when high schools do offer computer science courses, it can be a struggle to get students to enroll in them.[1] Shaun had the right motivation to learn to code, but he was also in the right location for that motivation to matter, with successful goals close enough for a teenager to aspire to and reach. Take note of that gestalt of

DOI: 10.1201/9781003589112-4

motivation, environmental opportunity, and expected success—we'll be coming back to it.

Shaun excelled at programming and decided that he had a goal: becoming a software engineer and continuing this form of problem-solving he so enjoyed. Shaun's rapid ascent through Computer Science undergrad and into a big, glamorous tech organization immediately after graduating felt like a dream coming true. As he described it to me, "Not trying to boast, but I always got that A." And, Shaun told me with a sideways smile, it felt like he was fulfilling his parents' dreams too. "They called me gifted, I think it's a little more complicated." He worked hard and cared tremendously about succeeding. Rather than gifted, Shaun preferred to describe himself as interested in a lot of things, and perhaps unusually able to focus. He admitted freely that focus had been on accruing external markers of success, first degrees, and then promotions and commendations in his work. Being a high performer was an identity that was important to Shaun for good reason: it continually unlocked the next opportunity on his path.

However, as Shaun hit his mid-thirties, he began to experience a relationship with success that felt more complicated. He told me: "Success . . . just stopped feeling like a win and started feeling like a test I kept taking and never finishing." While he maintained high achievement in his job, being a high performer all of the time began to feel like, well, a performance. It felt like he was on stage every day, stuck inside of a play reading lines that he no longer believed in. Always worried about the next step up the promotional ladder, Shaun had stopped feeling motivated by the puzzles and problems of code. He described this as a "treadmill . . . maybe a hedonic treadmill, where I'm never quite as happy as the moment when I get a new promotion, but it fades away." He reached for his reliable, career-long pattern of planning the hard work around explicit achievement goals, but each achievement seemed less fulfilling than he'd imagined. When Shaun got the title of Staff Engineer—a moment he'd imagined since joining his company years earlier—he woke up the day after the promotion feeling shrouded in darkness.

All of this took a toll on Shaun's well-being. For the first time in his life, Shaun felt his performance beginning to slip. He'd become increasingly worried about making mistakes in front of his colleagues and leadership. Even though he readily told me he'd never experienced a significant failure, when it came to his technical work, he imagined that failure all the time. "It feels like every win I have disappears in my hands," he told me, "And even though I always get it, I'm so tired of being afraid of not getting it." With these worries about performance filling his mind, Shaun found it understandably difficult to invest in his own learning, which began to make him less creative at work, too. He started to actively avoid any situation in which he feared he might not look like the most competent developer in the room. "I ask myself, what happened to that motivated kid?" He finally voiced to me, a plaintive question that went right to the heart of Shaun's dilemma.

Performance is a concept that's everywhere in our organizations. Businesses create endless verbiage to describe wanting high-performing teams, leaders admonish teams to invest in performance cultures, and HR departments set performance-based reward structures that impact the trajectory of developers' careers. Helping you become high-performing seems like an obvious goal for this chapter. After all, becoming a "high performer" is the focus of endless self-help books. But if sustainable performance were as easy as telling ourselves to *just perform*, we wouldn't need to talk, think, and worry about performance so much. The truth is that finding a balanced strategy for *sustainable* performance is more complicated than we make it out to be, particularly for demanding, creative, and ambitious knowledge work like software development. And we need to face cultural barriers in tech that can trip teams and developers up when they try to invest in their own motivation. In Chapter 2, when we explored the limiting belief structures that keep Brains-in-Jars organizations from unlocking software development innovation, we learned about the Brittle Productivity Trap: the sticky belief that keeps organizations that primarily focus on maximizing individualized short-term performance miring themselves in future failures. This cycle happens because forcing people to maximize for short-term performance introduces fragile psychological trade-offs that eventually rupture under stress. Optimizing *only* for explicit demonstrations of performance in the short-term is also directly in conflict with the psychological and cognitive demands of software development problem-solving, meaning businesses fail to protect the path to innovation.

Shaun was enmeshed in his own personal version of this conflict. Despite his many on-paper strengths, accomplishments, and work ethic, focusing entirely on demonstrating external performance had pushed Shaun to lose sight of one of his most precious resources: his own motivation and self-efficacy, the psychological powerhouses that keep us reaching forward to achieve difficult goals over time. Shaun's story shines a light on the fact that our internal motivation system is far more complex than just winning and losing. Even though he continually achieved many of the extrinsic rewards that organizations prize and by all organizational "performance" measures was a successful engineer, Shaun had to confront a very real psychological challenge with how he conceived of his own work. This challenge had a concrete impact on his intrinsic motivation, getting in between Shaun and his own capacity for problem-solving, innovation, and joy. In this chapter, we're going to focus on that complex system.

Shaun's story is a poignant one, but I didn't find it surprising. Because many of the strategies we rely on to reach Brittle Productivity look better than the long-term and more lasting strategies, Brittle Productivity can seem like the right choice when we're in the dangerous lead-up before its breakdown. It's possible to miss the toll this dynamic is taking on developers' motivation and an organization's future innovation until it's too late, particularly when the most immediate costs are borne by individuals. But the cost eventually comes to organizations. I've seen many individuals and teams get stuck inside of what I've jokingly named Cat's Law in an homage to the many "laws" that software practitioners love to use to help describe the paradoxical experiences of software development, where many of the solutions we reach for can exacerbate the very problem we're trying to solve. Here's my contribution to the library of laws:

> Cat's Law: The more a software team fixates on demonstrating short-term performance in their environment, the less they are able to protect the foundation on which long-term performance depends.

Please know this is just a tongue-in-cheek "law," and I don't mean this as a true scientific law for all contexts. Psychologists hate to say an approach is right or wrong. Psychological processes, and our behaviors, can almost always be either adaptive or nonadaptive for us depending on the specific situation. But Cat's Law is meant to draw your attention to the psychology that powers motivation and long-term, mastery work and the paradoxical impact of "performance thinking." I've presented Cat's Law to thousands of software practitioners, and the moment it flashes up on the slides those audiences frequently erupt in recognition and laughter, which more than anything has convinced me that software folks are curious to learn more about our amazing motivation systems. To further unpack this Performance Paradox, we need to understand the social contexts that shape our beliefs about striving and success.

SOCIAL COGNITION SHAPES HOW WE SHARE PERFORMANCE

For three years of graduate school I sat in a large upstairs play space in a science museum and asked hundreds of children between the ages of 3 and 6 to sit down with me and listen to a storybook. To the children, they were sitting down with a friendly neighborhood psychologist to enjoy the familiar ritual of story time. But with their parents' consent and the children's assent, we were actually investigating the development of social cognition. Together, we looked at illustrated[ii] storybooks of children facing dilemmas about performance and talked about what choices the protagonists should make.

Across multiple studies, each child was randomly assigned to hear subtly different stories. In one of my studies, for instance, two key differences were varied across our storybooks: whether the protagonist of the story succeeded or failed at a basic puzzle task, and whether a friend character in the story reacted with a supportive or a judgmental statement. From there, I asked each child how they think the character would respond (asking about other people's behavior is a delightful way to learn about children's social expectations—try it with the young children in your life!). Would the protagonist tell their friend about a failure? Would they tell a friend about a success? In further variants, we asked additional questions about whether children expected the character to ask for help and how the friend's performance might impact those expectations.

Our studies revealed the immense power that social information has on our choices about performance and disclosure. This capacity also develops over time, exactly as children are developing their capacity to imagine the minds of others. While the youngest children in my studies gave similar answers regardless of the performance of the friend character, children nearing kindergarten were already pondering the weight of that social context and using it to change their expectations. Those kindergarten-age and older children scrutinize the social context of performance and adjust their expectations to try to suit that social context. I remember one thoughtful 5-year-old who gave a succinct observation: "Friends have feelings." Young students are more likely to engage in performance disclosure when they know they're sharing positive information about themselves, and they're also more likely to do it in an environment of social support, a finding that has implications for how we all decide to navigate our classrooms and eventually, workplaces.[2] At the same time as most of us start learning to read and write, our decisions about the disclosure of performance are already infused with a heartfelt need to be accepted by others and a keen sensitivity about how social context changes how we demonstrate our performance.

These differences also vary by culture, showing even more evidence that social context shapes what people internalize as the "rules" of disclosing performance and failures. Psychologists like Gail Heyman (one of my collaborators on the disclosure studies) found that young children in the United States, for instance, are more likely to interpret disclosing high performance as a boast compared to children in China, who are more likely to interpret the disclosure of high performance as an implicit offer of help.[3] What I think your performance says about me, in other words, can be meaningfully different depending on our social context. Disclosure is a fascinating place to begin to understand performance beliefs, because talking about what we've done is a precondition for deeply important moments in learning and work, like obtaining help at the moment that we need it, or getting credit for our contributions.

Five-year-olds are sometimes still puzzling out the nuances of playing hide and seek and whether or not other people can lie to them, but they're already sensitive to the difference between successfully solving a puzzle and failing at it, and they hesitate over the choice to tell their friends. In our earliest encounters with the concept of performance, we forge a perspective on how we think our performance will impact our social standing with others. To go back to my friend Shaun, his relationship with performance had become so entangled with a network of beliefs about the social and performance consequences of failure that it had begun to block him from focusing on the work in the first place. In trying to restart his motivation engine, Shaun had to confront the mental model that he was carrying about performance itself and how it had limited him to one specific goal: avoiding failure.

Moving from our earliest development of beliefs to the lifespan, when psychologists study how people's beliefs about success and performance relate to their achievement over many years, a discernible pattern emerges from the types of goals that people prioritized in an achievement situation. Drop a hundred random software developers into a challenging achievement situation (let's say, a new development project!), and we might see some of them primarily approach the challenge with a focus on gaining mastery, centering on increasing their own level of understanding, achieving task competency, and expanding their knowledge. Folks who operate with this mastery orientation often think more about the long-term development of future skills than their current performance. For a person who's internalized a mastery orientation, deep learning, intrinsic enjoyment, and taking on new work that expands their knowledge and exposes them to novel challenges can be key achievements, even when it opens them up to making more mistakes or looking worse than others. In contrast, some of our hypothetical developers are likely to approach their goals with a performance orientation. This stance toward achievement maximizes demonstrating performance in the present moment. For instance, these developers might be more likely to focus on goals like excelling against a normative standard, seeking out opportunities to show their work to others, and demonstrating competency in front of others.[4]

It's important to note that these different "goal orientations" can be functional strategies that help us meet real and meaningful needs. While life is about more than grades, meeting deadlines, and promotions, it's an unavoidable fact that moments of short-term performance can be critical turning points and real achievements that unlock future opportunities.[5] The practical business of software development often demands that we think about comparison and performing better than others: for most organizations, building a competitive product and successful businesses inherently requires competition. But it's also the case that focusing on learning, creativity, and mastery experiences for their own sake has immense psychological benefits. As we learned in Chapter 3, deeply engaging in problem-solving is core to the behavioral investments that result in innovative breakthroughs—creating future experts in a domain area requires junior people to be allowed to pursue mastery goals and supported in long-term learning. From a career-level perspective, many developers report that mastery goals (such as deepening technical craft or exploring new technologies) not only are fulfilling in the moment but also function as a key feature in maintaining their passion for programming work.[6–8]

Although our minds like clean binaries, like most psychological constructs, mastery and performance orientations are not truly cleanly divisible into "good" versus "bad" mechanisms. Rather, psychology challenges us to recognize which processes we are defaulting to and what that balance adds up to over time. Our own individual answers need to come from understanding the balance of how much we pull on specific strategies and whether these patterns are truly serving us as we try to meet the challenges of life. Shaun, who agreed with me that he had primarily landed in the performance orientation camp throughout his career, had thrived and succeeded with this orientation in ways that he found meaningful and important. However, this thriving had proved brittle. Research has consistently found that mastery orientation is strongly associated with durable performance and recovery from mistakes, which originally led psychologists to argue that this was the default frame we should encourage for learners. However, as more evidence was gathered, it became clear that performance goals are not always the bad guy. The evidence for how successful learners with performance goals can be has been puzzlingly mixed, with some people still achieving continuous success while others struggle.[9] What, then, explains why some performance goal orientations sour?

Psychologists studying the dynamic trajectory of people's achievement outcomes over the long run have a theory: accessing long-term performance is steered by both our internal strategy and our wider social context. On the internal strategy side, while mastery goals associate most strongly with long-term achievement, there's a further nuance that can help protect our learning even when we need to meet performance goals. For both mastery and performance orientations, people who prioritize challenge-seeking and reaching outside of their comfort zones to meet either type of goal (an *approach* strategy) have better resilience and better outcomes than people who primarily focus on avoiding any scenario that could circumvent their goals, such as moments where they could be asked to perform in front of others (an *avoidance* strategy). Ironically, in the performance-avoidance mindset, our very focus on not looking like a failure increases our chances of failure. This makes sense when we remember that failing is a necessary part of learning, which is easy to *say*, but hard to accept. As we learned in Chapter 3, desirable difficulty consistently sharpens our minds' problem-solving and metacognition, maximizing both the efficiency of our learning and the amount we engage in learning at all. When we make performance goals more important than anything else, we start to minimize risk and challenge in our lives, dragging down our long-term performance.[10]

Psychological scientists now layer the approach-avoidance dimension into how we characterize people's achievement goals. When we do need to focus on performing, having an approach strategy helps correct the imbalances that performance goals can set for us, driving us to enhance our effort and ensuring that we continue to be exposed to skill-building opportunities.

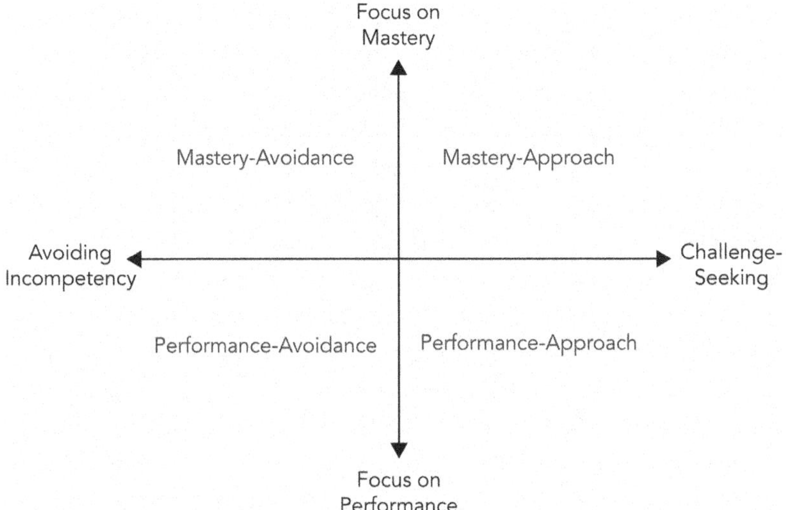

Achievement Goal Strategies.

Over the course of the challenges he navigated, Shaun had been clear about his performance goals. He and I agreed that in the past, he had tended to have a performance-approach orientation. However, over time, he invested less and less in effort-focused and psychologically nourishing goals of mastery, and began obsessing over the possibility of making a mistake, a classic avoidance pitfall. As Shaun fell deeper into making his goals about avoiding all failure rather than finding goals that did not rely on performance demonstrations, like his own learning, his performance-approach orientation had begun to shift into performance-avoidance. With the threat of other people's judgment clouding his choices, Shaun started to avoid much of the challenging and rewarding technical work that he had previously tackled, which set off a vicious cycle of decreased self-efficacy, further worsening his worries about performance. He was living out the consequences of the Performance Paradox.

With this new vocabulary in hand, take a moment to think about your own organization and the messages it sends about performance (a fun way to do this: search for the word "performance" across your email!). What assumptions are encoded in those messages? Recognizing that our social contexts interact with the powerful individual factors that we bring into them (such as whether a developer is high in performance orientation or high in mastery orientation) can help us begin to understand why so many initiatives that aim to inspire high performance workforces can end up doing the exact opposite. Because social context matters deeply to how we interpret performance messages, and because mastery goals are essentially for long-term learning, leaders who want to build a sustainable achievement culture need to respect this critical interaction. Without enough room to pursue the mastery goals that define technology learning, leadership messages about performance culture can evoke the fearful expectation that only short-term, immediately measurable outcomes matter. This may lead developers to short-change their own learning cycles and disinvest from the collaborative work necessary for innovation, even if this was never what leaders intended. Likewise, when a manager tells a software team it needs to "perform at all costs" or "focus on excellence," this might feel to the manager like motivating, energetic, and passionate language. But to a developer who is already struggling with the performance-avoidance fear of failure, such a message might only reinforce the wrong strategies.

Even when we as individuals value mastery, what we think our organizations value can change how we present our performance at work, disclose to colleagues, and choose our goals. In a series of laboratory studies, psychologists Mary Murphy and Carol Dweck simulated this experience by presenting undergraduate students with examples of organizational messages that endorsed different theories for what mattered. Specifically, one organization endorsed the idea of people having a fixed intelligence that they were born with, while the other endorsed the belief in people's capacity for intellectual growth over time (you're probably familiar with these belief systems being called having a growth mindset or a fixed mindset—psychology also calls this an *entity theory* of intelligence, when intellectual ability is considered an unchangeable belief fixed at birth). They found that despite individuals' incoming beliefs, people shifted how they presented themselves in an application to align with the organization.[11] They also found that organizational messages went deeper than just how people performed those beliefs externally: exposure to a different organizational theory for success and ability shifted what people later rated as most important in their own self-concepts.

With a larger group of researchers, this work was followed up by a series of three studies, including a field study of more than 500 employees across multiple companies, which reinforced the laboratory findings by showing that how employees perceived their organization's beliefs had a measurable impact on whether they thought collaboration, teamwork, innovation, and intellectual risk-taking were acceptable in that company's culture.[12] Our shared organizational belief systems shape the opportunities we see for ourselves and the rules we internalize about how we demonstrate performance. And for developers who already have reason to feel vigilant about how they are being evaluated, the burden of constantly monitoring for unfair beliefs from people around them can directly impair the same resources needed for problem-solving (more on this in Chapter 5, where we dive into groups).[13]

We're so attuned to others' beliefs about success and performance that we can even take in subtle messages about what matters for our performance from the way work is praised, or the mere expectation of evaluation. When people receive praise that centers on the process they used to obtain an outcome or solve a problem ("I loved that interesting approach you tried in the code!" "I noticed that you tested and discarded a couple of less efficient ways to tackle this, great diligence"), rather than praising them as a person ("you're a great engineer!" or "you're a rockstar!"), a mastery emphasis strengthens intrinsic motivation and people's sense of their own competence.[14,15] Process praise sends the message that on *this* team, we care about quality problem-solving. It can even help developers grow those critical metacognitive skills we covered in the previous chapter.

On the other hand, messages that reinforce the fears of people with performance-avoidance strategies can directly degrade their motivation to solve problems. In a series of studies, Corwin Senko and Judith Harackiewicz manipulated whether or not people solved a puzzle in one of two conditions: an evaluative condition, where the experimenter would time and score each puzzle and evaluate their performance, or a non-evaluative condition, in which participants were simply told they'd be solving a puzzle.[9] They found that the evaluative condition dampened the intrinsic interest that people felt in the problem-solving challenge, but only for people who already reported being prone to avoiding challenge. Organizational researchers have argued that creating an organization capable of adaptation and self-improvement requires a collective goal orientation that allows individuals to invest in mastery-oriented exploration, whereas a performance orientation culture incentivizes people to invest primarily in exploiting already-known knowledge.[16] For technology organizations, which demand that people engage at the edge of knowledge, it's particularly important to ensure that the balance between knowledge exploration and exploitation isn't stifled by an organizational norm that encourages avoidance.

I've seen many organizations and leaders unwittingly create feedback cycles where nearly all the praise and motivating messages that developers hear are centered on fixed mindset messages about who a great developer is, rather than drawing attention to developers' effort, strategies, and improvement over time. Leaders are often focused on achieving outcomes and frequently monitoring them under a time crunch—more code written, higher quality, better features, delivered within timeframe. It can feel natural to reach for praise that emphasizes performance goals and innate talent. But if that's all our conversations emphasize, we are often reinforcing Performance Paradoxes across the cultures of our technological organizations.

THE BUILDING BLOCKS OF MOTIVATION

How do we start solving the Performance Paradox? Like swapping productivity for problem-solving, another construct swap can be very helpful here. When a developer tells me that they're struggling with their relationship with performance, the first questions I ask are usually about how they experience motivation. For my friend Shaun, once he'd determined that he wanted to learn to look past conceptualizing his software developer life as a long series of tests that would never end, we sat down to talk about what it felt like when solving software problems brought him joy. What held his interest? What had drawn him into programming in the first place?

Intrinsic motivation is a consistent predictor of both performance and engagement across workplaces. When people experience intrinsic motivation, they often report high curiosity, enjoyment, and a sense of fusion; when we're intrinsically motivated, doing the task becomes the same as accomplishing a goal itself. The reward becomes intrinsic, a property of the activity rather than something that's achieved externally.[17] This self-fulfilling quality of intrinsic motivation helps people persist, fostering important approach strategies that maximize achievement. It helps keep us persisting in a single domain because we stay optimistic about early failures and also helps us reach more diverse kinds of success. When we're motivated, our increased challenge-seeking broadens how and where we apply our talents. Converging across different schools of thought, many psychological theories have considered intrinsic motivation central to a psychologically rich, individually fulfilling life. For instance, self-determination theory, which emphasizes people's need for autonomy, competence, and relatedness, considers intrinsic motivation a critical part of what moves people to sustain performance.[18,19]

It can be easy to overlook this mountain of psychological evidence when we hear cynical messages that people only make their choices based on external incentives, like we're robots running on coins. Of course, our material needs matter deeply, and meeting them may be a precondition for seeking out meaning in our work. But it's a mistake to think that meaning and motivation don't matter. Meeting these psychological needs matters even for people experiencing great adversity and our motivational mindsets structure how we see the world and rise to challenges.[20] Feeling motivated carries enormous benefits that resonate with the ways that software developers have described both their happiest and most productive days.[21–23] For instance, in experiential accounts developers have described days of high autonomy and enjoyment including experiences of persisting to the completion of tasks and achieving goals, and being able to flexibly adapt their work time to ensure that they are able to match their highest-priority productivity demands with their highest-motivation moments.

Software developers who have always counted on their own passion to provide constant fuel can take motivation for granted. Caught up in imagining the importance of external achievements, Shaun agreed that he hadn't spent enough time even asking what motivated him in the first place. Without that knowledge, nurturing his intrinsic motivation had been neglected for too long. Understandably, Shaun's performance strategies were also shaped by environmental factors like the expectations of people around him, his desired promotional trajectory, and the very real psychological pressure to get good grades and a good job, performance goals which our minds associate with our very survival. Plus, his technical environments hadn't emphasized developers' motivation as a shared value, either. While I don't have the numbers on this, my guess is that the number of organizations that describe themselves as a "high motivation" culture is far fewer than those that would claim a "performance" culture.

Few leaders would disagree that they'd like a motivated workforce, and few software developers would disagree that they could benefit from being able to rely on a strong and renewing feeling of motivation as they go about their workdays. Yet even though motivation is a central part of staying engaged in achieving complex goals, measuring and monitoring a healthy motivation culture is strikingly absent from most HR surveys and businesses' people operations, which tend to instead center on employee performance. And while many of the applied research studies on software engineering have been curious about characterizing software developers' motivations, a systematic literature review conducted by Tracy Hall and collaborators on software research studies between 1980 and 2006 revealed that many of these studies neither mention an empirically tested theory of motivation nor use robust and long-standing theories about how motivation works to interpret their findings.[24] Luckily for us, there's a rich vein of empirical evidence about how motivation functions from the social sciences that we can draw on.

Kristy Robinson is one psychologist who has studied how motivational belief networks function over years-long achievement pathways for engineering students.[25] For most challenging goals, we know that motivation frequently decays over time. Tracking different components of people's motivation over time has revealed that we are subject to many inhibiting (or negative) and promoting (or positive) factors that interact to change our motivational state. Critically, studies like these also reveal that key trajectory-changing supports promote long-term sustainable achievement, helping slow the decay of motivation, or supercharge it over time. For example, in this research, engaging in a supportive gateway course in students' first semester of study predicted a slower change to specific facets of motivation: how useful students felt the challenging work would be to their future self, and the level of effort they felt would be required.

These ongoing appraisals about the future and the utility and cost of our current behaviors shape our motivation day by day. One central theory that psychological scientists like Kristy Robinson and her team draw from to measure and track the dynamics of motivation is called the *expectancy-value theory.* Just like the children in my dissertation weighing the storybook character's disclosure choices in the upstairs of the museum, as people think about a goal and the tasks that could lead them to achieving those goals, they appraise both the value of completing a goal, and their expected likelihood of success, along with the future effort's associated costs.[26,27]

Distortions or changes to any piece of this equation can sabotage our goal pursuits. When Shaun was imagining taking on a new and challenging area of technical work, he undermined his motivation by continually imagining the possible social cost of failure would be far larger than reality. He'd also underweighted that activity's value to him: "I forgot that I used to love experimenting with new approaches," Shaun recalled, reflecting on how rewarding no-pressure coding used to be in his life, "I stopped making time for it, and kept thinking it would be a lot harder than it was to make time for it." By resetting his beliefs about the value of experimentation, and reflecting on whether its cost was truly prohibitive, Shaun started to find small daily ways to take time for the learning that nurtured his intrinsic interest and the self-fulfilling rewards of his technical work even without changing anything larger in his environment. How we set and refine our personal expectancy-value mental models also steers which long-term goals we commit to in the first place, for example, early expectations about both the cost and value of completing tasks in a given domain can predict long-term career aspirations.[28] As a bonus, Shaun's small daily exercises helped him challenge his performance-avoidance narrative that said his team might think he was a failure if he took time to have fun, experiment, and try things that might not work.

Beyond individual benefit, for the technology leaders and organizational influencers who have a responsibility for the design of the larger environment around software teams, the expectancy-value theory provides a useful framework for reflection. Think about using each aspect of the theory as a possible intervention point to help improve organizational and team-level motivation. When a team is faced with a new, challenging, and ambitious request, motivational support can come from leadership increasing their expected likelihood of success or from leadership decreasing the imagined costs associated with trying to meet the goal.

THE MOTIVATED SELF

Another signal for a "motivation culture" that leaders can protect and developers can nurture is a strong and consistent self-efficacy for solving technically demanding problems. First proposed by Albert Bandura as a critical determinant for the motivated self, self-efficacy has been a powerfully influential concept in the psychological sciences, where one classic paper has over 37,000 citations![29] Self-efficacy is a core belief we have that we can do something, and critically, it can be specific to a given setting, domain, or skill area. We form self-efficacy beliefs based on both external information, such as the social models we see from others, as well as internal interpretation. One of the reasons mastery-approach strategies work so well to prepare newcomers in a domain for future challenges is that pursuing challenging learning situations is a recipe for increasing self-efficacy. By continually confronting and finding ways to succeed over friction, we build our internal belief in our own ability to overcome unanticipated and novel challenges. These adaptive psychological strategies can have a cascading benefit for organizations. For instance, employees with high self-efficacy in new jobs prefer to have less prescriptive training, and instead want training that emphasizes letting them design and add new elements to their own jobs, bringing creativity and improvement to the business. For software development, healthy self-efficacy is a critical part of the toolkit for dealing with constant change in technologies. In fact, studies have documented that high self-efficacy seems to directly increase people's problem-solving efficiency in the moment of working on a hard problem, likely by helping ensure that we're using better strategies and freeing our working memory from the demands of managing our fears about our performance—once again underlining the direct causal connection between healthy psychological conditions and the outcomes we want our teams to achieve.[30,31]

When I set out to measure a few key psychological factors that I believed we should make more legible to software teams in the research project we named "Developer Thriving," I knew that developers' self-efficacy and motivation had to be on the list. To break through the Performance Paradox, software organizations need to create environments that help protect all of the powerful behaviors that lead to innovation over time: seeking out challenge, trying new things even when the outcome is unclear, and empowering their creative technical contributors to build and experiment. While there are many possible elements that can be measured here, developers' self-efficacy and motivation provides one strong signal that a team is on the right track. Across an observational survey study, we adapted efficient but empirically backed research measures from psychology to software development contexts and asked developers to report how strongly they felt they had access to learning culture, agency, sense of belonging, motivation, and self-efficacy.

Then, we asked developers to rate their last month of productivity.[32] The Developer Thriving project did indeed find that developers' self-efficacy and motivation (along with all the factors in our Thriving model) were associated with higher rates of productivity for those developers (while productivity is complex and impacted by many factors, overall, we were able to estimate approximately a 25% increase in developer productivity was seen for every increase in a software developer's Thriving score!). This connection held when we tested it again across the many diverse people and situations sampled by our study—more than 1,282 software developers working in over 12 industries, and around the world, representing a wide range of backgrounds and personal characteristics such as age, race, and gender. Why does a psychological factor like self-efficacy provide such a reliable predictive signal for developers' productivity? Likely because self-efficacy is strongly associated with the positive cycles of motivation, trying harder in the face of challenge, and interpreting setbacks as new opportunities rather than as signals that a certain future isn't possible. Over time, all of these moments of micro-motivation create problem-solving momentum in our lives.

Our results also demonstrated the power of incorporating developers' core psychological needs into how our organizations measure the developer experience. Individual developers' productivity is a massively complex outcome, and research across all forms of human knowledge work acknowledges that what we call "productivity" is always the result of many variables and factors that range from the individual, team, organizational, to societal and even global levels.[33,34] Developer experience practitioners have often wryly observed to me that their initiatives can get bogged down in an organization's quixotic quest (or a leader's unreasonable demands) to capture all possible variables around software teams. Our Developer Thriving project was not designed to capture all possible effects that impact individual productivity. Instead, we aimed to show that teams could rely on rigorously tested empirical theories from psychology and use those constructs to gather practical observational evidence about the organizational gaps that leaders can quickly address. Starting with core building blocks of developers' psychological needs is a powerful first step to learn what needs to be improved and provides needed context for why interventions might fail to reach resonance with developers or produce desired change in our environments. Building developer experience measures on robust psychological concepts and the core mechanisms of our motivation can help us identify connections that will be useful and detectable across industries, demographics, and a wide range of organizational contexts.

BETTER PSYCHOLOGICAL FRAMEWORKS HELP DEVELOPERS FACE CHANGE

Across 2022 and 2023, while post-ZIRP layoffs rattled the tech industry and developers and their communities were still reeling from and experiencing the impacts of the Covid-19 pandemic, AI had come to the forefront of everyone's worries about software development. While speculation swirled about how AI worked, the best way to design these tools for programmers' needs, and the break-neck pace of new models, I wondered about a slightly different question: what was happening for developers themselves?

In particular, I worried that charged debates about what it meant to be a developer were creating a psychological storm for many people in software. When we worry about demonstrating our performance and productivity, it can heighten the Performance Paradox. In particular, when people feel that an important identity is being threatened, and that they'll lose it if they look incompetent, it can lock us into feeling like we're not allowed to learn new things for fear of looking like we're not those magical, know-it-all top performers. For developers, AI tools presented new ways of working but also a potential threat to feeling competent and respected at work. In keeping with how I'd seen software development teams struggle against the Performance Paradox, I wondered whether cultures that focused on whether developers constantly demonstrated short-term performance might actually exacerbate technologists' threat in the midst of rapid skill shift, making them *worse* at the very learning and upskilling they needed. Conversely, could we find any clues to what would help developers reframe the challenge?

I had an educated hunch (scientists like to glorify these by calling them hypotheses) that we could understand how developers were experiencing AI by learning more about the mental models software developers had internalized about what makes people good at software work in the first place. This was based on an emerging area of research into the power of our field-specific ability beliefs, or "FABs." As we surveyed in the Brains-in-Jars thinking traps in Chapter 2, people navigate their complex lives with a suite of beliefs, social norms, and both explicit and implicit expectations about how things work. We also put this theory-building to work as we attempt to enter specific professional fields and learn what drives success in them.[35] Over time these can begin to cement as collective, group-level beliefs, networks of stereotypes about who can succeed at a certain type of work. One noticeable way this shows up in my own personal life is that despite our similar training, and overlapping areas of expertise, people often react to finding out that my wife is a neuroscientist by saying "she must be a genius!" People hold a strong field-specific ability belief that succeeding at neuroscience requires genius. Sadly, this is not the stereotyped field-specific ability belief I usually hear when saying I'm a psychologist!

FABs can look different for different fields, with large consequences. Andrei Cimpian and Sarah Leslie and their collaborators have uncovered a particular dynamic that they've termed The Brilliance Trap: when our stereotypes make us think the highest forms of success in a certain field can only come from innate brilliance (such as a stereotype about "genius"), we often don't recognize people who don't match our genius stereotypes even when they do excellent work, leading to worse outcomes for the whole field. The damaging connection between these belief networks and the long-term innovation and diversity of different fields has been uncovered across multiple fields, like physics and neuroscience. These beliefs show up early in our cognitive development, and a stronger endorsement of brilliance deals damage to the behaviors that promote long-term performance, like challenge-seeking.[36–40]

Curious about how software developers dealt with massive technological shifts, or even just the threat of *imagining* them, I began to suspect that brilliance beliefs about programmers might drag teams down if developers felt that their own status as "brilliant people" was threatened. In classic Brains-in-Jars fashion, valuing the idea of innate brilliance (and watching for it from our colleagues) feels very enticing in our technical organizations. Particularly in a business where every conversation you have with your boss might be about today's metrics or team velocity, organizational messages continually underline performance goals over mastery. Influential figures in software are often exalted for their individual success and individual genius, and as we learned in Chapter 3, the "10x Developer" myth is alive and well in the attribution errors we make about what drives technological progress. It can be hard for developers to not scoff at the idea that it's dangerous to celebrate brilliance. But a constant narrative about software that constantly pushes "innate brilliance" explanations to the front of our minds, isn't neutral. As we learned in Chapter 2, brilliance explanations also foster an environment where people engage in constant, damaging technical contests that ask people to constantly prove that they belong.

For software developers dealing with AI augmentation and generated coding practices, I was curious whether we would see that strongly believing that innate brilliance is both (1) rare and (2) required for exceptional software development outcomes would trap developers in avoidance strategies, and whether we would see the same connection between contest cultures and negative outcomes play out during this high stakes moment of change. The causal connection between brilliance beliefs in software development and negative outcomes for technical organizations had also been proposed as a future research direction by at least some software researchers who suggested that field-specific ability beliefs around brilliance might be one possible explanation for the effects they observed where marginalized developers, who are less likely to be seen as "brilliant" because of our pre-existing biases, grapple with more hostile feedback during code reviews compared to majoritized developers.[41]

But to my knowledge, at the time of our study no software research group had actually developed and directly tested a measure of brilliance beliefs and contest cultures for professional software developers, and specifically looked at how these beliefs affected the way software teams dealt with brand-new technologies that threatened the role of a software developer with change. For this project, we recruited over three thousand software developers who were experiencing the ramp-up into generative AI coding into an observational research survey.[42] Developers answered a battery of questions that we'd developed based on the psychological literature, and we carefully analyzed the results across many demographics including age, gender, self-reported identities, and important contextual factors like different engineering areas, years of experience, and industry.

Looking at data from thousands of developers, the findings matched our hypotheses. Developers who strongly endorsed brilliance beliefs about software development, and who believed that ruthless contest culture behavior was a defining feature of software development, were about twice as likely to report significant threat and anxiety about whether they would be able to keep up, and whether they would be fairly evaluated, when imagining an AI-assisted coding future. And being highly effective at coding couldn't protect developers from the negative effects of a contest culture: when I looked just at developers who reported many years of experience and strong confidence in their coding skills, the negative impact of feeling like they were inside of a contest culture was just as strong. Troublingly, AI Skill Threat was particularly salient for racially minoritized software developers, who as a group reported significantly higher AI Skill Threat when compared to their majoritized peers, even accounting for other factors like industry, experience, and type of engineering work. Remembering the social context of performance helps us understand why: one driver of this difference is likely because minoritized software developers have systematically greater experiences of unfair evaluations of their performance, which can directly exacerbate their experience of threat during change.

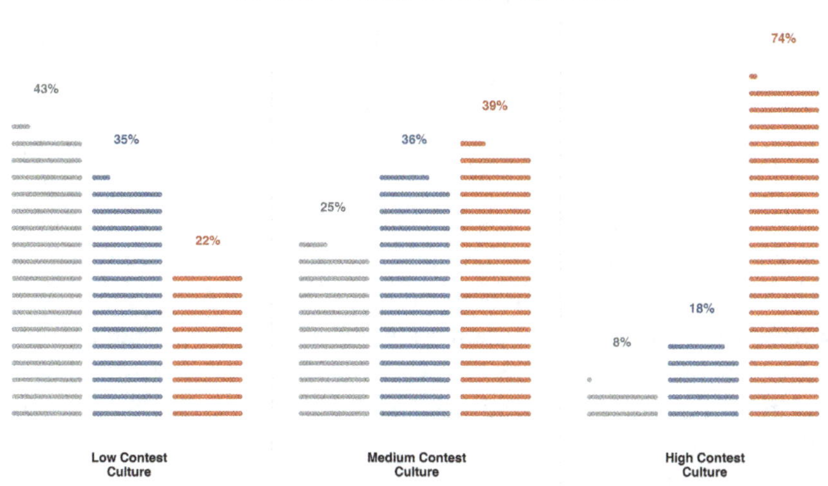

Contest Cultures Drive Up AI Skill Threat.

However, we didn't stop at measuring the threat. To identify signals for where teams and organizations could turn to protect developers' experience during rapid technology shifts, we also measured two key alternative psychological factors that research suggests provide a mastery-oriented alternative to the dual threats of brilliance beliefs and contest cultures: cultures of learning and belonging. Both of these factors provide a strong counterweight to the innate brilliance story of software development. A team with a strong learning culture emphasizes that learning is an expected and socially shared part of a developer's journey, and rewards its contributors for sharing and supporting mastery goals. A team with a strong belonging culture emphasizes creating a space where different people, with their diverse strengths and abilities, can belong and are welcomed in software development, and where people's uncertainties about whether they belong are met with support and reassurance that their contributions and identities are welcome. On a team that can offer a strong belonging culture, struggles and worries during change are less likely to graduate in developers' minds into proof that "someone like me" does not belong in software development. As we'll explore more in the following chapters, our sense of belonging has been a powerful research measure in psychology, and increasing belonging has frequently been the target of social-psychological interventions at scale which have produced measurable change in durable, long-term achievement outcomes.[43] Just like our other measures, these constructs aren't usually translated into the realm of software development, but emerging software research has suggested their powerful predictive value for technology teams, including finding associations between low belonging and developer burnout.[44–46]

Using these measures, we were able to place software developers on a map between contest cultures (that endorsed brilliance and contest mental models for successful software development) and thriving cultures (that endorsed learning and belonging mental models for successful software development). Of course, some people hold mixed beliefs, and as we've seen, our organizations and teams can shift how much we endorse them. But in general, these two different belief systems are negatively correlated. Our results strongly indicated that developers with access to a thriving culture reported a significantly lower experience of identity threat when they imagined AI changing software development. In fact, on average 63% of software developers who reported contest culture beliefs had AI Skill Threat, while only 32% of software developers in a thriving culture reported the same. For comparison's sake, most medicines that can reduce a patient's relative risk of experiencing a disease by half would be a triumph. Just as we found in our Developer Thriving project, in the real world, the software teams that do a better job at meeting developers' human needs win out over Brains-in-Jars models.

To come full circle from the empirical and back to the personal, I also saw my friend Shaun benefit from letting go of the Performance Paradox. After Shaun practiced reinvesting in his own intrinsic motivation, he began to get back in touch with the other goals that his younger self had imagined once he had reached all those exalted goals. For example, he remembered thinking that once he got the fabled promotion, he might spend more time mentoring junior developers and lead group sessions with his team to explore interesting and creative uses of technology. Shaun reflected that perhaps his many achievements and promotions could take on new meaning if he used them for something. In a gratifying moment for me as a psychologist, our AI Skill Threat study provided Shaun with concrete inspiration for this step. Shaun told me that he used the learning materials we released with our study, and the highlights from our empirical evidence, to motivate his team to join him in a learning-culture-building day as they confronted their internal questions about how they were going to audit security risks and come up with thoughtful shared values as they considered new AI-assisted workflows. And as he led the event, Shaun bravely shared the ups and downs of his own performance fears, a disclosure that his more junior colleagues found deeply meaningful. Shaun had gone from being fearful of looking incompetent in front of his work community and feeling stuck on a stage, to boldly and authentically modeling the value of a mastery-approach mindset to his team. And his motivation had never felt stronger.

QUESTIONS TO ASK TO START SOLVING THE PERFORMANCE PARADOX

- Do we think about whether we're a "motivation culture," not just a "performance culture?" What questions would we ask if we were more concerned with software developers' motivation?
- Are software developers encouraged to develop approach strategies?
- Are organizational leaders and technical influencers in our organization sending messages to software and product teams that encourage mastery? Are we incorporating process praise in how we give each other feedback?
- How can I use the components of expectancy-value theory to help my teams? When we ask a software team to dig deep and work hard, have we helped developers have an accurate and encouraging expectation of their likelihood of success, a large enough value attached to the goal, and is the cost they anticipate less than the value of the goal?
- Is my team or organization falling into the patterns of a contest culture? Do we foster comparisons, litmus tests, and dog-eat-dog "contests" around technical topics? Have we considered the long-term cost of these practices?
- Where might it be possible for my organization to use targeted, actionable measures of self-efficacy, motivation, learning culture, and belonging culture to improve software developers' experience?

NOTES

i. While his name is anonymized for the sake of his inner peace, "Shaun" is a software developer friend who kindly volunteered his real story to me for this chapter.

ii. Amazingly, the undergraduate research assistant who helped make these pictures that I used in my grad school experiments would later become an exceptional scientist, and a founding member of one of my software research labs. Dr. Carol Lee, my frequent co-author on the research mentioned throughout this book, was that research assistant.

CHAPTER 5

Conflict or Coalitions?

THE GROUP THAT WASN'T

As we met for coffee, a friend who was a user researcher at a large company described a dilemma. She was part of a cross-functional team working on a new feature for the company's flagship product. This team was also the first attempt at a culture change. Across the company, employees had felt that teams were too siloed; in particular, many had noted the need for software and product teams to collaborate more closely. Now, having survived the gauntlet of planning to emerge with a sanctioned place on the roadmap, the new team was ready to model this collaboration. They seemed to have the preconditions for success dialed in. Everyone agreed tighter feedback loops would move the business toward its goals, including increasing the value delivered to customers. Team members had contributed to setting shared objectives, managerial chains were deeply supportive of the new initiative, and work started with enthusiasm. But just a few weeks into the project, the mood had drastically changed.

The two sides of the team were subtly but pervasively at odds. While meeting separately, the product side would make comments about whether developers truly cared about product priorities or were fixated on enjoying clever engineering with no external value for the business. Some implied developers were intentionally misleading product folks with imprecise and variable estimates. "Those engineers," a designer scoffed, "Always going down technical rabbit holes!" But when my friend sat with the developers, she heard a mirror-image tale. Developers showed visible impatience and irritation when she presented their product colleagues' work in engineering meetings and implied the other half was obscuring *their* estimates.

DOI: 10.1201/9781003589112-5

A representative comment from one developer: "product people" had to be "kept in check" because they were "easily distracted by artsy stuff." Developers felt that only *they* understood what it took to focus on value for customers.

Whichever side you sympathize with, you can probably recognize features in this story. Perhaps you've been on a team (naturally the one with the most righteous and hard-working individuals!) that felt grievously wronged by another team (a collection of no-good slackers!). Or perhaps you resonate most with my friend. Perhaps you've also taken on a role with cross-functional impact, only to realize that a history of separation—or outright animosity—between collaborating groups meant every action was scrutinized so closely that it felt like partnership was impossible. As one of the only people who worked closely with both sides, my friend was caught between two groups with sharply different perceptions of the same situation who were unwilling to find a path forward. She had entered the tumultuous land of intergroup conflict.

In this chapter, we'll take what we've learned about how individual psychology impacts software development and move upward and outward to see how group psychology impacts whether we work well together. This is a complicated realm, with powerful effects that change who we listen to, believe, and trust. The groups we identify with shape our thinking, our behavior and even our moment-by-moment perceptions and memories of the events we witness, often without our realizing it. That's why group psychology sheds light on some of the most difficult questions people face about collaborating in the workplace. For example, how is it that alliances between people help us achieve so much in the world, while at the same time, create so much conflict between and within groups? What helps people unite into a supportive team, and what makes those attempts fail? How can teams prevent the conformity of groupthink?

As we'll see, paying attention to the people who have learned to operate at the margins of existing groups can reveal these hidden forces. So does noticing what helps some teams form a coherent identity with shared goals, while others splinter. My friend had a unique window into how a conversation that seemed uncontroversial to one half of the team could be taken as a personal insult by the other half, but she wasn't listened to. And while the product and development folks had been thrown together with an ostensible shared goal, leadership missed a critical step of helping them access a *new* team identity that could repair past conflicts and bring both sides together with empathy. It probably won't surprise you to learn my friend accurately predicted that the ambitious goals of the project would never be realized. When we got a second coffee months later, she told me the project had been dissolved, leaving the tensions between functions worse than ever. And she was planning an exit to a new company. Whether or not we successfully come together to form healthy groups has real consequences for our work.

Brains-in-Jars models pressure many technical leaders and technical people into minimizing the importance of group cohesion and collaboration. Even when we acknowledge it's important, software advice tends to stop at "and be sure to collaborate!" Yet software professionals report that agreeing on group goals in the first place is one of their hardest challenges, taking up an enormous amount of time and attention.[1] One of the most influential revelations across psychology has been that the groups we identify with shape our perception of the world, often more than we realize. That means when we see conflict with other people as being a threat to a *group identity*, we tend to grip tightly to our point of view, and can fail to see the other person's whole humanity.

Leaders who discount the importance of understanding group coordination may find themselves continually wailing, "*why on earth can't you all just get along?!*" It's not that simple, because the same psychological architecture that helps us mobilize together ("we're a world-class engineering team!" "We are obsessed with the quality of our product!") can turn against other people ("they couldn't possibly understand engineering problems!" "They're asking us to compromise because they hate quality!"). But when you learn to recognize what flips this switch, you can identify important moments to guide your teams toward becoming a united group that still values and allows for dissent and creativity.

In this chapter, I want you to keep two things in mind. First, we need to think expansively about what defines a group. Second, we'll remember that while teams let individuals achieve amazing things, groupthink can also create harm. On the first, I've noticed that many leaders assume a "group" means the formal team, usually a collection of individual contributors aligned under a single manager in a reporting chain. However, real groups aren't always best represented by formal hierarchy. Tremendous variance in how teams operate impacts people's closeness. Some teams have daily stand-ups, while others hardly talk. As a developer told me, "I see these people twice a year—at our off-site and the company holiday party!" Plus, software's complexity means that developers work across formal team lines and frequently coordinate decisions across emergent groups (picture an incident response, or a new feature initiative, or even simply when context from original authors is needed for code written long ago). Over 60% of developers in my research say they work closely with people who report to another manager.

In fact, as anyone who's worked on a complex project can attest, knowledge workers resist rigid bureaucracy which bogs down problem-solving and instead need to flexibly trade and shift responsibilities.[2] Organizations frequently have shadow hierarchies in which strongly networked individuals who coordinate important information wield an implicit social influence that's different from hierarchical, formalized power. These are often more predictive of people's real patterns of communication and decision-making than the org chart. Shadow organizations help communication across teams and influence whether and how information is taken up and used to change practices.[3] Outside of organizations, communities of practice also provide developers with group identities. For instance, technology practitioners who steer public conversations around everything from tools to tactics influence what people internalize as the prototypical *software developer.*

On the second point, I've often been struck by how much conversations and commentary about software teams shy away from acknowledging that a united team isn't great if it's pointed at bad outcomes. Groupthink can amplify negative stereotypes about others and suppress empathy and open-mindedness. Learning to recognize in-group bias and damaging norms doesn't mean that we need to take a nihilistic view of the people around us. Rather, it's worth it to engage with the reality of our minds' capacities for groupthink because that's what will help us design more beneficial strategies. To bring group psychology into focus, I like to pay attention to the liminal *moments* when we're likely to double down on conflict or break through to new coalitions. Moments when groups of people need to commit to joint goals, share information, and coordinate are moments when we can see and shape our choices. Developing a vocabulary for these moments will not only help you understand and empathize with your colleagues but also think more expansively about the many groups in the world whose lives are impacted by the software our teams build.

THE SWEEPING POWER OF THE IN-GROUP

Throughout history and across cultures, people form collectives. This also happens in technical cultures. A software developer in your organization might identify as a user of a certain programming language, an adherent to a tool, or a believer in a set of programming practices. Developers self-organize into professional societies, open-source projects, and alliances in the workplace. This isn't surprising when we have so many good reasons to work in groups. Tightly connected groups often outperform individuals at challenging cognitive tasks, collective breakthroughs often outpace individual work and define modern knowledge work, and team coordination is an unavoidable step in accomplishing workplace goals.[4–6] Because groups are so commonplace, we often underestimate just how fluid they are. But as you begin a new project, join a meeting, or meet potential collaborators, you are likely engaging in a constant process of deciding out whether the people around you feel "like you." Shared identities help us feel more certain about how to act and reassure us that we will make accurate predictions about other people's behavior. In psychology, a core insight called *social identity theory* argues that we don't just layer on group belonging to our sense of self, but that our individual identities are derived at least in part from the groups we identify with.[7] Our groups change our thinking because when we're on a true team, our teammates feel like they *are* us. In fact, researchers have proposed that mitigating uncertainty about ourselves is one big reason people seek to join groups.

One proof point for this comes from the fact that the more our sense of self needs bolstering, the more intoxicating merging with a group becomes. Uncertainty-Identity theory, proposed by psychologist Michael Hogg, argues that joining a group ameliorates the stress we feel in uncertainty. Under this theory, we'd predict that people will tend to form stronger group bonds when something is leading them to question who they are, and when a possible group presents a compelling opportunity for certainty. That's what Hogg and collaborators found across several studies where they directly manipulated identity uncertainty.[8] In one study, participants engaged in a brief manipulation intended to trouble their personal identity, reflecting on aspects of their life that made them feel uncertain. Participants who'd been shifted toward self-uncertainty reported identifying more strongly with a political party. In a second study, participants were brought into a lab and assigned to a group for an experience that they believed was a study on decision-making. Unbeknownst to the participants, however, they were randomly assigned to experience a combination of two different conditions: participants who were told their group was highly cohesive and different from other groups, *and* went through an uncertainty manipulation identified more strongly with their group compared with participants who were not given the uncertainty manipulation and who were presented with a more loosely defined group. In uncertainty, we gravitate toward compellingly coherent groups. This is one reason that old group biases can get hold of teams when uncertainty about what we actually need to solve comes bubbling up to the surface and a new team identity hasn't truly been invested in at an organization. Brains-in-Jars organizations downplay social collaboration, and in doing so, rarely craft an alternative group that people can join.

To learn about the basic cognitive building blocks of those biases, psychologists developed a clever set of methodologies called the minimal groups paradigm.[9] In a classic minimal groups study, people are sorted into groups based on novel and arbitrary assignment. In other words, people have no prior reason to expect to be grouped in this way, and no history of previously identifying together. Early examples pioneered by Henri Tajfel and collaborators grouped people based on their supposed "guessing accuracy" when confronted with clusters of dots or on preferences for painters such as Klee or Kandinsky (for the record, I'm in the Kandinsky group!). What's remarkable is how much the minimal groups paradigm pulls a fast one on our social categorizing. People assigned to arbitrary groups immediately form strong allegiances, even though they haven't been given any other psychologically meaningful cues about their group. Our ability to create an in-group is so strong that even when people have a new group identity that didn't exist in their minds minutes earlier, they discriminate in favor of it. To ensure this isn't just the result of the social interactions between people that happen *after* group assignment, researchers have tested many variations of this method, including methods where participants had no face-to-face interaction within their own team or with the other team in the experiment, and replicated the same results. Mere assignment is enough to start an in-group bias.

When people in these studies compete, they systematically try to reward their group more. In fact, not only do people prioritize maximizing their own in-group's profit, they also try to ensure their newly formed in-group has the largest possible *difference* from the other group's profit. Research has revealed that even when the choice is between getting the most profit at all or winning against the out-group, people choose winning. Maximizing the difference between the two groups' outcomes is frequently preferable to people to simply optimizing for the greatest profit. In other words, we might choose for our group to get 9 points and the other group to get 7, rather than an outcome where our group gets 10 and the other group gets 9.[9,10] When we're worried about how our group is doing, we judge this based on its relative status, even if that actually means our group gets *less*.

In-group allegiance is so strong, it can even change our memories. In a demonstration of this, Alin Coman and William Hirst conducted two studies in which participants were brought into a lab to study materials about a student exchange program and then listened to another person talking about his or her experiences in the exchange program.[11] However, this second person was actually a confederate and intentionally emphasized only a selected subsample of the previously studied information. The experimenters manipulated whether the participant shared an identity with the confederate, in this case going to the same school. With an in-group member, the participants were more likely to selectively remember the materials recounted by the other person and forget the materials that were not made salient. You may have even experienced this on a team yourself, if you've ever noticed the people around you rehashing past events and unknowingly aligning individual recollections with a single, shared in-group narrative. This is called *memory convergence*. While the best versions of group reflection and information-sharing can create the productive cycle of social learning, unchecked in-group biases on a team might trap us in endless battles about what *really happened* on that one nightmare project. In-group bias, coupled with that powerful capacity for social learning, can also supercharge the transmission of prejudices. In six experiments, David Schultner and collaborators documented that even just observing interactions between someone expressing a prejudiced belief and in-group members influenced observers to incorporate that prejudice into their own thinking and erroneously attribute it to their group.[12] This suggests that our strong proclivity for social imitation can warp our sense of our group's values and that ambiguous moments when our in-group seems to tolerate prejudice can have big consequences for organizational culture.

In-group bias shows up across a wide range of behaviors. We evaluate in-group intentions more charitably, attribute greater morality to our in-group, work harder to accomplish goals for our in-group, are more likely to cooperate with in-group members when it conflicts with our own personal needs, and expect greater reciprocity from our in-group.[13,14] Scientists have also directly measured differences in our neurobiology that shape how we react when we classify others as *like us*. Our minds quickly respond to in-group and out-group categories, even when the categories are novel and not based on existing group differences in the real world. For instance, neuroimaging has found that people's brains activate more with pain when they see an in-group member experience failure but with pleasure when a competitor experiences failure, a feeling also linked to reporting more acceptability of harming rivals.[15,16] A further body of research has found that groups supercharge competition significantly more than individuals, and that groups can get locked into even fiercer competition when there's a power imbalance between the groups.[17] When the idea of intergroup competition is activated in our minds, especially when there's explicit conflict between groups, it changes the way we process other people's experiences and whether we truly feel for them.

Going back to my user researcher friend, I suspect that if we were able to sit down and speak authentically with the product and developer sides, we might learn that a history of perceived inequitable resources and competition for relative status within the company set the stage for their hidden conflict. While it seems paradoxical that our psychology can make us sabotage a goal we really do care about, wanting to protect our group during conflict makes our minds rationalize this loss as worth it. As we learned in the AI Skill Threat study, our minds push us toward more extreme appraisals when we feel threatened. One strategy for my friend's organization might have been to try to encourage the formation of a *new* in-group, perhaps by acknowledging the past histories of division and offering the two teams the opportunity to forge a new identity as a project team. However, this coalition can be significantly more difficult to access for people in our workplaces who have experienced the worst sides of group psychology.

BELONGING UNCERTAINTY

I've played lever harp for over 20 years. I love my instrument. I've moved with the same harp from tiny apartment to tiny apartment; played my harp at campfires, on sidewalks, and on video conferences with new teams; taken years of harp lessons; and once qualified for the annual Fleadh Cheoil, a music festival in Ireland that welcomes lever harp players from around the world. I can even claim an extremely niche folk instrument badge of honor, which is that I primarily learned by ear and imitation with a harpist who taught not with sheet music, but with the aural tradition. All of these memories and experiences shape my expectation that people who play lever harp (there are dozens of us!) could see me as one of their own.

On the other hand, sometimes I negotiate differences between me and others who might belong to in-groups of "harpists." Because I play for myself and rarely keep a serious practice schedule, I often disclaim that

I'm a hobbyist, not a "real musician." I've also never been bold enough to play in a session (a celebratory tradition where folk musicians get together and jam, typically at lightning speed, playing jigs and reels). When I question whether "real harpists" would accept me as a member of their group, I might ask myself whether they would believe that I'm competent enough to clear a threshold that the group expects. One day, on a trip to Ireland, I walked onto the grounds of a castle and saw a woman playing the exact same type of lever harp that I had grown up playing. I tentatively told her that I played too. She was overjoyed, insisted that I sit down and play, and we shared some harmonies and favorite tunes. In that moment, it was clear that neither the differences in our relative competence nor our differences in background mattered next to the shared identity we were able to experience.

This particular identity of *harp player* is one I cherish, but it's also malleable depending on the social context. My sense of belonging to the world of musicians is a little bit uncertain. As we've learned in the previous chapters, belonging is a fundamental psychological need. We look for belonging from the groups that are around us and the environments we inhabit, scanning around us all the time for clues about whether we can and will continue to belong. Our beliefs, thoughts, and feelings about whether or not we truly belong in an environment are dynamic, pushed around by the actions of the people around us as well as by how we interpret the situations we're in.

My joyful experience with the harpist echoes a very large body of research that has found positive associations between how strongly people model and encourage belonging for us across our environments and our long-term outcomes. In far more serious contexts than my hobby, belonging is a powerful predictor of both achievement outcomes and psychological factors such as intention to persist, including in technical and STEM fields. While I'll likely never pursue a career in music, I felt buoyed by that harpist's welcome enough to imagine that I could have if I'd wanted to. Likewise, research has found that when people training for careers in STEM have been encouraged and supported in seeing themselves as having a shared identity with scientists, they're more likely to stay motivated, cultivate networks of belonging, and experience adaptive cycles of positive reinforcement.[18] In my Developer Thriving study, developers' overall rating of their sense of belonging on their software team was significantly associated with higher self-reported productivity. Estimating the sizes of these effects is complex because team context is so variable, but our statistical models for both Thriving and AI Skill Threat showed that when we looked across thousands of engineering roles, every increase in Thriving could be associated with an average estimated increase of between 25% and 35% in self-reported productivity.[19,20] This aligns with randomized-controlled trials of direct interventions to increase sense of belonging in education, which, when deployed well and thoughtfully, have been able to halve achievement gaps and significantly increase retention.[21,22]

This is the upside of our group psychology. The downside is that if our workplaces and colleagues make us constantly fear we'll *lose* our in-group status, particularly if there's a conflict between who we are and what our groups seem to value, we experience a potent psychological threat that can dramatically change how we think and act. While interviewing a handful of experienced software engineers, I once experimented with asking them to define what "being technical" meant and whether they would self-define as a "technical person." Across the interviews, almost every single engineer admitted that they debated mightily over what that word meant and shared how much they felt uncomfortable with how exclusionary the term could be. This was striking because in my experience, both engineering organizations and our public conversations about software love to sort people with "technical" and "non-technical" labels. You can probably guess I'm about to tell you this is yet another Lone Genius trap, a moment we should be careful about the potential cost of attribution errors.

In Chapters 3 and 4, we learned that entity theories (for instance, that technical ability is fixed and innate rather than learned) and attribution errors (for instance, that outcomes are attributable only to individual ability, not structural, collaborative, and social factors) can be dangerous explanations to reach for. They distract organizations from environmental drivers of success and wreak havoc on our intrinsic motivation. In the context of groups, constantly policing who belongs to the *technical* group can also erode people's belief that they can successfully navigate new technologies and be welcomed by other technologists as their roles expand and shift. Psychologically speaking, when we shift a label from an action-oriented description of people's choices, effort, and behaviors, and instead use it like it's a fixed label about who someone *is*, this shift makes people assume that you can only be born good at something rather than learn it.[23] People in authority often pass along these messages and keep reinforcing in-group and out-group divisions without even realizing it. Having an entity theory doesn't automatically make you a bad or unfeeling person, but it can give you a distorted lens when you're trying to encourage and motivate people who feel they're on the outside. People with entity theories may often try to comfort others in ways that actually *discourage* cross-field collaboration and dampen engagement and collaboration by saying things like "oh that's ok, not everyone is a technical person!", which just reinforces the belief that you have low expectations for them and won't support them if they try a new challenge.[24]

Psychologists Katherine Emerson and Mary Murphy conducted three studies which explored the impact of an organization that used "entity" language across their mission statements and websites (e.g., "we hire employees who have the intelligence and abilities that we are looking for") compared to an organization presenting a malleable, or growth theory of intelligence ("we motivate employees to find environments and working strategies that will help them learn, discover, and grow"). They found that the entity messages pushed women (but not men), who generally have more initial reason to fear being negatively stereotyped by entity theories, to expect to be perceived as less competent, to feel more disengaged when they imagined a negative interaction with the organization, and to report lower trust in the organization.[25] Companies and teams who continually remind people of in-group bias threats are unwittingly signaling that the organization as a whole believes in an entity theory about who's allowed to belong in technical work.

Connecting deeply to the identity of being a technical contributor can give developers a strong sense of belonging as long as things are going right, but without a healthy and inclusive group, that gift can become a double-edged sword. When the idea of being rejected by our technical community looms over us, threat drains our cognitive, attentional, and emotional resources. Scientists call this being in a state of *cognitive vigilance*, and the more people believe in entity theories, the more they feel it.[26] As we learned in Chapter 2, decades of barriers created between people and their technical potential, including our stereotypes about who can be part of technical groups, take a mounting toll on organizations' capacities to form coherent, trusting, inclusive teams. When software researcher Bianca Trikenreich and collaborators synthesized guidance on how to reduce burnout risks for developers, they cited increasing people's belonging in technical groups as a core strategy leaders should use to improve well-being.[27] Both the Chilly Climate and the Lone Genius thinking traps reinforce entity theories, positioning technological skill as the attribute of a small, select, and homogenous group. When developers in Brains-in-Jars organizations are pressured to continually question whether they truly belong, and these thinking traps make it more likely that technical groups engage in constant "competence checks," developers are constantly thrown back into cognitive vigilance rather than being able to work on forming a strong, shared group identity.

A study from Will Hall and colleagues surfaced an example of the toll that competence threat can take on people in something as simple as day-to-day conversations.[28] These researchers were curious whether task-based conversations could be a threat trigger for people who already had reason to doubt their in-group status in an engineering workplace. Given the highly collaborative nature of engineering, daily conversations form an obviously crucial part of both team solidarity and getting the work done. However, without healthy group norms around belonging, the meaning and impact of conversations at work can be experienced very differently for people who face the background radiation of threat. In their study, Hall et al. recruited men and women from a male-dominated engineering office for a diary study. This research methodology is one of my favorites: in a diary study, people report many samples of their daily experiences over time, which allows researchers to look more deeply at overtime patterns. In this case, the researchers explored the relationship between engineers' feelings of burnout and conversations that elicited worry of incompetence. While people of *all* identities experience negative impacts from threats to their competence, this study found that such conversations created a particularly potent identity threat for women, which was associated with greater burnout. Findings like this align with a large body of research in psychology that has found the signaling that happens inside of our organizations about who is at risk of exclusion can have much steeper costs when a developer is part of a group that regularly faces adversity. When people have lived through unfair group conflict and inequity, as has been the experience for many marginalized people in tech, they can learn to make highly unfavorable inferences about others' intentions because of a justified fear that status and belonging are always at risk. Psychologists Claude Steele and Geoffrey Cohen called this a "barrier of mistrust" and describe repairing this trust as a central goal for mentors and leaders who want to resolve group conflicts.[29]

Many developers tell me they identify strongly with being a developer and find profound meaning in connecting with their technical communities. However, just like my belonging uncertainty with harpists, developers' trust in their in-group status can be shifted from certainty to fear when we allow bad psychology to define a technical culture. Despite how solid and fixed identities often feel, we constantly ask how other people see us ("perhaps they wouldn't really call me a software developer"), we can feel more or less close to one of our identities ("I take a lot of pride in being a software developer!" versus "I am not sure I take pride in this"), and we can question whether we are allowed the same identity as others ("I love being a developer . . . but I do not get the message that people like me belong in software development"). In a Chilly Climate, developers who've experienced repeated threats to their belonging may feel even more sensitive to the risks of landing on the wrong side of a perceived in-group and have stronger reasons to fear inequitable evaluations of their competence. As we learned in Chapter 4, these pressures also drive people to double down on the *avoidance strategies* that also interfere with getting technical work done.

Threats to belonging give us a new lens for technical debates that may seem frivolous and are often used as tongue-in-cheek examples of outrageously pedantic arguments (tabs vs. spaces, anyone?). In-group and out-group signaling can be seen throughout technology communities' long-standing arguments about the tools of the trade, and even marketing (remember those commercials about Mac vs. PC?). Picture how strongly people might debate which programming language to use when the choice is framed as an allegiance to a certain side of software development, instead of representing a diverse set of choices, trade-offs, and individual preferences. Even when we acknowledge these debates can be arbitrary, their intensity makes sense when we realize they trigger very loaded, real emotions and social meaning about belonging and competence for people in technical worlds. If *tabs vs. spaces* is not just about my preference but about what our group believes *all competent developers* prefer, being afraid of landing on the wrong side of the debate makes sense.

CRAFTING BETTER GROUPS

In the middle of conflict, it can be tempting to feel like opposing groups are fixed in stone. Just as we struggle with the fundamental attribution error when thinking that differences in developers' output must come from immutable individual traits, in-group bias makes us think people on the other side are fundamentally different from us. But a famous (and controversial) demonstration of group identity paints a very different picture, one that's much more malleable. In the 1950s and 60s, psychologists Carolyn and Muzafer Sherif conducted a series of studies with young boys that have become known as the Robbers Cave experiment.[30,31] Unbeknownst to the campers, their "summer camp" was actually a research study, carefully designed to provoke intergroup conflict, and staffed by researchers. First, two groups competed with each other over multiple days, winning and losing prizes. Prejudices quickly formed between the groups, who chose group names and symbols, and quickly escalated into taunts and conflict. But the most remarkable thing was what happened next, as the researchers tried to design for resolution between the groups. First, they tried to rally the groups together with fun activities like movies and shared meals. But merely socializing with the other side wasn't enough and didn't remotely change the relationship between the campers (this may sound familiar to any engineer who's been promised a pizza party at the end of a death march project). The next tactic was an unusual one: the warring boys were given *joint problems* that could only be solved by working together. For instance, they had to work together to clear rocks off the water supply and work to help unstick a truck carrying their food on the road. These shared and high-priority dilemmas worked unlike anything else, leading the campers to reconcile and celebrate their victories together.

It's important to note that this old era of social psychology is now rightfully criticized for manipulating people, putting them in too stressful situations, and applying researcher pressure to participants. But modern research has reinforced the key findings that people really can connect and resolve group conflict—as long as they have a reason to recognize common problems and form coalitions to solve them. Psychologists call this having a *superordinate goal.* Superordinate goals help us break through in-group biases as we both realize that cooperative problem-solving is truly necessary and help us see the humanity in the folks solving next to us.[32] As further proof of this, how strongly people believe they share a "common fate" with others can predict whether they decide to invest in prosocial and mutually beneficial responses despite initial differences, particularly during high stress situations. We're not mindless automatons in our groups. Despite our tendency toward in-group bias, most people also care deeply about unfairness, are highly sensitive to disparities and inequities between groups, and at least aspire to distribute resources equitably. People are more likely to resist in-group bias when they're asked to explicitly punish an out-group member or assign them negative characteristics.[33–35]

In my friend's story, without an explicit identity reset, shared fate, and commitment to superordinate goals together, those warring product and engineering teams stayed locked in their initial conflict. Individual developers and product designers felt encouraged to rehash and feed off negative stories about the other side. They were constantly tuning their behavior toward conflict, rather than coalition. One strategy to prevent this from happening is to inject new superordinate goals at particularly powerful moments of early team formation, when people are more open to change. Summarizing years of research on team dynamics, team researchers Ruth Wageman, Colin Fisher, and J. Richard Hackman described impactful leaders as cultivating a sense for detecting predictable times when teams are *open* to helpful interventions: beginnings, midpoints, and endings.[36] At beginnings, establishing a strong shared fate is important pre-work that a team can invest in to forestall future conflict. Project midpoints and endings are also potent moments to align what we really *want* to achieve together with what we're doing as a group. Beginnings are powerful for calcifying who we see as "like us," whereas midpoint check-ins are times we raise our heads from the noise and remember what we pledged to build, as well as do some detection on whether we're falling into in-group/out-group traps. Finally, at project endings, people have time to reflect and carry forward the lessons of collaborative work, which can have enormous organizational ramifications on who we identify with and see as a potential collaborator.[31] Each of these moments works as a group formation point because they're times when our sense of *who we could be together* is more fluid.

Learning to notice norms is the first step to creating those intervention moments. Scan around you at a conference, and note how similarly people behave, share jokes, and organize. Think about the way you might speak at an all-hands, compared to a small team meeting with trusted colleagues. In both cases, a big part of what shapes your behavior choices is likely your awareness of situational and group norms. Norms reflect what we believe to be prototypical about a group or a setting and exert a powerful impact on individual behavior.[37] Many people constantly modify their behavior to try to express themselves within the parameters laid out by the people around them. For example, a developer who strongly internalizes the idea that their engineering team has a norm of giving harsh public feedback to all technical ideas might write cold, factual code reviews regardless of their own personal beliefs about it. That same developer may be far warmer when they're volunteering at a local library. And as organizations are shifting even more dramatically to multi-team systems where technologists need to negotiate simultaneous membership in many groups, situational team norms play an even bigger role in shaping behavior.

But norms steer us wrong when groups on the conflict path get rigid about them, policing people's behavior with backlash. Picture a developer who's a long-standing member of an open source project and decides to try a different approach to their shared project, one that isn't endorsed by all members. Now picture an outsider, perhaps a new contributor to the project, proposing the same idea. Who will receive harsher pushback? Given in-group bias, we might assume a group is always less likely to welcome new ideas from an outsider. But research has found that people sometimes react *more* negatively to their in-group members when they are seen as explicitly breaking norms. This is because of something expressively named the *Black Sheep Effect*. While we may be less empathic to outsiders in general, outsiders also don't violate our expectations when they behave in counter-normative ways. In-group members are a different story. We react to in-group members with both more positivity when they conform to our expectations and harsher punishment when they violate our normative expectations. Conscious of the discomfort of acting in opposition to the group, norm breakers themselves feel powerful self-directed physiological responses of anger, blame, and fear.[38–40]

Our beliefs about group norms come not just from the actions we see people around us take, but also from our subjective inferences about what we think other people *intend*. For example, when we think that other people are taking actions for prosocial reasons, we're more likely to think those actions are a group norm, and we should do them too. This is another reason that actively encouraging prosocial actions on software teams, such as asking senior technical staff to model mentorship and collaboration out loud in the workplace, has group benefits that can be larger than just the impact a single moment of mentorship has for the people directly involved. Seeing trusted colleagues take action can be a more powerful norm changer for developers than top-down instructions from leadership.[41,42]

On the flip side, although we're constantly being influenced by norms, we're also taking noisy guesses at what other people really think. This can lead to a fascinating group-level phenomenon called *pluralistic ignorance*. Pluralistic ignorance happens when people in a group make a collective error about their fellow group members' beliefs, in particular, that the group's beliefs do not match their own. A frequently cited example of this phenomenon is the overall positivity of people's beliefs in climate change policies versus what we guess; in one study, a majority of people in the United States supported climate change mitigation policies but erroneously estimated that a minority of their fellow citizens shared their views.[43] Pluralistic ignorance can be a powerful blocker of positive change because it might keep us from expressing our true views out of a distorted sense that we won't receive support for them within our own group. When we mistakenly believe that other people act and think differently than we do, this can also lead us to over-conform, dragging the group's norms further away from what we truly want.[44]

As you start to question the Brains-in-Jars assumptions around you, you might begin to notice patterns of pluralistic ignorance. As we saw in the AI Skill Threat study, a sizable percentage of software developers (although not all of them) internalize the belief that *other* software people as a whole will expect software to be a place where we engage in ruthless competition, try to detect impostors, and undervalue collective problem-solving. But many developers lean into the alternative cultures of open learning, sharing, and valuing mistakes, and valuing warm and inclusive teams that have learned to cultivate belonging. Many software developers, engineering managers, and tech leaders have quietly shared with me that they have burning questions about how we can improve technical environments. Decades of commentary on what creates beneficial software outcomes have continually surfaced the need to loosen the grip that competitive and individualistic defaults have on software.[45] And when I've asked developers in my research studies whether *they* consider "helping others" to be "an important part of the role of a software engineer," more than 90% of them say yes. Many leaders also tell me that they understand that patterns of isolation and competition create burnout for developers and ultimately make their businesses more brittle in the face of challenge, yet fear that their fellow leaders might not feel the same.

This matters because once cemented, these erroneous beliefs can keep us from trying to change our groups for the better. My user researcher friend likely experienced this in her group conflict: it's very likely that, individually, some of her engineer colleagues and some of her product colleagues could have recognized the same tensions she did and wished for a better working relationship. But the situational norms of those development and product meetings may have kept them from reminding the group of their superordinate goals, fueling the cycle of conflict. Remember the Black Sheep Effect and pluralistic ignorance the next time you find yourself unusually offended by a disagreement with someone in your group and ask yourself if your reaction contains a tinge of the desire to punish their deviance from the norm. Focusing the conflict on the *tasks* in front of them, rather than emphasizing their different role identities, could have helped. Groups who use structured strategies to surface dissenting viewpoints and affirm that dissenters are still valued members of our group, can break through conformity pressures. For instance, teams can explicitly acknowledge many points of view in the room and invite alternative perspectives to be shared before decisions.[46]

If teams can set new norms for valuing dissenting points of view, they increase the chance that positive change will surface. Leaders in particular should pay attention to who is most likely to change their groups from the inside. We might often assume that the people questioning our group norms are troublemakers, or at the very least, that they are people who don't care much about the group. Dissenters can face harsh criticisms that question their loyalty (have you ever pointed out a problem your team is failing to address, only to be told you're "not being a team player"?). However, care for the future of the group may be the very thing that's behind many dissenters' motivation to try to push their groups toward change.

Across four studies, Dominic Packer and Alison Chasteen uncovered that *strongly* identified group members were willing to dissent from a group norm when they reflected on possible harms to the group created by the norm.[47] Crucially, this effect did not emerge if the harms from the norm were merely individual, suggesting that loyal group members' dissent was primarily motivated by a prosocial desire to shift the group toward a better alternative. Packer developed a theory to explain these findings called the normative conflict model of dissent: when strongly identified group members are closely tuned in to possible problems their group is steering into, it's *because* such dissenters are motivated to help their group that their conscientiousness leads them to take action, even when the individual penalty is costly.[48,49]

If we're interested in encouraging the divergent thinking that leads to better technical problem-solving, we should take heed of the lessons in the normative conflict model. Contrary to our knee-jerk fears about them, the people most willing to vocally oppose group norms that go unquestioned may in fact care the most about our group's future thriving. Principled dissenters who break down in-group and out-group assumptions and question groupthink make their groups more adaptive. Minority dissent increases creativity, and open debate between dissenting viewpoints can drive expert triangulation of technical problems.[50] Another thing that happens when teams show they can welcome productive dissent is that this behavior signals to people that group norms are capable of being dynamic at all. This belief can be a powerful intervention lever. Research on signals that encourage people to make more sustainable choices even when they're seen as counter to group norms has found that increasing people's beliefs that norms could be dynamic in the first place shifts individual behaviors, even before the group norm has shifted. And when we watch people break social rules specifically to achieve ends that benefit others, we're more likely to attribute power to those individuals.[51,52]

And dissent has a powerful effect beyond better bug triages and project discussions. More evidence of the power of courageous dissenters comes from research on prejudice from Aneeta Rattan and colleagues, who studied the belief-changing impact that confrontation can have for people mired in group conflict. Across a series of ten studies conducted with over three thousand people, these researchers synthesized diverse evidence from hypothetical scenarios, retrospective reflections, and in-laboratory manipulations to show that observers of a confrontation conclude that someone who is willing to confront another person in their group about their racially biased behavior is modeling the belief that poor behavior can actually change.[53] People who are willing to call out destructive behavior from within their group are doing something uncomfortable but also signaling that they believe their fellow group members are capable of positive change. Leaders who create a safe response to these dissenters, celebrating their courage, shape their teams for the better.

COALITIONS IN CRISIS

We might think of an "internet mob" as inevitably instantiating the worst possibilities of group behavior, intensified by the relative anonymity of the internet and conformity. But in the summer of 2021, a moment of group psychology took technologists by storm in a very different way when an empty test email was mistakenly sent out to subscribers by an HBO Max intern.[54,55] Swiftly and humorously acknowledged in a post by the streaming service's social media, what happened next was a groundswell of conforming to *support*, not persecution. Under the hashtag or phrase "dear intern," hundreds of technologists, and eventually, people from all types of occupations, began to share their own stories of early job mistakes and failures. The group norm for these posts quickly converged on a tone that was celebratory, laughing, and compassionate, and the vast majority of posters reaffirmed that the intern belonged and still had a bright future in tech.

Multiple factors were likely behind the unlocking of empathy over censure in this moment. Making a mistake in a first job or internship is a highly relatable experience. In 2021, the streaming service landscape was a fast-moving and competitive space as many services vied for attention, a dynamic that likely meant technologists who had lived through previous product launch seasons could sympathize with the pressures facing these teams. The modeling of "dear intern" responses from senior people in respected technology positions, sharing their own mistakes, created a humorous frame that others could echo, as well as a reminder to readers of their shared humanity with the mistake-maker. Rather than responding with objectification and anger, people imagined a real person on the other side of the mistake as "one of our own" and acted accordingly. Humor is one of humanity's oldest tools for breaking down silos between people, and humor can often serve us as an emotional regulator, particularly when it is used for self-enhancing goals rather than self-deprecating goals—for instance, in creating a cognitive reappraisal of a difficult situation.[56] Recognizing that mistakes are a common experience is also a core component of self-compassion.[57] In many of the "dear intern" responses, I noticed technologists using strength-based framings on their experience, pointing out both the absurdity of large technology systems and human mistakes, but also validating that things could and would be ok after a distressing experience, and that making baffling mistakes in technology was part of our shared humanity, perhaps even a rite of passage.

Despite groups' potential to lock us into in-group bias and narrow thinking, large groups of people can and do also come together to rapidly respond, triage, problem-solve, and scale help in a way that individuals couldn't accomplish alone. While not every crowd response is a viral moment, you can probably think about moments in your team or technical organization when you felt your group cohere around conflict or coalition. Those moments can provide guidance to the group-organizing features that we often don't realize we're choosing. Another example of choosing coalitional thinking is the technical community habit of sending "HugOps" (a delightfully human-centered play on DevOps and all of the other -Ops addendums that are so popular in tech) to working teams when public incidents and breakdowns occur.[58] "HugOps" messages are kind-hearted, but they also play a normative role for groups by modeling an explicit statement of empathy with the human experience of the people working to respond under the pressure of public scrutiny. I find this type of collective psychological action tremendously poignant, and an important counterexample to the group conflicts that can divide us and the Brains-in-Jars models that ignore human needs. As tough as crises are, they can remind us of how much we're connected by shared humanity, even in technical spaces.

As group reactions are forming, we need early moments to set the narrative that catalyzes more coalitional reactions. For example, groups of people are sometimes less likely to act to help others compared with people alone, a famous phenomenon repeatedly found in psychology research called *the bystander effect.* However, recent large-scale meta-analytic examinations of the bystander effect, with a new understanding of our dynamic evaluation of the world, have revealed the more hopeful view that the bystander effect is less driven by lack of empathy than it is by lack of *information.* Bystander effects are ameliorated when people can easily recognize that the situation is an emergency, and one person who takes action, clarifying the situation to others, can start a chain reaction of aid.[59] When groups of people fail to respond to emergencies, it's often because of lack of certainty and lack of clear information, rather than lack of compassion. This is a much less depressing view of humanity.

As with internet crowds, many people assume that in aggregate, groups of people are prone to panic, take only self-centered actions, or even devolve into irrational violence during crises and emergencies. But many real-world studies of crowd behavior show the opposite. Across crises and emergencies, social scientists studying collective behavior have noted that most people are remarkably calm, rational, and prosocial during moments of crisis. Rather than turning on each other or taking an "everyone for themselves!" attitude, people in emergencies frequently act with tremendous empathy toward strangers and rapidly organize groups to coordinate care, rescue others, and minimize harm. Survivors frequently act as citizen responders, can be highly effective at both directly saving lives and offering social-emotional support, and because of their location at the center of events, can often have a more immediate impact than highly trained emergency personnel.[33,60–63]

This collective resilience that emerges from groups of people facing adversity has given researchers important new evidence about why and how we can rapidly form coalitions, a capacity that counterweights the old, entity theory idea that we're locked into unchanging group identities forever.[64] When we're united against a shared threat or motivated to achieve a collaborative goal, people can quickly craft a new common identity, able to rely on mutual support with the others around them. Working with, rather than against, our social identities can help this process. For instance, studies have found that when we're told that our group prizes empathy, we show more empathy to out-group members and their experiences.[65,66] Rather than being locked in an eternal battle between in-groups and out-groups from which we can never escape, we form diverse and novel group alliances based on our belief in the likelihood of others' coordination with us, and that we are remarkably adept at doing so. Our tendency toward intergroup conflict in the face of competing goals or threats to our group's status is an unfortunate downside of our deep desires to protect the people that we care about and guard our group against threats.[67] Psychologically healthy teams with supportive processes have a better toolkit to guard against these downsides of group thinking, by fostering dissent, setting norms around empathy, and breaking down conflicts in search of superordinate goals.

But hope is not lost if your particular in-group is struggling with elevating empathy. Emerging research on self-compassion has also suggested that people who are able to more strongly connect to a shared sense of humanity in how they think about themselves are also more likely bring that empathy to out-group members.[68] I find this uplifting because it reminds us that the connection between our individual psychology and our group psychology is a two-way street. As we saw with my friend Shaun's journey in the last chapter, the self-concepts we invest in for how we see ourselves can also shape the possibilities our minds are able to see for others. And this means that if you are a developer struggling inside of a "Chilly Climate," the work that you put toward cultivating self-compassion can result in benefits for yourself but also for others as you gain and model a deeper ability to recognize the humanity of your peers.

Increasing a team's collective awareness of their shared values can also matter deeply to the paths teams take. One example of this comes from the research on *self-affirmation*, which despite its use in pop psychology, has a serious meaning in psychological science. The scientific version of self-affirmation isn't about mantras or telling ourselves what we want to hear. Self-affirmation happens when we "firm up the self," described by psychologist David Sherman as taking action to demonstrate one's adequacy, inviting people to express and remember what's important to them. Reflecting on our values, why they matter to us, and actions we can take toward them helps us realize when we're unwittingly narrowing our identity and gives us a more expansive frame. As evidence toward this, intervention studies have found that engaging in a values affirmation exercise can promote large and immediate behavioral changes such as more prosocial actions, improved achievement under stress, and uncoupling of people's self-concepts from a threatening external situation.[69,70] Drawing on self-affirmation during moments we feel threatened reduces our defensive thinking, making us less prone to cognitive biases like rationalizing our biases or being defensive about how we're seeing other people's actions. You may even already know how to take advantage of activating self-affirmation: a developer who takes a moment to remind themselves of their values of security, or their care about an infrastructure project, or their love of programming exploration and problem-solving, is exercising self-affirmation.

These individually good factors associate with team impacts, as well. When my research team created a psychological intervention to directly improve developers' *individual* self-compassion and tested its impact in a randomized controlled trial, we found this directly improved developers' ability to participate in code reviews, providing *group* benefit.[71] In our studies, we've consistently found that developers who feel a greater sense of belonging on their teams, are statistically significantly more likely to rate their teams as collectively effective. Across many areas of the behavioral sciences, reframing people's appraisals of threat and helping them craft better tools for handling it, such as self-compassionate mindsets, and reinforcing those strategies with supportive environments, has been the core logic behind some of the most successful interventions on psychological outcomes. Psychologically healthy groups that promote adaptive mindsets are a huge part of that supportive environment; this is likely why we see that psychological and productivity outcomes for teams move together.[72] I believe that building team norms that genuinely reduce the threat that people can feel at work—either to their belonging or to their competency—is an underexploited but transformative goal for organizations and leaders. We'll explore this interaction between individuals and environments more deeply in Chapter 7.

Let's go back to those developer and product teams that couldn't stop seeing each other as the enemy and see if we can imagine a different path for them. A wise project leader, noticing the conflict, could have intervened on it in the beginning of the project, rallying the two sides to a new, shared identity. Inviting members of the groups in to actively set a superordinate group goal might have helped—a mounting body of evidence suggests that leaders who *share* leadership with empowered individual contributors achieve more effective teams.[73] Reminding the teams to triage emerging conflict at a crucial solidarity moment, like the midpoint of the project, could have helped to repair past hurts. Likewise, setting aside time to explicitly ask for diverging points of view (to which my user researcher friend could have contributed) could have interrupted the cycles of in-group bias on either side. And investing more deeply into lowering the threat temperature by ensuring all team members felt like they belonged and had opportunities to feel valued for their competence could have helped new coalitions emerge. Our groups shape our thinking, but they also aren't unchangeable destiny. Across both our work and personal lives, we continually adapt, cement, or shift our sense of what groups we belong to, and our actions are part of what sets our norms. That also means we have the power to make our groups happier, healthier, and more productive.

QUESTIONS TO ASK ABOUT CONFLICT AND COALITIONS

- What are groups that exist among developers in my organization? What groups have influenced how I see myself?
- Does my team treat other teams like an "out-group"? Is there a history of conflict between our groups?
- Can I look for "beginnings, midpoints, and endings" where I can help encourage healthy group norms?
- When have I seen someone in my organization dissent from a prevailing viewpoint? How was that received? Have I ever experienced being a dissenter?
- Where might it be possible for us to think about the "shared fate" we have with other people in our organizations? What practices reinforce this message, and what messages pit us against each other?
- Does my organization reinforce the "shared humanity" of people across different roles and functions during a crisis? Do we reward and recognize the prosocial actions of developers during incidents and other collectively stressful situations?

CHAPTER 6

Becoming an Organization That Wants to Understand Itself

WHY MEASURE? EVIDENCE STRATEGY AND BULLSHIT DETECTORS

"Numbers mean nothing," an engineering manager told me. "Businesses don't care what the data says. All data can be fudged. You're better off spending your time in some other field."

I was at a tech conference as the leader of the new, scrappy applied lab that I'd founded to create empirical evidence about the connection between developers' psychological environments and software development outcomes. In other words—we were numbers people. Maybe even worse, we were *numbers about feelings* people! During the break between sessions, I'd been describing my mission to a group of leaders. It was a tough moment to be challenged. I can still remember the conviction in this person's voice that *data = fake.*

But as a social scientist I've also seen how much evidence shapes our world. Empirical evidence had helped me steer schools toward prioritizing programs with lasting positive effects on learning, win grants for nonprofits serving rural populations, and test whether investing in free and open educational resources could boost learners' achievement on a national scale.[1] Here's the answer I gave that day: just as code can be used to create massive harm or extraordinary help, so can measurement. Measurement

DOI: 10.1201/9781003589112-6

is a tool. It's possible to get it right, and important to care about not getting it wrong. We need evidence to understand the world, and I want to be part of helping organizations use evidence well.

This isn't an easy challenge. Even after dedicating our lives to it, whether we're accurately measuring human experience is something social scientists fiercely debate. But measurement in workplaces is doubly hard because hypocritical uses of data cause so much damage. In an era of big data (but not necessarily *meaningful* data), many of us are deeply aware of measurement failures around us. Employees monitor what data is used to justify decisions to gauge whether they believe leadership cares about fair outcomes.[2] And when software work has been measured, it's frequently been with a narrow focus on punitive individual stack ranking, which further damages the trust that developers have in their organization's use of evidence.[3] While new frameworks for measuring software work emerge steadily, they often falter in the real world. As we found in our No Silver Bullets study (Chapter 3), simplistic averages from narrow software metrics like cycle time can have little comparative value between teams and organizations, and most likely capture many unmeasured environmental factors much more than individual effort. At the same time, vendors promise to pin software development down once and for all with magical benchmarks for developer productivity, justifying their claims with everything from brain scans to eyetracking to black box algorithms, all conveniently available for an annual fee.

This mess foments fear. Skeptical technologists who feel little input or agency over the ways they're measured correctly identify that numbers are often used to bullshit. Being mismeasured is a fundamentally threatening experience because it means that we feel misrepresented to others. Mismeasurement in our work introduces conflict between what we know we *need* to do to produce good outcomes and what we feel we need to perform. As we've been exploring, even small triggers that lead us to question whether we belong or will look competent to others can provoke an outsize reaction in our psychology, because these are important signals to us about whether we'll be seen for our true selves, get credit for our work, or stay in a treasured community.[4] Frequent disappointment with how leaders actually use organizational evidence also fosters deep cynicism. After one talk I gave, an anonymous employee dropped a confession in the Q&A chat: "I work with customer survey data all day long . . . but I've never answered a single one of our internal surveys. They say it'll give us a voice but never make a change based on our data. I assume the point is just to make leadership *look* like they're doing something."

I bet you've heard the same and felt the same. Across dozens of interviews, I've heard developers voice profound experiences of disappointment, fear, and anger around how software work gets measured. I love statistics, and I find the puzzles of measurement profoundly useful and fascinating (believe me, nothing else would've motivated me to get through the hazing ritual that was the graduate statistics sequence during my PhD!). I have a firm conviction that we can use data as a powerful force for positive change. Still, these feelings make a lot of sense to me. Turning complex human experience into compressed numbers is an imperfect process. We can and do make mistakes with it. When our institutions use data poorly and we experience the harsh effects of being mismeasured, we're not likely to forget it. But I don't think we're struggling with this because, as that manager suggested, "no one cares." In my experience technologists care deeply about what we measure, how we measure, and why we measure. This is *because* they know evidence matters.

Swiftly and accurately accessing evidence across our organizations can especially matter in high-stakes moments. This fundamental insight drove Amy Edmondson and collaborators to investigate whether the "psychological safety" in teams could be a reliable predictor of safety and performance outcomes across groups like surgery teams, manufacturing workers, and airline employees, among many others. If there's one concept from psychology that tech folks have heard before it's probably this one, thrust into the limelight by media coverage of an observational study at Google which reproduced the strong connection between team outcomes and team psychological safety.[5] Despite its fame (or maybe *because* of it!), engineering teams I work with often have a misconception that psychological safety just means everyone acts warm-and-fuzzy during interpersonal interactions. They're surprised when I say that as a psychologist, I think about psychological safety as being less about feelings, and more about teams' mindsets around evidence.

In the research, psychological safety is defined much more precisely than "being nice." It's a group-level belief that we'll face less interpersonal risk with disclosure, particularly for sharing negative information. As we learned in Chapter 5, groups that allow diverging perspectives to surface can avoid the groupthink traps of conformity and bias. Psychological safety reassures us that divergence is allowed and tells us that on *this* team, we won't risk dire interpersonal consequences when contributing a perspective.[6] Having access to a state of reduced risk makes us feel better personally, but it also unlocks information flow across the group. This is especially impactful because *without* a strong norm for psychological safety, negative information naturally faces a steep penalty in moving across an organization. We don't like to share bad news, and we're worried we might get blamed for it, particularly when we need to share organizational errors with people who have power over us. In fact, given the difficulty organizations already have understanding their software and IT projects, some researchers have suggested that it's *especially* hard for software experts to navigate disclosing the failures of software projects.[7–11]

This drag on reporting negative information leads to errors in our models for how *much* failure happens, because we think shared outcomes are representative of the outcomes that actually happened. Our bias against both seeing and sharing failure is big and consistent. For example, people systematically underestimate the true rates of negative outcomes in a wide variety of contexts, from health outcomes to business failures. In a series of seven studies, Lauren Eskreis-Winkler and collaborators documented that failure is underestimated and underreported across more than 30 domains, including national outcomes like healthcare and education, international failures in human rights and pollution, and individual negative outcomes like relationship breakups and medication failures.[12] This underestimation phenomenon is so consistent and consequential that they've given it a name: *the failure gap*. Psychological safety isn't a silver bullet that totally reverses the failure gap, but it does remove a major source of friction from the transmission of challenging information by reassuring us that our colleagues understand and value hard conversations. This increases the probability that we'll not only get *more* evidence flowing toward our decisions but also get more *diverse* evidence, yielding categorically different insight. Psychologically safe teams can learn from failure, while teams that can't tolerate facing failure won't. On a long enough time frame, and especially when quality and safety are included in measures of performance, psychologically safe teams not only outperform less psychologically safe teams but also see more innovation from employees.[13–15]

I keep the lessons of psychological safety in mind when I work on making *data = meaning* for software teams. To get to effective evidence, we need to create measurements that developers trust, take seriously harmful histories that have prevented them from trusting measurement in the past, and show developers that participating in our requests for evidence will benefit them and their teammates directly. To do this, we need to de-risk sharing good evidence. Thankfully, whenever I've helped teams embrace evidence strategy, this is a challenge they recognize. Every time we've dug deep into a team's most heated debates about how to do development, we've usually discovered we're having a conversation about evidence:

- If we had a good quarter, do we know what features drove it?
- Are we measuring the right things when we hire?
- If I'm setting a metrics target for all the software teams in my organization, can I justify that decision?
- If our leaders aren't seeing our impact, can we make that impact visible and undeniable?
- If we've measured something in a certain way in the past, will it work for another team in a different context?

Creating an evidence strategy is less about introducing something completely new than it is about taking notice of these already-present questions and motivating colleagues and teams to come together to invest in systematic information that fuels progress. I call this *becoming an organization that wants to understand itself.*

If that's not enticing enough, evidence literacy also builds you a great bullshit detector. The tech industry (and the world) is full of proliferating claims full of intimidating data about how software should work, who developers are, and what teams need. These can sound suspiciously like supplement ads at the end of a wellness podcast: *Buy this tool for your developers, and expect 500% productivity gains! If you don't work with our (proprietary) method you'll never understand your team! We are the only source for benchmarks for elite teams!* It's not shocking that in a world with as much money and stakes as software development, plenty of people are hoping for a gullible audience under pressure. Data literacy and a healthy skepticism about claims help you navigate through the noise and make your own judgments about what counts as strong evidence. Having even a few thinking tools you use to break down specious causal reasoning can defang claims and protect you and your organization from evidence snake oil.

Rather than trying to stuff a research methods textbook into this chapter, we'll explore foundational concepts to give you a starting place for an evidence-based practice that generates more reliable insights. The goal isn't for you to learn every statistical technique or become a quantitative scientist—a good evidence strategy will also help you recognize when you need to bring in experts to tackle complex measurement problems. You'll also notice I'm not endorsing a specific software metrics framework. That's because of two things: there isn't much robust and replicated empirical evidence around which ones produce the best outcomes for organizations, and I firmly believe you'll likely need to assess many metrics, frameworks, and measurements over the course of your career for goals that only you will be able to determine. This chapter is about evidence strategy, not metrics. Evidence strategy focuses on what it takes to motivate creating evidence and validate our theories about what causes what. An evidence strategy will strengthen your decision-making and give you a structural foundation for evaluating the causal stories we tell about software teams. Just like maintaining software, maintaining a healthy evidence practice is a constant practice. The reward is seeing more about the world around you and a better map for creating change.

MOTIVATING EVIDENCE-BASED PRACTICE

The first study I designed to learn how software teams used evidence was, in true psychologist fashion, very meta. I wanted to know how developers *perceived* their organizations' attempts to measure their work. Did developers think leaders were making good choices? Did developers even know what their leaders used as evidence? What advice would *they* give to their organizations?

Software research documents a lot of misalignments between developers and their managers on this. In a survey study, Margaret-Anne Storey and collaborators documented just how differently developers and their leadership looked for signals of productivity, with developers focusing more on *activity* and managers more likely to focus on outcomes like performance and efficiency.[16] However, sample sizes from studies like these are often small (only 34 managers were included in that study) and shaped by being entirely from a single company, with all of its existing norms, histories, and shared context (in this case, Microsoft). Perhaps not surprising given the Brains-in-Jars models that keep organizations from inviting their developers into these decisions, it's hard to find studies that share developers' judgments of measurement practices with a public sample recruited from diverse organizations, industries, demographics, and countries. Because of this, I turned to the lived experience of practitioners to design our questions. Eric Bouwers, Joost Visser, and Arie van Deursen had summarized 11 years of advising software organizations into practical guidance for avoiding pitfalls in measurement.[17,18] I used this guidance as inspiration to create our own lightweight *Measurement Pitfalls* scale. With my lab's researchers Carol Lee and Morgan Ramsey, we pilot tested these new measures to ensure developers felt they were accurate to their lived experience. Here were our four pitfalls:

1. We tend to measure things without enough context.
2. We're concerned about the appearance, but not really the meaning, of what we've measured.
3. We have not measured enough things.
4. We measure many things, but they do not feel related to each other.

Developers could select more than one option or indicate when they believed none applied (and write in their own answers!). Developers also answered a battery of items about their team's practices around data. Inspired by research that proposed both the perceived utility and perceived value of software metrics could predict their adoption, we also asked developers to rate how *useful* they thought software metrics were, along with how much they felt that tracking and quantifying their work helped them and helped their teammates and managers have a shared understanding of how work was progressing.[19]

Surprising us, across our sample of more than one thousand developers of many ages, genders, countries, racial identities, career levels, and industries, developers had very positive attitudes toward measurement. Eighty-seven percent of developers agreed that tracking and sharing patterns in software development could help their teams make trade-off decisions, increase the visibility of technical work, help them understand teammates' work, and help individual developers reflect on their own progress. Interestingly, when we examined them separately, even developers who reported that their teams were falling into a pitfall remained strongly positive about the benefits of measurement in general. At the same time, we surfaced warning signs: roughly 70% of developers reported that they believed their team was falling into one or more of the four pitfalls (the most common were "we have not measured enough things" and "we tend to measure things without enough context"). Even on the simplest questions, we were alarmed to see that 26% of developers reported they didn't even *know* if their managers and leaders used measures (survey design protip: you learn a lot from including an "I don't know" response option!). We explored but found no evidence for statistically significant differences in how likely developers were to report experiencing measurement pitfalls by engineering role, industry, and other demographics.

Because our project was so explicit about centering the developer point of view, it gave us not just a measure of how many teams used measurement, but what happened when developers were truly bought into it. In a category we dubbed "healthy metrics users," we explored when software developers reported that their teams (1) had consistent measurement practices and (2) agreed that those measurements were "right for us." Only a small group (14%) were healthy metrics users. But the benefits of being in this category were striking. Alongside the powerful effects of the human-centered factors of learning culture, agency, belonging, and self-efficacy (our Developer Thriving model), the developers on Healthy Metrics teams reported greater productivity than comparable developers.[20] And because of our diverse sample, we were able to test that this connection was present when controlling for many demographic, organizational, and industry variables.

You may have noticed our Healthy Metrics study is descriptive rather than prescriptive. When we're struggling to understand conflicting evidence ("measurement helps software development!" "no, measurement harms software development!"), it usually means we haven't specified our questions precisely enough. If our study had just asked developers to rate how satisfied they felt with their team's use of metrics without layering in more multidimensional information *about* that usage, I might have come out of it saying, "well, some developers love measures and some hate them," failing to reflect the reality that many developers found value in measurement but also had meaningful critiques of how their teams were implementing it and where it should be used. By separating out the situation into components that we had reason to think might change the picture, like developers' buy-in to how measures were being used, we found pointers toward what leaders should think about.

When teams are divided on the right practice, I usually find it's better to start by getting a clearer picture of what's really happening rather than charging ahead with a one-size-fits-all answer. Our Healthy Metrics study validated what I'd already heard from developers: unlocking the benefit of measurement is complicated. Whether developers agree with an organizational measure depends on the context of its usage as well as the content of the measure. Another evidence tip: nearly every complex topic can be understood better when we try to layer in categorically different kinds of evidence. For example, in psychology, mixed methods studies bring together qualitative and quantitative data to look at the same underlying phenomenon. Roughly speaking, quantitative evidence = translated into numbers. Qualitative evidence = everything else not easily viewed as numbers, from open text to interviews to focus groups.

In our Healthy Metrics study, people also shared their in-depth perspectives in qualitative form. An engineering manager with 15 years of experience managing teams described the context dilemma of measurement eloquently: "If a manager makes a certain metric important, software engineers will learn how to game that metric. That is ultimately where [software measurement] falls apart. However, if a serious engineer or a team with a really good culture takes metrics seriously, they can improve themselves and their process dramatically."

This manager's comment echoed an adage often attributed to both the economist Charles Goodhart and the social anthropologist Marilyn Strathern: "When a measure becomes a target, it ceases to be a good measure" (fun fact, Goodhart did not precisely say this. Apocryphal quote websites can perhaps be forgiven for seeking something pithier when his actual work reads like this: "Any observed statistical regularity will tend to collapse once pressure is placed upon it for control purposes"[21]). I've always favored the eponymous law of Donald Campbell, a social scientist, which describes the human behavior change we're usually most worried about: "the more any quantitative social indicator is used for social decision-making, the more subject it will be to corruption pressures and the more apt it will be to distort and corrupt the social processes it is intended to monitor."[22] Unlike rocks, galaxies, trees, or cells, human beings are conscious of being measured and adapt to how measures about them are used, which makes measuring human behavior incredibly tricky. But neither of these observations proclaimed that measurement was always *meaningless.* Rather, they both point out that we need to be precise and careful about knowing what our measurements truly mean.

To me, measurement needs to be a collaboration. Getting a good measure to *stay* a good measure becomes about creating the context that rewards good evidence for emerging, mitigating the perverse incentives that discourage authentic participation, and setting outcomes that we actually want to achieve, rather than thoughtlessly defaulting to just measuring the thing that seems easiest. Measurement tells people what we have chosen to care about, and good measurement invites them to decide it's worth it to engage authentically in our evidence process. Both our engineering manager and developers' perspectives on measurement point toward what that context needs to have: a demonstrated and shared commitment to using evidence for real understanding and culture improvement. In fact, a supportive context might be what psychological scientists call a *mediator* for obtaining the benefit of using metrics: a third variable that changes the direction of the relationship between x and y.[23] Because of our findings, but also because of mountains of empirical research that tells us people need to buy into interventions for them to work (more on this in Chapter 7), I believe a focus on collective learning and co-design of evidence is the right mediator to unlock.

Difficult though it may be for some individual contributors to believe, in my research I've found that managers *also* feel frustrated by the limitations of the measures their organizations use and worry about how to represent developers' effort, learning, and progress correctly. When I gathered qualitative examples from 112 engineering managers describing how they would advocate for their teams to get more time and space for learning, a key theme that managers emphasized was translating developers' effort into protective measures (for instance, extended timelines, or measuring learning outcomes or code quality improvements) that would defend the value of their time.[24] My lab and I developed an exercise in which we asked leaders to sort examples of different software metrics and describe what their organization *did* measure, versus what they *wanted* their organization to measure. When we took it to a technology conference, managers made rueful faces and jokes as many of them shared that they wanted to decrease how much their organization used measures of "production," simplistic metrics like number of tickets closed.[25] I adapted our card sorting exercise into an evidence ice-breaker and still use it when I work with software leaders designing new evidence strategies. It's remarkable how much opening up the discussion about whether we're really getting from our metrics can yield new points of view in the room.

What we can change *within* a person, especially by presenting them with opportunities to use more adaptive strategies, is an area of psychology I love about because it's a powerfully effective way to create cultural change. Just like teams can overcome conformity pressures by committing to moments to bring dissenting perspectives to the surface, when working through challenges, people often learn best with a little structure.[26–28]

If you're a manager, leader, or someone trying to design a new measurement approach, I encourage you to use scaffolding to drive a conversation with your team about co-designing for shared evidence goals, perhaps in the form of a team conversation. Like those critical moments of team formation, the beginning of an evidence project can be a moment that reinforces a group value around evidence. Demonstrating a commitment to psychological safety is especially important if the evidence process uncovers times when people felt their work was misrepresented. In the spirit of all those measurement "laws," I encourage you to explicitly acknowledge the existence of common measurement pitfalls, like always assuming any number should always go "up and to the right." Ask your developers to weigh in on times a metric can be misleading, and important variables that aren't captured in it. You will likely learn that important types of work are less legible to the organization, weakening its decision-making and observability across software development. One developer in our study described the ways that focusing on tracking code production can systematically give more credit to individuals in certain roles while ignoring the collaborating work of others:

> On highly collaborative teams or teams where individuals may wear a lot of 'hats,' just tracking code is only one slice of the picture. It can present a false metric on productivity. For instance, if you are great at looking at the big picture and remove obstacles from others' paths, you are benefiting the team as a whole but the reflected code metrics are not attributed to you and the other individual.

When I shared this quote with a professional development group for engineering managers who had invited me to talk about evidence, one manager had an epiphany. Her senior contributors were expected to aid others, but this wasn't represented in any of the metrics that went into performance evaluation. Fired with resolve, she went back to her workplace and created a new performance category to specifically recognize mentorship. Performance evaluations were something she had previously considered boring and unchangeable—but after working with her organization's learning and development function, she was able to introduce this small but meaningful change. The evidence for mentorship was kept intentionally broad (for instance, qualitative feedback from peers about impact counted) but formalized her commitment to rewarding those activities. With human goals in mind, we can use structured approaches to evidence to broaden our organization's attention.

As we learned in Chapter 3, approaches that assume developers work in isolation won't accurately capture the mutually interactive nature of software work. Putting too heavy a hand on this type of measurement, with a simplistic theory ("everyone should increase velocity forever!"), incentivizes the wrong behaviors for actual innovation. However, given a demonstrated commitment to safe listening, I've always found developers incredibly willing to openly share and even offer potential solutions to gaps in incentive structures. If you're a measurement decision-maker for your organization, the collective evaluation of measurement is where you can iterate on a shared evidence strategy together *with* your teams. Doing this can be more than a bit terrifying because it requires you to have some collective intellectual humility; in other words, a culture of admitting out loud and in public that you don't know everything, and that you need other people's help. But these moments of courage give us the chance to shift our groups toward psychological safety. Leaders who consistently demonstrate humility can start a domino effect on their teams, as people begin to believe that collective striving toward improvement will truly be rewarded.[29,30]

I've had to face this challenge myself trying to serve technical communities, so I know it can be scary. I've long been inspired by a research philosophy called *participatory action research*. Action research springs from many traditions, but at its core it seeks to affirm the value of people's lived experiences in shaping science and sees research as most valuable when it helps a community actively move forward. In action research, scientists work as partners in dialogue with communities, rather than acting as isolated authorities.[31] Action research also suggests that empirical studies need to have direct benefits for the people who participate in them. Toward these values, I've worked to ensure the studies I've led have design components that help participants reflect on and improve their experience. Where possible, we've released open workbooks and coupled our recruiting with a donation from the research team to an open source software foundation chosen by our participants. But inviting the community in has also had its tough moments. Like that manager who told me numbers mean nothing, I've fielded feedback from developers that criticized every word of our studies, or said we were studying the wrong topics altogether. But I've never regretted opening up our work to technical communities.

The powerful insights we've gotten from our community, which have deeply improved our work, are more than worth it.

Likewise, in a company, the developers whose expertise, experiences, and insights you need are critical stakeholders in designing evidence about software development. Leaders need to establish that measurement practices will have benefits for the people trusting them with data. In my studies, I have often used *co-design* practices, such as pilot testing our ideas with a small collection of developers, or inviting developers to comment on the validity of our language and concepts before we finalize our study materials, or even taking in study requests from many people across my public audience, which helps me learn about where their greatest needs lie. Co-design is remarkable for creating more valid measures because it challenges us consider how people might have experienced being excluded, misrepresented, or harmed by measurement. When I sit across the table from a developer and hear her tell me about a team where she felt forced to close tickets rapidly against her own judgment because she was being pressured by her manager to not drag down a team average, I don't hear someone who's complaining, "gaming the metric," or being oppositional. I hear someone communicating a vital piece of information about what system is forcing individuals to do, as well as pointing to the solution (figure out why managers are doing this, and change their behavior!). Developers will often be living and working the closest to the actual effects you're trying to generalize about in your organization and have powerful intuitions about what we should expect an effect to look like. While I've seen many organizations invite developers to suggest content for their evidence strategies, such as lists of pain points in the software development lifecycle, I've rarely seen organizations invite developers to weigh in on measurement misconceptions, such as a reasonable threshold for a given team's context, an inappropriate benchmark source, or effects where they see nonlinear relationships that have more complicated patterns than simple positive correlations.

Another powerful culture lever is transparency in the early stages of evidence planning that allows for traceability between evidence and the changes we want people to make. This empowers teams to take an active role in evaluating conclusions. One example of this for scientists is open pre-registration. Just like sharing a product roadmap with a community of users, pre-registration is a practice in which we share a public "plan" for a research study *before* we do it, including what we're hypothesizing and why, and how we're going to analyze the data. For researchers, this pre-commitment helps to guard us against the temptation to report only the findings that best match our hypotheses. For readers, it means that you get a backstage pass to the thinking that inspired a project and choices made about what to report. I've found transparency practices inspired by pre-registration to be surprisingly beneficial for internal teams working on standing up a new evidence plan. Showing developers the design of a project and committing to a plan that shows them how you'll go from data design to decision points establishes trust even when plans are imperfect. It gives you something to refer back to and helps guard decisions against slipping away from the actual evidence and what we decided it would mean. The simple step of pre-committing to an evidence and analysis plan can show that we care about reporting what the data really says, even when it contradicts our beliefs.

LESS BIASED TOGETHER

In a classic piece of experimental psychology known as the Marshmallow Study, Walter Mischel and Ebbe Ebbesen tested whether young children could wait alone in a room with a marshmallow. Waiting children who were able to refrain from the temptation to scarf the treat as soon as the researcher left were promised a *future* reward that the child thought was more valuable than the tempting, and present, treat (depending on the child's preference another possible future reward was a pretzel, but I guess "pretzel study" just doesn't have the same ring to it). The Marshmallow Study aimed to measure *delay of gratification*, our ability to push off an immediate reward for the sake of a delayed outcome. Mischel and collaborators went on to propose that children's results on the Marshmallow Test were associated with better long-term life outcomes such as academic performance and stress coping.[32,33]

People *loved* the Marshmallow Study. I learned about it in my first college psychology class, and you'll find *delay of gratification* in thousands of thinkpieces about parenting. The Marshmallow Study was an evocative and appealing experiment that has direct resonance with childhood experience (many people can remember a childhood struggle to resist stealing treats from the kitchen counter). Its conclusions are neatly packaged into a theoretical story that feels pleasingly coherent and matches our desire for science to yield interesting but sensical discoveries: better achievement outcomes are driven by our capacity for self-control, and one clever test could detect individual differences that added up over a lifetime, explaining major differences in life trajectories.

The problem is, that story was wrong. In 2013, a study by Celeste Kidd and collaborators took a fresh look at the Marshmallow Test and revealed that children's responses changed if they were put in environments that were shown to be unreliable.[34] In other words, children don't wait for a future reward if they have a rational reason to believe that promised reward will never materialize, because previous promises went unfulfilled. It turns out the Marshmallow Test isn't a pure, unbiased measure of self-control. Rather, wait times are a noisy signal that can be shifted by multiple factors, including children's rational judgments about what is most likely to happen in their environment. And because some children experience more unstable environments than others, it's possible that the original connection between wait times and future achievement was actually picking up on a third variable outside of the study: the less predictable rewards experienced by lower-income children. More rigorous analysis went on to show that performance on the Marshmallow Test does not seem to reliably associate with achievement by adults.[35]

When we set out to create evidence, we're typically operating with a theory in mind: a proposed explanation for why a set of things we observe allows us to predict future behavior. In order to put evidence behind our theories, every time we design a measure, we collapse a small piece of our complex world down to a tangible thing we can grapple with. Psychologists call the process of defining a measure *operationalization*. When we operationalize things into variables, we usually do so because we hope they will point us to *constructs*, the unmeasured phenomena that we think are important to the part of the world we want to understand. *Minutes-before-snack-gets-eaten* is an operationalization. *Delay of gratification* is a construct. And theories give us the story that justifies caring about our measures, proposing explanations that unite constructs and their interactions into a coherent system.[36]

Making sure that our operationalizations actually correctly point to our constructs, and that our constructs are coherent, takes expertise and effort. Figuring out how to craft better operationalizations is a constant living and breathing work, and construct validity (or whether we're really measuring what we claim to be measuring) is a massive debate for most areas of science.[37] But it matters, because vagueness in how we've actually matched our underlying construct to its operationalization is an evidence killer. For example, in a project that had 15 different teams come up with tests for five hypotheses that were only described conceptually, highly varied operationalizations produced contradictory evidence.[38] Crucially, getting more concrete and transparent about theories, constructs, and operationalizations makes them actionable because this allows us to test our theories in systematic ways and unlocks the potential for others to test our ideas as well. The original theory for the Marshmallow Study task didn't hold up against better evidence. But scientists could introduce a new variable ("environmental stability") to test the theory, which makes this story more a scientific success than failure. When we build with evidence strategy that lets us systematically update our beliefs, we're always improving how clearly we see the world. You might not always be in a position to seriously test the theories around you. But anyone can adopt the "test/retest" mindset of a scientist to assess evidence and strengthen *what* information you're using to explain your experience. In fact, in-depth field studies suggest that highly creative development teams are marked by deliberate practices of systematically generating and discussing alternative explanations for why things went the way they did, engaging in constantly refining theories.[39]

Another powerful benefit of the test/retest mindset is that it can help you realize when you're filtering evidence through cognitive biases. Our minds love to interpret evidence in systematically skewed ways that feel right in the moment, but actually exclude parts of the picture.[40] There are dozens of possible cognitive biases that people might fall into when evaluating effects in the world, but here are the umbrella categories I've found most useful for software teams thinking about their evidence:

- Anchoring bias: overweighting the first piece of information we get (e.g., our manager throws out a tentative benchmark for a certain metric, and that sticks in our minds as the reasonable value simply because it's the first one we heard. Future targets are now limited to a window around that first value).
- Availability bias: when we believe that things that more easily come to mind are more true (e.g., individual effort explanations for software velocity are more familiar and accessible to our minds after we've read a lot of social media chatter about individual developer productivity. When we look at financial outcomes, we assume that our quarterly performance must be the result of our coworkers' slowness, because their actions are more tangible to us than the macroeconomic forces impacting the industry).

- Confirmation bias: searching for evidence that confirms our already held beliefs rather than considering alternative explanations (e.g., a leader who believes that remote work damages collaboration only notices moments of friction from her remote team, rather than their many moments of collaboration. Even when evidence of collaboration is presented to her, such as senior developers holding virtual mentorship sessions, she interprets this as proof that developers struggle with remote work).
- Framing bias: making a different judgment when information is framed as a loss or a gain, even when the information is the same (e.g., choosing a method when we hear it has a "60% success rate at detecting defects" but not when we hear it has a "40% failure rate at detecting defects").
- Hindsight bias: believing that past events were more certain or predictable than they were because we know the outcome (e.g., concluding that an incidents team "should have known" an outage would happen because of a small spike in error rates, even though the error rates were within normal variation and such small spikes are frequently not followed by an outage, so a small spike is not a reliable signal).
- Recency bias: overweighting recent events or current experience and underweighting less recent information, making our predictions distorted by current trends (e.g., panicking when we see our team's velocity slow down, rather than realizing it always slows down during quarterly planning, and that the slowdown is reliably cancelled out by a future uptick in velocity).
- Selection bias: when what we are able to observe is systematically shaped by factors in how our observations are chosen (e.g., because people are more likely to voice feedback when they experience strong emotions about what they've experienced, when we examine customer satisfaction that comes only from customers who reached out to voice feedback, we don't hear from quiet but satisfied customers. Or when a hiring requirement demands experience with a certain tool, but that tool has missing accessibility features, meaning that any role requiring this tool will always exclude people with these accessibility needs).

This might be starting to feel like a lot of scientific jargon (psychologists like naming new technical terms just as much as engineers!). But think of these terms as conceptual handles, helping you carry evidence strategy into your conversations. Evidence concepts are especially useful for diagnosing what a measurement argument is truly about, and therefore, how to resolve it. For example, a team that can agree that they all care about improving collaboration, but disagree with how it's being measured, has an operationalization issue. But a team that doesn't agree on whether collaboration is really part of developer productivity might have a theory argument. And many arguments are hiding in the methods we use to collect our data, meaning that you can improve your decisions greatly by bringing some thoughtfulness to addressing biases in what's getting represented in your evidence. Are we operating with a selection bias because it's simply easier to record certain activities in our organization, or somebody else built a system for it, and now we feel beholden to that? Naming this can help identify when we need to invest in gathering new examples or developing a better theory in the first place.

Our biases are often strongest when we try to design and interpret evidence alone. This is another reason designing for evidence over time as a collective practice helps our teams avoid the perils of skewed information. Biases in *who* we ask and measure, like the selection bias, can warp our view. So can *what* we ask and measure, including the types of methodologies we use to gather data, which is why most teams are best served with a diversity of approaches. In my consulting with organizations, I've often found that when software teams are given permission to imagine designing new fit-for-purpose evidence targeted at answering specific questions rather than warping all their questions to fit convenient pre-existing data, developers show a renewed sense of agency and accountability. Investments in evidence strategy can have a ripple effect in unexpected places, including how developers invest in the broader insight strategies of the company. One developer put it like this: "I realized we could do better in hearing from our users, who are people like us, not just datapoints."

EVIDENCE LADDERS

The moment I started sharing open science about software teams, I began receiving emails from practitioners asking if I had evidence they could use to argue for the adoption of any number of trendy software development methodologies or best practices. At the same time, I started getting emails from software practitioners bemoaning the *introduction* of that very same methodology and asking if I had any evidence to disprove its efficacy. Memorably, I once gave a talk after which I fielded two different conversations, one from an adherent of a methodology and one from an opponent of the same methodology, who each believed their methodology was the obvious path to the good psychology I was talking about!

The truth is, I can rarely answer these types of requests because, while it's possible that one side is wrong, it's *also* possible that both folks are accurately seeing different things happen in their local context. Requests to prove whether one approach "always wins" for all contexts in the universe are often impossible for your beleaguered researcher friends to answer because the question is too vague, big, and messy. This is something that we call *underspecified:* it's actually many different evidence questions hiding inside of a big question trenchcoat. In order to study what effects really exist, such as that "team uses x method" is associated with more "profit" (or "customer value" or "satisfaction"), I would need to create a great deal more measurement precision and often unlock a chain of answers that let me drill into not just that something works, but under what conditions. Usually, the answer I would actually give to these two practitioners is a frustrating one, but a scientist's go-to answer: *it sounds like it depends.* Senior technical practitioners can probably relate.

But we can study what works and why as long as we're willing to think carefully about it again and again. We need a thoughtful evidence strategy that includes *it depends.* When we see opposite outcomes from the same set of practices, it's often because we're missing an important piece of context that shapes whether or not teams are able to get the benefit from that method. Identifying that missing context could unlock the answer. For example, teams in a small company might respond to practices that emphasize taking individual initiative, while teams at a large company might need practices that emphasize mutual persuasion. Making our lives even more difficult is the fact that there are different types of causal relationships. A *necessary* cause is something that absolutely must be present for our event to occur, like a genetic mutation that's necessary for a certain disease. However, necessary causes aren't inevitable. Much of the time not all the people who have a genetic mutation will end up developing the associated disease. A *sufficient* cause, however, tells us that X will definitely result in Y, but it may also not be the only way to get to Y. Death is an example of an outcome with many sufficient causes, from accidental falls to drowning. On a more positive note, you can keep in mind that many *different* software methodologies could each be a sufficient cause of better outcomes for a software team, assuming they all allow developers to work in alignment with their core psychology. Identifying those core psychological features is where the theories you've been learning for this entire book come in handy.

Effects can also be real, but downstream of other factors. Does a specific software methodology *always* produce an effect, or does it only produce an effect *if* it fills a gap that a team was struggling with? Is it possible to get to the same good outcome with multiple paths? The *it depends* evidence strategy recognizes that to trust an answer about team practices for *this time*, and *this place*, we might need to go out and gather much more information about the heterogeneity in the environments that developers inhabit and the diversity of strategies that can work. Across the behavioral sciences, researchers recognize that for pretty much every intervention we design and implement, successful change emerges under a certain set of conditions, and likely fails to emerge under other conditions. We call this *effect heterogeneity*, and accurately modeling it can save us from accidentally throwing away real solutions just because they fail to emerge universally.[41] We'll explore more examples of this in the next chapter as we learn about the hard-won lessons of intervention science. But for now, keep in mind that an evidence mindset means learning to recognize moments of underspecified questions and the reality of effect heterogeneity, and making a plan for how you can more precisely specify within your local context.

Even a small amount of pushing yourself to make this plan can greatly clarify your causal reasoning. When we're casting about for causal stories, we usually start too big: what methodology is *best*, what makes work *work*, *who* should I hire? We often *think* we're evaluating the whole picture when instead we're imagining simplified concepts at a high level, making fuzzy generalizations about ill-defined and abstract categories. Without better specifying your causal model, you'll likely end up frustrated by data that turns out to not feel very relevant to the actual decisions you must make or falsely confident about a misleading theory that misses an important factor. To avoid this fate, I recommend being able to answer three questions: (1) what kind of specific effects are you interested in, over what timeframe, and for what outcomes?, (2) how can you refine and then use the evidence that you'll be able to actually get in the real world?, and (3) can you design to reveal *counterfactuals*, or alternative explanations for the things you're observing? When we force ourselves to get specific about the questions we want to ask as well as our real constraints, we frequently reveal hidden assumptions and constraints in our mental models. For example, while you might start with a high-level question like "does a practice work," specifying the question will often reveal that you really care about something like, "will introducing this specific practice, which we've defined as working in this way, improve our sense of autonomy, and speed up our delivery?"

With unpacking and specifying, you now have something tangible to build with: a couple of possible outcomes ("delivery speed" and "sense of autonomy"), and maybe even the beginnings of important implementation ideas and mediators ("I'm going to try to get the team to do this practice for a long enough time that it's reasonable to think it'll have an effect" and "I better test this practice not just when we've got slack, but also when we're pushing under deadlines"). And if you realize that you have an alternative set of practices as your opposing decision path, that could give you a counterfactual ("is this practice uniquely important to gain autonomy, or do some teams in my organization have autonomy while working differently?" Or "can we try one practice and then the other, and assess them both for strengths and weaknesses?"). Now you're engaging in evidence strategy: *designing* to evaluate change and outcomes in terms of the factors that you can actually change. I find engaging in this question-unpacking process especially handy for moving any debate away from tired ideological battles and toward a plan for productive diagnosis of a team's specific situation. Much of the time, even opposing sides can be brought together to agree on an evidence strategy that gives each side the chance to see what approach wins out.

Don't have the power to really test things over time in your workplace? You can still build a better evidence strategy with an evidence *audit*. What do we currently know and use to inform our decisions, and how certain do we feel about it? Being able to categorize types of evidence and their strengths and limitations can help you assess how systematic (or chaotic!) the evidence around you really is for the causal stories you or others are telling about software development outcomes.

Consider the following examples:

- Controlled experiments that assess the impact of a specific intervention. For example, randomly assigning a large group of software developers to use a new tool for getting through tasks, measuring their ratings of their own productivity as well as measuring the quality of the tasks, and comparing these scores to a similar control group who did the same tasks without the new tool.

- Natural experiments or observational causal inference. For example, creating a staggered roll-out for an infrastructure change across a large engineering organization such that some software teams have access to a certain tool and other software teams doing comparable work do not yet have that access, and measuring differences between the teams' velocity over time.
- Observational or descriptive studies, such as running a survey on developer experience about various tools within your organization, examining developers' average scores of satisfaction, and looking at how those averages vary between teams and engineering roles.
- Qualitative inquiry—which could be the topic of an entire book in itself. For example, conducting conversational interviews with senior members of the technical team and writing up a document that lists key "themes" from the conversations. Looking back at the recorded comments across incidents, and reading the text for patterns. Interviewing customers and summarizing themes about their perceptions of your product.

Which type of evidence feels the most compelling and convincing to you? Which feels the most open to interpretation or preliminary? If you're like most people, you probably have an implicit hierarchy for strength of evidence in your mind that roughly corresponds to the order of these bullet points. Each method has strengths and weaknesses. Controlled experiments are often considered stronger and more robust evidence than observational studies because when we can design and learn from controlled manipulations, we are able to directly examine whether changing something in the world affects our outcome in the way that we've theorized, and hopefully, control for the many other factors that might be hidden in an observational study. Qualitative inquiry is rich and detailed but also open to many different interpretations, and because it's quite labor-intensive, often more limited by sample size. Observational studies are informative and can help us reach large groups of people, but don't always give us that clear test for a counterfactual explanation, or can pick up on effects from unmeasured variables, so it's important to gauge whether they're backed by a solid theory and keep those limitations in mind. Like it is in our problem-solving and our groups, diversity is a strength when it comes to evidence strategy.

In a set of recommendations developed by a team of social scientists who work directly on helping governments and organizations use behavioral science, Hans IJzerman and colleagues cautioned against making sweeping decisions on incomplete evidence.[42] They proposed that behavioral science take inspiration from an unusual source: NASA. Modeled on the "Technology Readiness Levels" developed to provide a benchmark for how ready technologies are for implementation beyond their development context, they put together an "Evidence Readiness Levels" framework for evidence about people, where each step up the ladder guides us toward more supported decisions.

Level	Description
ERL 9	Use the solution to successfully address a crisis situation; feedback evaluation to expand evidence
ERL 8	Conduct large-scale testing of the solution in settings as close to the target settings as possible
ERL 7	Test the solution in a variety of settings and stimuli in a lab environment
ERL 6	Establish causal inference and potential side effects in a lab environment, testing replicability via cross-validation
ERL 5	Compare candidate solutions in observational settings (relying on data-driven techniques), generating formal predictions for positive expected effects and (unintended) side effects
ERL 4	Select measures; evaluate validity and measurement equivalence
ERL 3	Conduct systematic reviews to select potential evidence of candidate solutions
ERL 2	Consult people in the target settings to assess the problem's/problems' applicability
ERL 1	Define the problem(s) in collaboration with stakeholders

Evidence Readiness Levels for Social and Behavioral Science. Reproduced with permission from: IJzerman, H. *et al.* Use caution when applying behavioural science to policy. *Nature Human Behaviour* 4, 1092–1094 (2020). Springer Nature.

I see these steps as functioning more like mutually beneficial points of view than competing ways of knowing. We need them all. Different methods are appropriate (or may be our only choice) for different questions. Psychological experiences like a sense of belonging are mostly only reliably measurable by self-reports, but self-reports will also contain participant biases. However, contrary to popular opinion, people *are* quite good at many self-reports when you design the items well, and especially when you use validated, empirically studied measures. Most "implicit measures" that attempt to measure psychology in sneakier ways (such as error rates in perception) have turned out to be far less reliable and noisier than just asking people to report on their mental thoughts and feelings.[43] Every method has limitations to keep in mind that may help us choose what's most important for our particular questions. Controlled experiments are tremendously powerful but expensive, slow, and often out of scope for everyday questions, making them suitable for high-stakes topics. Descriptive and exploratory qualitative evidence, on the other hand, is uniquely valuable for surfacing discounted explanations and new theories that can turn out to be central turning points for what we learn. By bringing diverse sources of evidence together, we shore up our confidence.

Software researchers such as Marian Petre have used rich qualitative approaches to surface many evidence stories from real software workplaces. In two years of work with 12 IP-generating engineering companies, Petre conducted field observations and interviews to explore how experts pursue out-of-the-box thinking with deliberate, systematic, and collaborative practices, as opposed to the Lone Genius notion that innovation is chaotic and individual.[44] One characteristic of high-performing teams was a hunger for input and updates to their knowledge base. And if you can't run a study, you can turn to evidence sources outside of your organization to ensure you're working from what's been robustly tested. One tactic to refine your sense of the "evidence readiness" behind different practices is to try to map where proof for their effectiveness lands on the evidence readiness framework. For example, a small case study can spark ideas and hypotheses, but most likely should be marked as more preliminary than larger-scale evidence systematically gathered across many types of teams and situations. Likewise, a piece of evidence that's only been found in an academic lab may need real-world testing before it's ready to change organizational policies.

If you're drowning in a sea of possible directions for things you could start measuring, I find it helps to focus on two characteristics of good targets: is it practical, and is it tractable. *Practical* targets are, quite simply, things we can measure that are within the scope of our resources, larger context, and strategic priorities. For example, sending every junior developer at a company to a six-month education curriculum at a local university is likely to produce a powerful and real effect on their knowledge but might also be pragmatically out of scope for your organization. A more practical approach might ask, what are the learning activities that we already invest in for our company, and can we measure the impact of those?

Tractable targets are dynamics where we have reason to think they can *change*. We have enough evidence (whether from understanding the underlying mechanisms that drive those targets or from documenting natural variation in how we see those targets emerge in the world) to believe they'll respond to our efforts more easily than other things. For example, psychologists believe that people's sense of belonging is a tractable measure because studies have shown we can shift it with careful interventions and that changes in local environments greatly change people's belonging.[45] Other attributes might be theoretically interesting in a science lab but incredibly difficult to change and ultimately have far less predictive value compared to measuring the aspects of people's experience that truly fall under leaders' responsibility (personality traits, I'm looking at you).

Finally, there are many causal effects in the world that might be real but simply inappropriate or unethical for you to include in your evidence strategy. As an example, imagine you've been tasked with monitoring some signal for productivity in your organization. We know from plenty of science (and basic biology) that the quality of people's sleep is a very powerful predictor of how productive they can be the next day. But let's imagine some of the problems that immediately arise from bosses trying to monitor people's sleep: it's invasive, it would automatically detect and penalize all the people in your organization who have young children, it could be fallible because of time zones, it's probably illegal in many places, plus embarking on a measurement plan of this sort would create an uproar in any reasonable group of people.

Once again, this shows us that evidence strategy is about the *context*, not just the *content* of our evidence. You might be willing to share data about sleep with a healthcare team, but sharing the same information with a manager has completely different implications. Without a structured approach and justified targets, we can demoralize our teams and colleagues by targeting the wrong change or failing to understand why they aren't responding to the change we're asking them to make. Your goal is not to measure everything there is. Start with the things you think you can change and that are important to make legible to your organization. Remember the precondition of psychological safety, and measure what people agree you can actually help with.

LEARNING FROM GOOD DAYS

An observational study by André Meyer and colleagues opened an empirical window into developers' perceptions of "typical workdays" in a large engineering organization.[46] Conscious of the need to not design their measure of developer activity from stereotypes, and wanting to surface categories of activity from developers themselves, they first conducted qualitative interviews with a small random sample of developers in the organization. These interviews were used to develop a taxonomy of activities. Next, these researchers designed a longitudinal survey measure that asked participants to report over a period of four months: (1) the time they spent across those activities on a previous day, (2) whether this day was typical or not, and (3) whether they'd judge this as a "good day."

Along the way, many details in this study give examples of motivating participation. The authors adhered to research ethics by securing approval from an ethics and privacy board (likewise, when I first began leading behavioral intervention studies, my research lab and I set up a federally registered Institutional Review Board to ensure all our methods would be approved by an outside panel). Additionally, the final design was pilot tested with 800 developers. Participants were also given an explanation of the purpose of the survey, and an explanation of how the data would be analyzed (in aggregate, with individual data not shared back to corporate collaborators). It's important to recognize the elements of a research project that make it work beyond items on a survey: what produces high quality evidence is careful, intentional human decisions that shape each stage of evidence creation, collection, analysis, and communication.

And those decisions yielded an interesting evidence story. Rather than matching the stereotypes of the dissociated, uncaring "brains" of the Brains-in-Jars model, only interested in the minutia of code, software developers in this study voiced a deep desire to contribute value through meaningful work and judged whether they'd had a good day by this standard. Among the many findings from this "good day" study, one that caught my eye was the powerful differentiator of experiencing greater agency. Across the four months of this study, better days were marked by developers feeling better control over their experience at work. James Moore, a psychological scientist who studies our sense of whether we control our actions, defines sense of agency as being "in the driving seat when it comes to our actions."[47] Increased agency is a consistent request from technologists, while the demoralization of feeling out of control creates many negative impacts.[48] Likewise, our Developer Thriving study found that higher sense of agency was associated with greater productivity for developers.[20] In our study, our operationalization of agency intentionally captured two things that are highly relevant to an evidence strategy: first, whether developers believe they're able to voice disagreements with their team's definition for success, and second, that developers believe they have a voice in how their contributions are measured.

It's easy to assume bringing data into complicated questions about work means being a cold, hard, unfeeling numbers person. But evidence strategy isn't about plunging thoughtlessly into "big data" or numbers for their own sake. Even relatively simple descriptions of human experience, if pursued with authenticity and transparency, can illuminate the right direction to move in for organizations. The authenticity is not optional; whether people trust your measurement process enough to join it will mediate everything you can find. Evidence strategy can help you think through how to motivate people to participate in a collective evidence-generating process and help you learn to invite others in to help you close the gaps between meaning and data. This might mean creating data collection moments that people trust and opt into or carefully evaluating the evidence readiness levels behind your biggest beliefs. Evidence strategy also means taking the limitations as well as the potential of the quantitative seriously, and investing in diverse method choices, like rich qualitative evidence where needed. Evidence strategy requires putting intentional and iterative work into developing team buy-in for the *what*, *how*, and *why* of what we're measuring (and often, what we're *not* measuring). With an evidence mindset, you can bring rigorous compassion together with empowering the teams around you to build an organization that wants to understand itself.

QUESTIONS TO ASK TO HELP ACTIVATE THE EVIDENCE STRATEGY MINDSET

- Have I "unpacked" my highest priorities for what I want to observe, evaluate, and measure in my workplace?
- Have I experienced being mismeasured at work? Do I feel skeptical, angry, or fearful of "data claims" about software teams? Can I learn what went wrong in those cases so that I can avoid recreating this feeling in others?
- Do we create opportunities to increase developers' agency and allow them to give us feedback about how we are measuring things?
- Do we tend to fall into one of the four "pitfalls" of software measurement? What can we do about it? Have we explored where cognitive biases might be filtering the information we're using to drive decisions?
- What aspects of our work are important to us, but difficult or impossible to measure? Have we allowed ourselves to learn from the qualitative along with quantitative? Where might we need more diverse forms of measurement?
- Do we have a sense of the "evidence readiness levels" behind our practices? Which software practices do we think need more evidence, and which ones feel solidly evidenced?
- Do we bring in outside expertise for ambitious and high-stakes work? Have we invested in growing evidence science skills for our engineering leadership?

CHAPTER 7

Fighting Dirty for Good Culture

BUILDING FOR A FUTURE THAT ISN'T HERE YET

My great-uncle Jerry was a retired doctor by the time I moved to San Diego for graduate school, close to his desert home. Jerry was a quiet, gentle soul. He lived a solitary life filled with hobbies he was unusually intense about, such as taking a telescope out to stargaze for an entire night while sleeping only in a camping chair. Having grown up on the other side of the country, I didn't know my great-uncle well. But when I reached out, Jerry and I forged a surprising bond across the many decades of life separating us. We both liked classical music, interesting facts about biology, and old books. Just a few years later, Jerry would pass away. But in that time, we spent many weekends together at the symphony and getting dinner afterward, memories that I treasure.

It was during one of these dinners that Jerry told me about why he became a doctor. As the son of an immigrant family in Philadelphia, life had been difficult. Jerry and his brother, my grandfather, both began working at a young age and coordinated their schedules so that they could always walk home together in order to protect themselves from being hassled by local boys on the way back to their neighborhood. The family weathered many adversities, from his mother's serious health conditions (dismissed by the doctors they tried to see) to threats to their small business. But these difficult experiences never turned Jerry's gentle heart against anyone. Rather, early experiences of watching doctors

DOI: 10.1201/9781003589112-7

fail his mother fueled Jerry's motivation to go to medical school. Always interested in the latest technologies, Jerry developed a keen interest in radiology, in large part because of its ability to provide objective and early evidence that could validate patients' accounts that *something was wrong*. Jerry's unique strengths, like being able to enjoy spending long hours alone in the dark looking at minuscule details, allowed him to quickly realize that widespread implementation of new technologies in medicine could unlock far better outcomes for difficult diseases that had been diagnostically invisible for centuries. He could, quite literally, see the future.

Not all of his peers could. Despite the efficacy of new tests, Jerry also watched many doctors struggle to integrate the new practices of *using them* into their actual day-to-day work with patients. Scans were variable, difficult to read, and often came with laborious and esoteric walls of text that doctors struggled to understand. Some even became contemptuous about the technology change, dismissing its complex interpretations. This gap between technology and practice frustrated Jerry deeply, but he wasn't in a position to institute policy change.

But he *did* have evidence and a mission. His expertise was in demand, which put him in the position to consult across many cases and organizations. One conversation at a time, he began the slow work of persuading colleagues that they were failing to fully implement good practices. And they remembered him. Years later, over one of our dinners, he told me that eventually finding himself in a position to advocate for more standardized use of tests to improve diagnoses and early treatment for women, including advocating for greater coverage for early diagnostics in undertreated cancers, was one of the greatest accomplishments of his career.

I asked him how he had persisted against so much discouragement. How had he kept the faith that a different future was waiting, and that all of those small, relentless conversations would go somewhere? In his characteristically quiet way, Jerry thought for a moment and then said, "I saw what people needed."

I've kept those words close to my heart. Positive change requires people to see past the limitations of their current world, have the courage to imagine a better one, and find their own unique way to fight for it. Jerry knew that the patients he had spent his life caring about needed him, but he was also capable of seeing that his fellow medical providers needed help, and that given the right support, they could change. Jerry and I shared the belief that scientific evidence was a way to reach people, and that if you had access to that evidence, you had a responsibility to try to teach it.

Treating developers as Brains-in-Jars creates a barrier between the present of software development and a future that's sustainable and even joyful. Untangling how we do software development from the stereotypes of Brains-in-Jars models requires challenging our ideas, resetting some deeply held norms about technical work, and designing for new behaviors across our teams and organizations. Shifting our technical culture is an ambitious mission to take on. But I think this different future is worth imagining, because it's what will keep us on the path to a technology world that works for all of us.

Running software teams with the short-term strategies of Brains-in-Jars fails to create our desired outcomes because they ultimately run counter to the core needs of our minds and our psychology, which is what we rely on to produce creative and effective technical work. Teams trapped in Brittle Productivity cycles burn out and generate quick but weak results that fail to stand the test of time. Lone Genius stereotypes keep people from harnessing the full power of collaborative problem-solving, exclude millions of people from being recognized for their technical potential, and make teams more psychologically brittle when they face change and threat. And Chilly Climates freeze the gears of positive change, cutting groups off from hearing their valuable dissenters and keeping developers from unlocking the joyful collaboration and psychological safety that guides breakthroughs and innovation.

But if you pay attention, you will also notice that the Brains-in-Jars model is being disrupted *all the time*. People working in software break through this limiting model to get things done and make their environments kinder. This makes software development rich with counterexamples of a different way to work, one that honors human psychology. Despite tough workplaces, developers still pursue mastery, value intrinsic motivation, and constantly share novel and amazing solutions, often out of the joy of craft and a commitment to just wanting things to work better. Thoughtful people dissent from their groups' bad norms to push for better team practices that lead to coalitions, not conflict. Teams and organizations who design for healthy measurement practices rise to the challenge of being accountable to evidence. You can probably remember at least a few of those functional, joyful moments and how different it felt to be part of an environment that saw you as a full person. When it all comes together, people working in technology have always found clever, compassionate, and strategic ways to pursue meaningful work, even inside of imperfect organizations. Those examples point us toward the counterweight to the Brains-in-Jars vision of software development, a model which has always been present in the working practices of real software developers, and which deserves to come out of the shadows. I'm talking about a *Thriving* model of software development.

In psychology, thriving refers to being able to live and grow beyond mere survival. It's a state in which people truly flourish, often beyond our previous assumptions and too-narrow expectations. Thriving evokes the possibility of unexpected growth and cycles that feed our resilience, rather than stripping it. Importantly, asking for thriving doesn't mean we're asking individuals to be unreasonably resilient without any accountability from the structures around them. In fact, individual growth often requires a thriving *ecosystem* to sustain real change. Thriving doesn't mean nothing bad ever happens—but thriving organizations, teams, and individuals are far better able to weather difficult storms.[1–4]

I know that you have to set this book down and go back to a world that doesn't always make it easy to believe there's a better way to build software. It's my hope that you'll now be able to take the many lessons of a psychologically informed approach to software with you and use psychology to make your next environment a little more human than you found it. Most importantly, I want you to know you're not alone. So for this last chapter, we'll focus on how people have used theories of change to move real-world communities closer to thriving.

CHAMPIONS OF CHANGE

Kurt Lewin was a force in the study of group dynamics and group change and is often recognized as one of the founders of social psychology. He also immigrated to the United States just ten years before my great-uncle and grandfather were walking the streets of Philadelphia. Working in the immediate aftermath of the Second World War, Lewin was deeply concerned with how psychological insights could change the real world and is often credited with saying that the best way to understand a phenomenon is to try to change it. He also proposed that once we learn to start seeing the conditions that *keep* organizations or cultures from changing, we will begin to understand what does produce change.[5–7]

Both of these ideas have greatly influenced me and, in my experience, affirm the strategies of the most effective culture-changers I've met in software. The developers, tech thinkers, managers, and leaders who have shared their stories of change across my research have diverse strengths and highly varied contexts, but across all their accounts I've seen the same themes surface again and again: We need to move past fear and toward action if we are truly committed to caring about changing things, and we need to give ourselves the space and structure to iterate and experiment on *behalf* of the people around us. Change agents relentlessly identify moments to take action, but they're also deeply open-hearted when it comes to listening to the experiences of the people in their communities, and course-correct constantly. For decades, scientists across the behavioral and psychological sciences have asked exactly how we can bring together science from researchers like Lewin and wisdom from community change makers to help groups to change for the better. You've seen this concept throughout the book, so it's about time we name it—it's called intervention science.

Out of the hundreds of research papers I read while writing this book, one of my very favorites was a sweeping synthesis on the psychology of culture change from a team of psychologists, MarYam Hamedani, Hazel Rose Markus, Rebecca Hetey, and Jennifer Eberhardt, who are no strangers to grappling with tough problems where change is deeply needed.[8,9] It lays out a vision for how intentional culture change happens with a framework that draws from both the empirical psychology of culture and inequality, and scientists' real-world experiences applying those evidence-based insights in partnerships with communities in many real-world settings. Drawing from themes identified across efforts to create change, such as health disparities, the economy, criminal justice, and discrimination in the workplace, and synthesizing findings across contexts as small as volunteer community groups and as large as international collaborations, the authors describe seven science-backed principles for intentional culture change. These principles reinforce many of the lessons we've already explored in the past six chapters. I've spotlighted a few of the connections that I see between these culture change principles and the foundational psychology of software development.

	General Principles	For Software Communities
1	People are culturally shaped shapers, so they can be culture changers.	Technical people are shaped by the cultures of technology (like Brains-in-Jars beliefs), but we have the power to change what that technology culture is.
2	Identifying, mapping, and evaluating the key levels of culture helps locate where to target change.	Identifying, mapping, and evaluating what's really happening for developers as people will tell us where to invest in change (for example, recognizing the need for mastery cultures around developer problem-solving).
3	Culture change happens in both top-down and bottom-up ways and is more effective when the levels are in alignment.	Changing our technical environments can happen from both top-down and bottom-up ways, the most effective change will happen when developers are empowered to contribute to the design of change (as in co-designing evidence practices).
4	Culture change can be easier when it leverages existing core values and harder when it challenges deep-seated defaults and biases.	We should leverage existing positive core values to improve software development, such as values of lifelong learning and building, and carefully study where deep-seated biases (such as "brilliance beliefs" about technical ability) will block change.
5	Culture change typically involves power struggles and identity threats.	Technology changes (even tool changes!) can introduce identity threats when they require developers to challenge deeply-held aspects of their identities (as with AI Skill Threat), and successfully navigating this requires mitigating the threat.
6	Cultures interact with one another and change can cause backlash, resistance, and clashes.	Recognizing the diverse and different cultures around software development can be key to seeing how to create coalitions between them. Protecting principled dissenters who are trying to move technical communities toward better from group backlash is important.
7	Timing and readiness matter.	Choose your time for an intervention wisely, identify preconditions for change, and take into account the existing "readiness" of your technical communities or organizations.

Seven Principles for Intentional Culture Change.

These principles can provide inspiration for any scope and authority. If you're a junior individual contributor, you may not be in a position to stop a senior tech lead from disparaging the new idea you raised in a meeting, but you can take pride in understanding that your moment of courage was a dissenting act and protect yourself from internalizing the backlash you experienced. Later, when you move up the ranks, perhaps you will remember that experience and work to make sure ideas from junior contributors are heard and honored. Through the years, you may add to your toolkit the observation that those backlashing senior contributors have often had careers where they wrestled with continual identity threat when changes are introduced. Perhaps this shapes your willingness to create space during technical change without leaping to doubting people's competency, and a culture of respect and psychological safety when idea clashes occur.

It's easy to think change must flow from the top and that only leaders and organizational decision-makers can make it happen. But I'd like to suggest that every person working in technology has a sphere of influence, often greater than they know. Developers influence the tools, workflows, and processes that impact millions of people all over the world, and that means that how we form our technical cultures matters. As we've learned, the social signals we send to people in our communities can matter greatly and can prompt others to think differently. While experience or power unlocks certain change possibilities, I've found over and over again that change agents can operate on many levels in organizations. One thing that distinguishes them? Change agents recognize, design, and creatively test interventions.

Across the behavioral sciences, an *intervention* is a specific, structured attempt to change people's behaviors, often by prompting a change in beliefs or the strategies people see as possible in a given situation. Many interventions also focus on changing the larger structural environment around people, giving people more support for the behaviors they're already trying on their own. You can think of most developer experience initiatives as interventions, but so are infrastructure investments, or changes we might experiment with in how we develop features. If we're deliberately changing something inside of our organization with a goal of changing people's behaviors, we're in the realm of interventions. The most impactful and successful interventions usually pull multiple levers, helping individuals and changing features of the environment around them. And good intervention crafters tune into the important outcomes in how different changes interact. To identify where we're working when we're trying to think about how our intervention might shift a software development ecosystem, I use a guiding map that the Culture Change Principles draw on called *The Culture Cycle*. This Culture Cycle framing has deep roots across hundreds of studies on the interactions between individuals and environments.[10–12] I often work through the levels of the Culture Cycle as an exercise for design and alignment when I partner with organizations, teams, and leaders who are trying to find their entry points for change and want to shift their cultures away from Brains-in-Jars and toward Thriving. The four levels of the Culture Cycle are: *Ideas*, *Institutions*, *Interactions*, and *Individuals*. Change can flow in either direction, and each level interacts with the other levels. That also means positive changes to any level of the Culture Cycle can provoke unexpectedly positive change elsewhere, an exciting feature of a complex system.

Take the Culture Cycle map as a place to start rather than a finish line. You can and should add your own experiences to this framework and use it to interrogate the environments you've encountered. You may find yourself drawn to work on or think about one particular level but don't lose sight of the fact that we often need to create change on many levels for transformation to really stick. And while each of these levels is a way of looking at culture, they're not always equally weighted in terms of how pivotal they are in explaining what's happening around us. It may be the case that we need to change on one level for our intervention on a different level to truly work. For instance, if institutional policies prevent developers from safely revealing to collaborators when they detect a security risk, that policy might need to change before individual developers will meaningfully change their behaviors to triage more security risks. Or if interactions between two different functions in an organization are full of conflict, it could be difficult for an institutional commitment to collaborative product design to be genuinely put into motion.

Respecting the inhibiting and promoting powers of the different levels can help us steer clear of hypocrisy and remember our accountability to ensure that people *can* make the changes we're asking them to make. Considering the relative impact of different changes should also be an important part of your decision-making. Empirical interventionists like me often talk about prioritizing interventions that have a large "effect size," which you can think of as the strength of the effect we're observing, or the size of the relationship between our change and its outcome. Checking for effect sizes helps us to remember we need to care about the *practical* significance of a strategy, not just its statistical significance. If the impact of one change on part of our culture level is much bigger than a dozen small changes on another level, leaders with the power to choose an area for intervention should throw their resources into that high-impact change. For individuals, staying aware of these relationships can help you stop blaming yourself when a change you tried was prevented and help you identify more tractable starting places.

Lining up the Culture Cycle against the evidence we've explored in the previous chapters, I've created an exploratory look at some of the

Using the Culture Change Cycle to Shift Organizations from Brains-in-Jars to Thriving Organizations

	Brains-in-Jars Organizations	**Thriving Organizations**
Ideas *Assumptions across the culture about what is good, moral, powerful, effective, and why*	Brittle Productivity is as good as it gets Lone Geniuses drive everything Chilly Climates are inevitable Learning: Learning is often an unproductive distraction and only an individual pursuit when it's necessary Agency: Developer agency is a threat that needs to be contained Belonging: Only mission-alignment matters, not personal belonging; if developers constantly fear being found out as imposters that drives up performance Self-efficacy and motivation: Developers are only motivated by extrinsic rewards and punishments	Sustainable Productivity defines success Collective Problem-Solving drives everything Supportive Cultures are possible Learning: Learning is a central productive activity and learning goals are a shared practice for teams Agency: Developer agency is a strength that needs to be cultivated Belonging: Belonging is a sign of success; when developers feel accepted as whole people that drives up performance Self-efficacy and motivation: Developers' intrinsic motivation is a psychological engine for outcomes
Institutions *The organizational and institutional practices and policies that shape formal and authoritative expressions of cultures*	Company policies use top-down mandates for how developers work without integrating real observation of developer needs and friction points Software communities have hard boundaries on sharing knowledge and resist sharing technical breakthroughs	Company policies regularly solicit bottom-up insight from developers and reward them for providing it Software communities have permeable idea boundaries, allowing technical breakthroughs to propagate

(Continued)

	Brains-in-Jars Organizations	Thriving Organizations
Interactions *The emergent informal dynamics of people, between groups, and between people and products or artifacts*	Teams have strong in-group biases and group conflict dominates work between functions and teams Arguments are frequently resolved based on the loudest voice in the room rather than shared evidence Developers are constrained by tool choices that design against their psychological needs. Tools and infrastructure mask real friction from organizational attention.	Teams actively listen to dissenters, foster coalitional cognition, and design for surfacing divergent perspectives Shared evidence is brought in to inform disagreements and shape decisions, and teams continually seek to improve evidence quality Developers are freed by tool choices that design for their psychological needs and have their thinking improved by the design choices of well-built tools. Tools and infrastructure surface friction to organizational attention
Individuals *People's thoughts, feelings, identities, mindsets, and individual behavior*	People pursue performance goals and get mired in the Performance Paradox because of their use of avoidance strategies People have poor metacognitive skills and default to illusory behaviors like cramming and overwork People fall into the Brilliance Trap, judging others' potential for technical success in terms of innate traits People primarily work in insular, narrowly focused areas and rarely get exposed to outside ideas	People pursue mastery goals, cultivate intrinsic motivation, and use approach strategies to take deliberate challenging risks People develop strong metacognitive skills that check illusory behaviors and create more robust learning and problem-solving People recognize shared environmental explanations for technical success, welcome diverse collaborators, and see technical success in terms of effort and learning People regularly seek out new creative directions and have structured practices to expose themselves to outside ideas

characteristics that can help Brains-in-Jars organizations and technical communities move away from limiting beliefs and toward Thriving.

For example, the belief that software development requires ruthless competition (as we studied in our AI Skill Threat study) is an *idea* that shapes the culture of software engineering. The empirical evidence shows that while these beliefs feel productive to us, they steer individuals toward less actual productivity and more threat in the face of technology change. If you're a public speaker in tech with significant influence in your technical community, you might rise to the challenge of intervening on this *idea* level of your technical cultures by sharing stories of collaboration leading to innovation, breaking down Lone Genius myths by presenting a counter-narrative that centers effort and skill growth, or taking a dissenting stand when you see the celebration of ruthless competition. An *individual* intervention for this problem, on the other hand, might invite developers to internally consider the negative consequences of contest cultures. Interventions might teach developers to diversify their own brilliance belief explanations with other important explanations when they see themselves reaching for it and help individuals build habits of activating alternative beliefs (for instance, "I benefit from collaborating" and "we can all succeed together").

As they're often easier to access and deploy, interventions that target individual beliefs are more common and have produced many powerful outcomes, including increasing people's perseverance and how they interpret setbacks.[13,14] But if you're on a leadership team concerned with making a smooth transition to new technology, you likely need to think about an *institutional* intervention. You could design and promote messages across your engineering function that collaboration and life-long learning are expected and welcome parts of technical success. You could further implement policies that reward developers for investments in learning, or ensure that managers are trained and regularly informed of their responsibilities to support team learning culture. Finally, I've often seen insight unlocked when teams learn to evaluate investments in software development processes, like redesigning code reviews or shifting to a new toolstack, by whether they improve the *interactions* level of the Culture Cycle. If you're an infrastructure team responsible for tool decisions that impact an entire engineering organization, it's important to notice when you're intervening on how developers interact across project tasks as they collaborate, as well as how a single developer works on their machine.

Even just expanding your thinking to add one other level of the Culture Cycle to your default may help you identify opportunities for change. The Culture Cycle also provides an important check on our cognitive biases. In Brains-in-Jars organizations, interventions are only ever done *to* the people in our organizations. Because developers are seen as interchangeable cogs in a machine, divorced from psychological context, they're nothing but the passive recipients of top-down orders from managers. Compounding this, seeing interventions purely in terms of individual developers is appealing to our minds because this narrative is tangible and familiar in software. As we learned in Chapter 3, we love to attribute success to individual effort or cast blame on individual failure, even when the true story is situational and environmental. But the idea, institution, and interaction levels pull our attention back to situations and environment. These interventions also often have a bigger effect size in the real world than interventions that just target individual change, causing leading researchers in the behavioral sciences to call for greater investment in structural interventions as a path to change.[15]

In fact, I've found that focusing solely on individuals *feels* like it'll be an easier route to change but, in real life, can be harder and far more prone to failure. Developers are primed to be wary of individualistic interventions because many of them have already experienced years of failed culture change. As we already learned when thinking about evidence strategy, collective buy-in is key for changes to really stick. People's prior beliefs about whether a change will be effective, whether the source of a change can be trusted, and whether they agree with its goals, all strongly predict whether or not people will agree to participate in a change at all.[16] But the biggest change killer of all might be when individuals see a change request as hypocritical. Attempting to command individuals to change without adequately structuring, encouraging, and supporting the preconditions for it—or worse, punishing developers who do try to change—shoves their brains back into jars, telling them there's no room for their human needs.

These critical levers are what you start to identify when you think about intervention effectiveness. In keeping with the pragmatic approach of comparing effect sizes, scientists who study real-world change distinguish between something working in an idealized and scaled-down model of the situation (intervention science calls this "efficacy") and something working at scale when it meets all the context, friction, and implementation challenges of the real world ("effectiveness").[17] Think about this like the difference between testing a medication in a laboratory versus making sure it works across an entire country of people. Efficacy matters, but it's not all that matters. *Effectiveness* is a critical bar to clear if we want solutions that work when we scale them up. For example, that medicine might very well produce a real effect in a clinical setting, but be so inconvenient or difficult to administer correctly in the real world that it fails to help the population of people we're most concerned with when we try to implement it at scale. Experimental economist John List evocatively named the phenomenon of small successful tests that failed to scale to big solutions a *voltage drop*. In List's voltage drop, the original cost-to-benefit ratio that worked in a small and local setting for an intervention idea falls apart at scale, often because we didn't include enough of the key frictions or barriers that our idea would have to address at scale.[18,19] To fix this, List proposes that scalable change needs to be designed from the very beginning to include, rather than ignore, the constraints we know we'll need to scale into. This also matches what we learned from the Evidence Readiness Levels in Chapter 6: we need diverse evidence, tested across many places, to show us if our change strategies have been rigorously designed *for* the people we want it to help.

As frustrating as effectiveness failures are, when you see change fail in the real world, this usually contains pivotal diagnostic information you can wrap into your future strategies. Learning to notice change failures can bust you out of the "it works on my machine" approach to culture change. What we're most interested in is usually not *just* the intervention in some idealized sandbox, but the interaction that happens when the new adaptive patterns we want people to put into practice meet an environment that affords specific opportunities for putting those patterns into practice (or blocks them). This is a lot to think about, but keep in mind it also means that the real people embedded into the cultures they want to change—perhaps that's you!—have a serious advantage. You might be the closest thing to a culture expert for the technical cultures you're in. It's worth spending the time to learn where you're positioned to precisely identify the blockers and enablers of change in a way that people outside of your organization, community, or team would need months or years to understand.

Psychology has learned the lessons of effectiveness failures and voltage drops the hard way. Psychological scientists Gregory Walton and David Yeager have each led years of intervention experiments with thousands of people aimed at transforming outcomes in real world contexts, from helping motivate patients to adhere to difficult medical regimes, to randomized controlled trials of both belonging interventions across dozens of campuses that improve student retention.[20–26] But they've also seen hundreds of hoped-for lab interventions fail to work in the real world. In a piece setting out a vision for why some lab-tested attempts to change behavior succeed and others fail, Walton and Yeager give an insight that I love: "interventions are done with people, not on people."[27] One of the biggest shifts in the social and behavioral sciences over the past few decades has been from framing behavior change as a problem on the individual level, to recognizing that interventions need to be designed with interacting *systems* in mind, responsive to groups' unique needs, and tested for local contexts.

For example, an engineering organization that places a high cultural value on innovation may be a place where we see that individual developers are highly responsive to an intervention from a manager encouraging them to seek out more challenge. But in a different organization that doesn't share this value across teams, even the most effective manager in the world might struggle to create a challenge-seeking team. Developing a good intervention isn't just a matter of shouting the message that you think people need to hear; they need to be able to interpret the message in light of their existing context, put your change to work for them, and see it succeed. Reinforcing this, when psychologists compare between intervention approaches for changing people's beliefs about ability and performance, we've often found intervening on the systemic factors *around* people is one of the most effective routes to individual belief change. Even who delivers the message can be crucial. For many interventions to work at scale, researchers have learned that trusted authority figures need to deliver the call for change in order for it to be truly heard.[28,29]

People aren't programs, waiting to run in a new direction as soon as we send them new instructions. What happens *after* we've introduced the possibility of change is that people monitor their local context and test our offered new possibility against it; in Walton and Yeager's words, an "*intersection of vulnerability and opportunity.*" Another intervention scientist, Geoffrey Cohen, has designed and tested psychological interventions at scale to move the needle on people's self-affirmation and belonging and produce positive effects that are reinforced for years, including improving incredibly difficult-to-change outcomes such as deeply entrenched societal achievement gaps. Cohen calls the art and science of creating successful interventions *situation-crafting*. He emphasizes that change makers should direct their efforts toward shaping the *situations* we place people in rather than imagining directly changing people themselves. A thoughtful intervention offers people the opportunity to see the world differently, and empowers them to develop their own, more adaptive narratives.[30–32]

I use a simple mnemonic from psychology to remind myself to think about situation-crafting: *Mindset x Context.* Mindset x Context theory says that people change not just because of the beliefs that they carry around in their heads but also because of the larger environment around them and how those two things interact.[33] We can bring the *Mindset x Context* approach to our organizations. Here's one example: many of the biggest and most important investments in developer experience that leaders attempt to make rise or fall not just because of the content of the change itself, but based on whether developers can easily implement and benefit from the changes. As another example, gamification approaches that aim to increase developer contributions to an open source project (like providing badges or other external markers of status) may produce a real effect—but only so long as there is a culture that welcomes newcomers and provides them with a minimum amount of psychological safety to take the interpersonal risk of contributing in public.

Intervention science also has a term for the psychological context that can explain why different teams and people might react very differently to the same intervention: we call it a *psychological affordance.* Just as a design affordance changes our ability to interact with the physical world, psychological affordances change what we see as possible ways of showing up for ourselves as people in a team, an organization, or a technology community of practice. Sometimes it's easier to recognize this intangible component of our lives when you imagine comparing and contrasting between your different contexts (like companies or technical communities). As you think about past contexts, ask yourself: Did that context allow you to show excitement? Take agency? Demonstrate curiosity? Did you feel allowed to be in a state of open and collaborative joint attention with your colleagues? Did you feel that your context rewarded challenge-seeking, or preferred that you operated like a cog in the machine? Your belief that your environment would want you to enter into those different states likely hinged on the psychological affordances you saw around you.

I think the psychological affordances around software developers are a missing explanation layer in how many organizations think about developers.[34] If you want to help the teams around you, learning to see even just a few key psychological affordances can give you x-ray vision. Why does adopting the same new software tool seem to work so well for Team A, but only brew frustration and resentment on Team B? Perhaps the answer lies in differences in their psychological affordances. Let's say the new tool has some design elements that allow for a lot more sharing of solutions between developers, and developers are taking advantage of that. Team A has a management chain that sees developer agency and experimentation as a fundamentally good thing, even when it gets messy in the short-term, and they tolerate some increased coordination and review time for the team. Team B, on the other hand, has a management chain that's stuck in the Brains-in-Jars belief that developer agency is a *threat* to leadership's control. Despite providing the teams with a tool that has given them new ways to share work, Team B's leadership culture manifests in managers anxiously demanding that Team B take no extra time to learn the tool, punishing them for spending more time than usual in code reviews, and making developers feel less agency over their choices. Mixed results that often seemed paradoxical without the psychology lens ("this tool only seems to work half the time in our organization!") resolve into actionable patterns when we can trace how different psychological affordances shape the technical environments of groups and individuals ("this tool works as long as developers' agency is rewarded").

Once you practice identifying psychological affordances, you start to see them everywhere. In a qualitative interview study, Courtney Miller and collaborators recruited pairs of developers from the same team at a large company adopting a generative AI coding tool. This team was curious about why there were such strong differences in who adopted the new tools, despite the fact that each person seemed on paper to have access to the same general technical resources and environment. So the researchers recruited people based on contrasting usage: one person in the pair was a frequent user of the tool, the other was not. Looking deeply at the accounts that practitioners shared, the researchers identified multiple psychological themes that shaped the way that developers viewed the same tools, including differences in learning strategies, social learning, and knowledge sharing within the team, and critically, the pressure induced by *unrealistic productivity expectations* from the local leadership that those developers were encountering.[35]

That last point provided a particularly important insight: when authority figures asked developers to both adopt new tools *and* signaled that they expected outsized productivity gains and would punish any indication of lessened productivity, it set off a negative cycle within organizations that caused developers to disinvest from their own learning. Even though it felt like developers were getting the same opportunities and resources for change, they really weren't because their choices were shaped by entirely different psychological affordances. This was the exact dynamic that my study on developers' learning predicted we'd see, where I surfaced patterns of *learning debt* (Chapter 2). Unchecked, learning debt leads to the Performance Paradox (Chapter 4) in action: overly fixating on always proving our performance can lead us down unsustainable and destructive behavioral paths that undermine long-term, real achievement. And as my AI Skill Threat study revealed, these choices are significantly worsened by the belief that software work is ruthlessly competitive and success comes only from innate brilliance. While psychological experience is enormous, learning to consistently pay attention to even just one core psychological need can give you predictive superpowers.

Psychological affordances help us make more predictions because they force us to include human behavior and outcomes, which we need to bring clarity and context to the heterogeneous, messy, and constantly shifting ways most organizations have measured software performance. Across my work, I've seen that good and bad psychological environments constantly predict how developers will access and use technology. In the spirit of Kurt Lewin, the best version of a behavioral intervention both directly benefits the people engaging with it in their real lives *and* improves our theories of change. Once I began incorporating scalable measures of learning culture into my research and testing them across more than a dozen industries and many types of engineering work, I discovered that learning culture was a consistently strong predictor of team differences in productivity and effectiveness. Human beings and technical work will always be complex, but focusing on foundational psychological affordances that tie into the architecture of human problem-solving can help us find the biggest levers for change.

Whether you're a leader, a technical organizer, or a motivated individual trying to help the people around you, how you see those people respond to the changes offered to them can help you test your mental model of what is driving the change you want to see in the world. This means that even when you fail, if you've identified structural blockers, you'll come out knowing how to change course and target a different part of the Culture Cycle. Hopefully, as we use evidence strategy, the entire organization gains a better shared model for how to help individual employees achieve higher-quality problem-solving, more cohesive coalitions, better daily meaning at work, and the goals of thriving. Psychologists call this adaptive recursion: when the new way of thinking offered by an intervention for one challenge goes on to strengthen your mind in new, unexpected ways, the next moment a tough moment comes up *outside* of the intervention, because it's taught you how to craft your own adaptive strategies. I like to call it a *virtuous cycle.*

A VIRTUOUS CYCLE: DOES SELF-COMPASSION HELP DEVELOPERS FACE TECHNICAL WORK?

Carol Lee is a psychologist I worked with for years as we collaborated on many of the open science projects you've learned about in this book. Across many tech conferences and other tech events, we were often the only "psychologists in the room," commiserating with each other as we tried to explain why we cared about psychology and thought it belonged in technical worlds. Carol not only has clinical experience but is also a clever experimentalist who's designed unique and creative interventions. She's studied how "Leave No Trace" reminders in the wilderness can prompt people to practice more diligence outdoors, and how changing our cognitive strategies can help people become more resilient during adversity and distress.[36,37]

Carol came to me with an unusual study idea: "let's study code review anxiety among software developers!"

At first, I was nervous. While I thought the topic was incredibly important, anxiety is hard to overcome, and I had never seen anyone in software research create a real-world intervention that actually helped people with it. As an applied lab leader with a small team, every investment we made in a new project always meant saying no to other things, so we were under a lot of pressure. Intervening on code review anxiety was an ambitious and important idea, and Carol had the expertise to pursue it, but my decision turning point really come when she made this point: "Developers talk a lot about anxiety in the tech industry, but the advice they give is always something like '*improve your code review anxiety by getting better at writing code.*' The thing is, that's not how anxiety works, and advice like this is never going to help people actually face it."

I recognized the specter of Brains-in-Jars, a limiting belief that the only thing that steers outcomes is writing more code, faster. *If only these developers were more productive, that would fix everything!* But that's bad psychology. That solution doesn't actually match what psychology knows about how anxiety and problem-solving really function, and so it wasn't likely to help developers face code review anxiety, and could even do harm. Anxiety isn't a skill issue. High performers, at work or otherwise, also experience anxiety. In fact, performance anxieties in particular (like having intense and disproportionate worry that if a co-worker finds a small error in your code, they'll decide you're incompetent and unwelcome on your team!) often have no relationship to the actual capabilities of the person experiencing it. But as we've seen across many contexts in the previous chapters, psychologically distressing experiences can short-circuit our ability to *access* the skills we do have, and those negative messages are worse inside of Chilly Climates that cut technical people off from support.

Carol had also seen just how much this was a problem for real developers. Whenever either of us shared that we were psychologists in tech, people across technical communities opened up to us about just how much code reviews felt like a barrier in their lives. Reviews felt like critical *interaction* points of the Culture Cycle, a time when developers found themselves surfacing and testing not just code but also important beliefs about who they were allowed to be on a team or project. People often described tough review environments as moments of heightened belonging uncertainty with their technical group: *Can I have a different approach? If I make a mistake, will they understand? Will I be met with help, or with contempt and coldness?*

It was impossible for us to peer over the shoulder of every developer as they went through a review, or directly change their entire organization's code review culture. But we both felt certain that some of the tools of psychology could help the people who were reaching out to us, and that carefully testing our ideas in an empirical intervention could provide people with a convincing alternative to the punishing, Brains-in-Jars messages they were hearing. We decided to study what code review anxiety looked and felt like for developers and ask whether providing some psychological boosts could clear away some of the burden they were facing during code reviews.[38] Even though the most direct thing we could do was build an individual intervention, we knew that we could strengthen its chances of success by making sure it was also an intentional intervention that acknowledged other parts of the Culture Cycle.

Drawing from years of empirical psychology research on anxiety and her expert experience as a clinician, Carol designed an intervention for code review anxiety that took the form of an interactive workshop teaching more adaptive approaches for facing down code reviews. Importantly, we also crafted carefully designed pre- and post-measures to test whether the workshop had a significant impact on developers' ability to face their code reviews. We recruited 59 professional developers to join us, all of whom reported significant anxiety about code reviews.

When we looked at their initial experiences of code review anxiety, we surfaced an alarming connection: every increase in how intensely they felt code review anxiety meant developers were also about 40% more likely to avoid engaging with code reviews, either by ignoring code reviews in the first place or by checking out and "rubber stamping" changes. Just as we saw with my friend Shaun in Chapter 4, these are avoidance strategies. In distressing moments, we often think avoidance will help. But in actuality, avoidance usually makes experiences like anxiety *worse*. Avoidance mires us even deeper in the spiral of doubt and anxiety and cuts us off from many of the key moments we might actually gain a new perspective.

Rather than benefiting from collaboration and shared problem-solving, anxious developers check out from engaging with their peers altogether. This is yet another concrete demonstration of the connection between negative psychological experience and the quality of the technical work that gets done. Imagine your team bought a new developer tool and found out that it dragged down your coding velocity by *40%*. Psychological factors may be less visible than software, but they're incredibly powerful. Scaled out over time, and over many teams, the cost of a bad culture around code reviews to the actual engineering output of an organization can be enormous.

Rather than lecturing developers about best practices or telling people to "just get over" their anxiety (the advice we often saw when we looked at software developers' online discussions of code review anxiety!), Carol provided science-backed scaffolding and support for the developers in our workshop to work through the facets of anxiety themselves. Anxious experience often floods us with "negative automatic thoughts," undermining messages that we *can't* do something. Our intervention acknowledged the true threat that developers can feel but gave them a path forward. Using an interactive set of exercises that guided developers through the process, our intervention helped software developers in the study write out their negative automatic thoughts, consider the realities behind them, rate their believability, reframe them with self-compassion in mind, and then plan for alternative strategies they could practice during code reviews. We encouraged them to actively reflect on whether they'd seen that these challenging experiences are a normal part of software development, and one that many of their peers might share and understand.

I've included a set of graphs of our findings. The big takeaway? This intervention *worked*. Developers in the workshop condition had a statistically significant reduction in anxiety and a significant improvement in both their self-efficacy and their self-compassion. Best of all, we have continued to receive many messages from developers after the study who have used our Code Review Anxiety workbook, sharing that the study helped them feel less alone and more seen by their colleagues.[39]

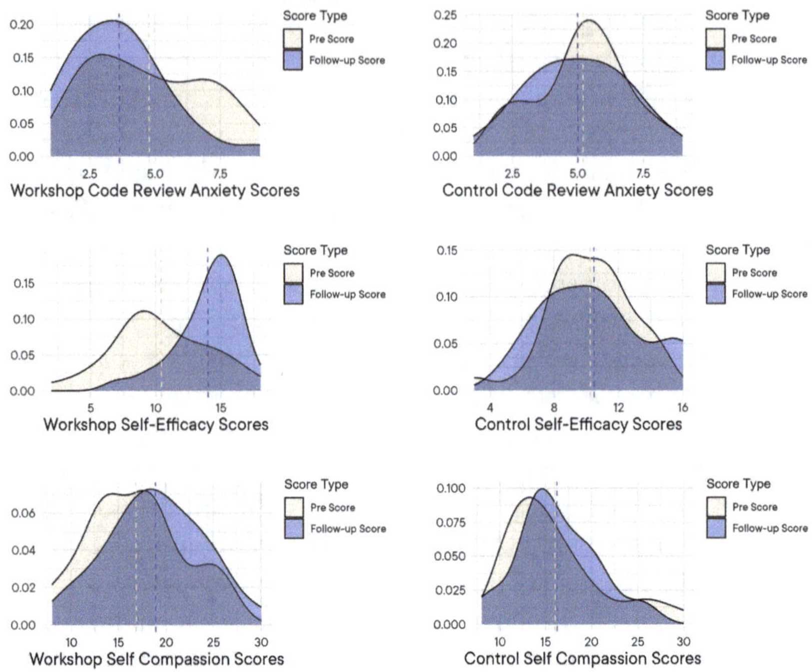

Code Review Anxiety Intervention Reduced Anxiety and Increased Self-Efficacy and Self-Compassion. Reproduced without change from Lee, C. S. & Hicks, C. M. Understanding and effectively mitigating code review anxiety. Empirical Software Engineering 29, 161 (2024). Licensed under CC BY-SA 4.0. https://creativecommons.org/licenses/by/4.0/

This design matched best practices from intervention science: people are better able to internalize new messages that they have an active hand in creating, something we call the *saying-is-believing* effect. The saying-is-believing effect is another reason that empowering technical teams to reflect on and become active contributors to the interventions you want to try will make them more effective. Plus, you rarely change anyone's mind by invalidating their current beliefs and telling them their experiences are wrong. For many maladaptive psychological beliefs, it's actually best to avoid flatly challenging them, as dwelling on the maladaptive thoughts can backfire by convincing our minds that those negative thoughts are common and reasonable. Instead of directly contradicting maladaptive beliefs, intervention science recommends providing people with careful reframes that show how alternative beliefs can work better and explain more, allowing them to reinterpret challenges in a new light.[24,28,40]

We doubled down on these themes of empowerment and agency by targeting two pieces of developer psychology that previous research told us were both amenable to change in a brief intervention and that also have a demonstrated relationship to anxiety and avoidance (remember the evidence strategy rule to pick *practical* and *tractable* targets!). Carol focused on helping people learn to activate their skills in self-efficacy and self-compassion during the moment of a code review, two psychological powerhouses that help us activate different beliefs to counteract the sabotage of negative automatic thoughts. In our large-scale Developer Thriving project, we'd already seen that self-efficacy was a strong signal for more productive developers, and years of studies have found evidence that self-compassion helps people reframe distressing circumstances.[41,42] We also used the methodological structure of a waitlist-control randomized controlled trial to create robust evidence that directly tested the impact of our intervention and followed the action research values we learnt about in Chapter 6 by ensuring that everyone who joined our study would get the support they needed. In a waitlist-control design, all participants in our study, including those in the control group, get the intervention—the control group just got it *after* they had already completed the post-test measures in our study.

Even though culture change can feel enormous, the first step toward change can be within the power of individuals on their next day at work. As part of his work on improving psychological experiences, Geoffrey Cohen has described successful interventions as designed to hit the "three Ts": interventions are *tailored* (it's the right message), *targeted* (given to the right person), and *timely* (the intervention comes at the right time).[43] I believe our intervention succeeded because it was designed to meet all three of these criteria. Developers needed to hear a message that affirmed their real fears and threats, and our intervention was tailored to give them an alternative to the Brains-in-Jars thoughts that struggling in code reviews meant they weren't good developers. We also targeted our intervention toward real working developers who had the opportunity to test out a new approach in their next code review and recruited people who were motivated to make a change. We provided saying-is-believing steps for what to try in the intervention by helping developers actively gauge the severity of the threat they were feeling and design their own next steps, empowering them to adapt our intervention to their individual experience.

Finally, our intervention was timely because it gave developers something to take action on right at the moment when they were being challenged by a scary code review. To validate our evidence even more deeply in the real world, we followed a small group of developers from our real-world study who generously volunteered reflections as they continued to use our code review anxiety intervention in their real workplaces. In these accounts, we were able to see that the intervention helped developers bring their new psychological skills to the surface in the middle of challenging work.[44]

Successful interventions work because they take advantage of common, naturally occurring situations in people's lives when they are considering their choices and open to change. That also means we need to hold ourselves accountable for evaluating whether what we've tried to change in people's lives really does help (remember, we want effectiveness, not just efficacy). When we've challenged ourselves to really do that work, even small improvements can lead to years of benefit because positive effects can be cumulative, setting off a cascade of next steps. For example, if succeeding in an early coding class predicts the difference between imagining that you could be a developer or not, we can create unexpectedly large changes by focusing on improving who gets invited into, supported during, and more chances to succeed at that coding class. If being able to successfully engage in technical collaboration and get feedback from developers is core to social learning, then mitigating code review anxiety with a culture that cultivates compassion during code reviews can create a cascade for your organization.

MEANING MATTERS

Throughout this book, we've explored a lot of examples of powerful empirical studies and impressive projects with thousands of people. It's my hope that this ecosystem of evidence helps you feel like you're not alone when you fight for thriving in software development, whether that's in your own career or as you make decisions for an entire organization. But none of this is easy; being inside an organization that needs a lot of change can be draining and isolating. How do we stay motivated to push for change when the complex challenges facing our technical communities feel enormous? I'd like to share something I truly believe and find personally motivating: working toward change *isn't* a self-sacrificial choice. Working toward change, even change that you'll never see fully realized in your own career or workplace, is good for *you* in the moment of doing it. It's worth it even when it's hard and imperfect.

One of the reasons I believe this is that advocating for change helps us believe that our efforts in the world means something. Our belief that our contributions truly matter is a powerful psychological affordance that helps to shape how much we consider our jobs worth it.[45] When I first started leading applied research projects, I often found myself spending a maddening number of hours on toilsome tasks. In one project, I was interviewing aging adults for a small healthcare company with a very small budget. I recorded audio interviews on tape, transcribed them by hand, and spent a laborious amount of time analyzing the themes from these interviews into insights without any software at all, a far cry from the highly resourced technology companies I'd worked at before. Yet because the work was meaningful—I cared deeply about what I was doing and believed it had the potential to help people—and I had high levels of agency, those hours of manual labor melted away against the meaningfulness of what I was doing. The joy of moving from an idea to a successful intervention that changed something for better in the world is something that psychologists and developers share. I still look back with pride at the results of that study, which shifted the choices of the healthcare company and improved the lives of the patients they served.

I've seen the same effect on many software teams. Of course, our basic resources, needs, and stressors shape what we think about and can do in the world. But the power of good psychology shows up whenever we consider the many rich examples in human history of people doing extraordinary things in constrained situations, because their work has psychologically rich meaning. Teams better navigate challenges and protect their values when they feel that their work and voices *matter*. Feeling out of control and subjected to the whims of a hostile environment is fundamentally distressing because it can make us doubt the connection between our actions and the outcomes that happen in the world, producing the powerless feelings of learned helplessness. But taking action can restore our sense of this connection between our effort and changes in the world, which is one reason that psychological agency is a core component in most models of human wellbeing and thriving.[46,47]

While Brains-in-Jars organizations try to cut us off from seeing ourselves as whole people in technology, I've consistently seen that developers who take steps to advocate for more humane development practices have a greater sense of clarity about their days and greater peace of mind, no matter how imperfect their organizations. I think this happens because when we continually reflect on whether we're aligning our actions with our values, we're giving ourselves more clarity and structure with deliberate practice and repairing the harms of dehumanization.[48]

Taking compassionate action on behalf of others has a similarly powerful protective effect on our minds. People who spend the time working out how their actions can contribute to a shared good are able to drive change and stay motivated for longer in their work. For example, research on the long-term effects of participating in communal volunteering examined 49 studies and more than 24,000 people and found that reflection on the meaning and goals of the work was a key predictor for which people unlock the lessons they learn from participating in communal volunteering and ultimately achieve higher levels of civic engagement throughout their lives. Intervention experiments across many domains and groups have found that guiding people to explicitly reflect on their values creates greater prosocial action. Even when the world around them dismisses their needs, people, communities, and teams that affirm their self-integrity and shared humanity are more resilient under threat. Self-affirmation and self-compassion broaden our perspectives, giving us a path to rehumanizing ourselves.[49–55]

Across this book, we've seen numerous examples of the illusion that our minds frequently fall into of assuming that *avoidance* strategies will make us feel more comfortable at work and protect us from pain. But taking action to improve our cultures can help us shift toward *approach* strategies. In fact, researchers have found that people who take an approach strategy toward problems at work report higher levels of satisfaction, less stress and depression, and engage more deeply and regularly in prosocial actions. These collectively mark behaviors that we call workplace social courage, which strengthens our belief in ourselves and our commitment to our professional fields.[56–58] We've also learned how deeply developers benefit from feeling a strong sense of belonging and community with those around them. While we might often focus on how we are being treated by others, what we *give* to others is an equally important part of changing culture. Psychologist Andrew Fuligni has named the psychological affordance here the *need to contribute*, a relational stance toward our community that we are able to access when we donate time, energy, and resources to the people around us. Contributing to our communities allows us to deepen and fully engage in critical social relationships and social learning. Being a community contributor is consistently associated with more thriving psychological outcomes, more adaptive behaviors, and even stronger health outcomes, from reducing cardiovascular risks to improving subjective life satisfaction.[59–61] As our Developer Thriving study also showed, developers who feel a strong sense of belonging and share goals around their human needs with their teams also see higher productivity. But I think that this connection goes deeper than moment-by-moment productivity. Developers who support their peers, bravely share learning, engage in open-source development, or simply help a colleague feel better after a difficult technical challenge are putting belonging into action. They're creating more meaningful possibilities for others. Taking action to help others feel *their* work matters may be one of the most powerful ways our minds have to repair and heal from the times we've felt dismissed by poor managers, toxic teams, or broken organizations.

Finally, I really do believe that crafting a better, more psychologically healthy culture is the most strategic way for our technical communities to achieve technological problem-solving and breakthroughs. Whether or not they'll say it out loud or even know that they endorse it, people who are still trapped in the old Brains-in-Jars model of software teams can often harbor an implicit belief that "nice software teams finish last." These beliefs go deep: think about the last time you heard someone say *no pain, no gain*, or overheard people at work boast about pulling an all-nighter. And when businesses are wrestling with the many-headed monster of organizational change, it can be even harder to believe that a communal, kind culture could be the one that survives. But this belief has been proven wrong time and time again. At the scale of culture, good psychology unlocks the mechanisms of human innovation and helps us cultivate lasting communities.

I think about technology itself as a collective outcome of good psychology. When you see it this way, you might start to realize that's what we've always been chasing in software development. The solution, innovation, intervention, or idea that feels small to one person may just be what the next person needs to solve a problem that the first person never imagined. Across our communities, as our solutions are passed forward, modified, and tested by others, they improve our lives in ways we never originally imagined. The evidence shows the power of technical communities that celebrate experimentation and scaffold developers to learn, create, experiment, and collaborate freely.[62,63] It's the group-level version of a virtuous cycle. Thriving technical communities achieve powerful goals because developers in them have access to something that's far bigger than the isolated capacity of their individual brains: a psychologically healthy culture that drives innovation and shared learning across software development. Brains-in-Jars models may have shaped our past in software development, but they don't have to shape our future. Exploring the everyday psychology of software teams exposes the mechanisms that have been there all along, hiding within our biggest technical triumphs.

CONCLUSION: SOMEONE BUILT THIS

When I decided to write this book, I decided to try an experiment tangibly documenting the ways that software shapes my life and the lives of my loved ones—not just in the obvious form of the computers and smartphones I've owned, the tools I use, or my workflows across statistical modeling and research projects. I knew that software was *also* present in the basic infrastructure of my life, relationships, and meaningful experiences, but before working with developers, I'd rarely cultivated a habit of paying attention to it.

As I was thinking about the psychological experiences of people in software, I wanted to actively practice that habit. We find software easy to ignore; in fact, we often prefer it to be invisible. If you aren't a developer yourself, the immensely complex and ever-changing interacting worlds of software can feel as remote as other solar systems, as if we can only observe their strange physics from a great distance, in the trace measures we detect through space. In many ways, the successful operation of these systems ends in them becoming invisible to us. Even for me, a psychologist working with software teams, it took intention to become aware of all the ways that technological systems sustained my day-to-day life.

There's a technique in psychology that I love called experience sampling. Experience sampling is when people report on their lived experience throughout the day, often in random intervals, so that we can get a much more accurate look at real life. I decided to try experience sampling my explicit encounters with software, and by extension, every time software developers' choices impacted me. For a while, I made quick, bullet-point notes in my notebook every time I thought about software choices that shaped my actions. As I did this, more software encounters became visible and real to me. Every day had mundane examples that read like this:

- Texted my mom
- Signed up for a workout class
- Used my bank app
- Met someone on a video call
- Recorded and saved the words going into this manuscript
- Read a research paper

- Recorded a podcast
- Checked out a digital library book
- Listened to music

The samples were ordinary and endless, but each one of them rested on so many people's technological work. Software development is everywhere.

As I ran the research studies about software teams that are in this book, I also lived through and recovered from a severe and very difficult illness. During this time, I continued to notice software. When I communicated with doctors, I thought about the many pieces of software that let me reach out during emergencies or the way that important diagnostic information was protected and shared so that more people could help me. When I underwent complicated testing, I recognized many layers of software that empowered and extended the powers of my medical team. Every piece of science that informed my recovery and my ability to do the things that mattered most to me had been touched by software, too—from the tools that scientists used, to the software that had helped manufacture my medicine or record and learn from precious data about patients, to the functioning of large, complex research institutions.

As I healed, I continued to try to see software. When I stopped at a nearby store after my errand to the pharmacy and bought a spontaneous bouquet of flowers for my wife, I did not need to understand the complexities of ensuring that both I and the florist could have a financial transaction based on the power of software, nor did I have to hold the fears and stress of making technological decisions about security in order to enjoy this privilege. When I checked my phone for messages and reached out to my long-distance family, I held conversations across time and space, untroubled by the existence of protocols, standards, and invisible webs of infrastructure that enabled everyone. I have lived my life supported, empowered, and rendered more capable because of the cognitive, emotional, and psychological labor of the people who thought about and made decisions within vast ecosystems of technology. I found myself continually thinking: *Someone built this. Someone built all of this.*

When I first joined tech as a psychological scientist, the beliefs I encountered about software developers were negative, full of the deficit mindset of the Brains-in-Jars approach. I was once told not to schedule interviews with "the engineers," both for the fact that their time was too valuable to spend on psychological topics, but also because it was muttered to me in an aside, "The engineers hate talking." Maybe, I thought to myself, it was because no one had really listened to them.

The human beings who interact with these vast technologies are not cold, controllable brains in jars, spinning out endless permutations of the commands we give them. They are human beings. In my listening, I've learned that for some software practitioners, their acute awareness of how much of the world is indeed built by software can be a burden. The feeling of being responsible for things that no one else is even aware of can be profoundly isolating. Nevertheless, it was software developers who welcomed me into their psychological worlds, who generously invited me to visit their castles of the mind, and who have been brave enough to share their fear, overwhelm, and the immense sociotechnical responsibility they feel in my research studies, as well as their tremendous experiences of awe, creative joy, and collaboration. Software is a vast network of human problem-solving. It's because of this that I think of all the work of developers, no matter how mundane, as a cultural heritage. In technology conversations, sometimes "legacy" is a bad word. But I like to think of our software legacies more like an ancient, treasured library we can learn from.

It's my conviction that a healthy ecosystem for software needs intentional protection to flourish. Because the problem-solving that is the living form of software is inherently shared, collaborative, and created between individuals, our technology needs good psychological systems. Like technological systems, the psychological systems you live inside can feel impenetrably complex. But here too, you can learn to become a builder. You can recognize what helps you thrive, and what holds you back, and you can share this knowledge with the people around you. Every day, people navigate a vast range of psychological input, create meaning out of layers of experience, and take action in the world. As a psychologist, I believe that we construct our worlds every day out of our beliefs, our hopes, and our moments of loneliness or connection with others. Psychologists cannot solve the same problems that developers can solve, but perhaps we can learn to listen, share, and ease some of the problems of developers themselves, and in doing so, help more developers help others. I believe so. I believe we owe it to each other.

To every developer who reads this book: let's build together.

Bibliography

CHAPTER 1 REFERENCES

1. Storey, M.-A., Houck, B. & Zimmermann, T. How developers and managers define and trade productivity for quality. In *Proceedings of the 15th International Conference on Cooperative and Human Aspects of Software Engineering* 26–35 (Association for Computing Machinery, New York, NY, USA, 2022). https://doi.org/10.1145/3528579.3529177.
2. Hicks, C. M., Lee, C. S. & Ramsey, M. Developer thriving: Four sociocognitive factors that create resilient productivity on software teams. *IEEE Software* **41**, 68–77 (2024). https://doi.org/10.1109/MS.2024.3382957.
3. Jackson, V. *et al.* The impact of generative AI on creativity in software development: A research agenda. *ACM Transactions on Software Engineering and Methodology* **34**, 1–28 (2025). https://doi.org/10.1145/3708523.
4. Storey, M.-A., Russo, D., Novielli, N., Kobayashi, T. & Wang, D. A disruptive research playbook for studying disruptive innovations. *ACM Transactions on Software Engineering and Methodology* **33**, 1–29 (2024). https://doi.org/10.1145/3678172.
5. Hicks, C., Lee, C. & Foster-Marks, K. The new developer: AI skill threat, identity change & developer thriving in the transition to AI-assisted software development (2024). https://doi.org/10.31234/osf.io/2gej5.

CHAPTER 2 REFERENCES

1. Hicks, C. M. 'It's like coding in the dark': The need for learning cultures within coding teams (2023). https://doi.org/10.31234/osf.io/nz8m3.
2. Van Bavel, J. J., Hackel, L. M. & Xiao, Y. J. The group mind: The pervasive influence of social identity on cognition. In *New Frontiers in Social Neuroscience* (eds Decety, J. & Christen, Y.) 41–56 (Springer International Publishing, Cham, 2014). https://doi.org/10.1007/978-3-319-02904-7_4.
3. Cheryan, S., Plaut, V. C., Davies, P. G. & Steele, C. M. Ambient belonging: How stereotypical cues impact gender participation in computer science. *Journal of Personality and Social Psychology* **97**, 1045–1060 (2009). https://doi.org/10.1037/a0016239.

4. Cataldo, M. & Herbsleb, J. D. Coordination breakdowns and their impact on development productivity and software failures. *IEEE Transactions on Software Engineering* **39**, 343–360 (2013). https://doi.org/10.1109/TSE.2012.32.
5. Berntzen, M., Stray, V., Moe, N. B. & Hoda, R. Responding to change over time: A longitudinal case study on changes in coordination mechanisms in large-scale agile. *Empirical Software Engineering* **28**, 114 (2023). https://doi.org/10.1007/s10664-023-10349-0.
6. Besker, T., Ghanbari, H., Martini, A. & Bosch, J. The influence of technical debt on software developer morale. *Journal of Systems and Software* **167**, 110586 (2020). https://doi.org/10.1016/j.jss.2020.110586.
7. Bredehorst, J., Krautter, K., Meuris, J. & Jachimowicz, J. M. The challenge of maintaining passion for work over time: A daily perspective on passion and emotional exhaustion. *Organization Science* **35**, 364–386 (2024). https://doi.org/10.1287/orsc.2023.1673.
8. Nielsen, K. *et al.* Workplace resources to improve both employee well-being and performance: A systematic review and meta-analysis. *Work & Stress* **31**, 101–120 (2017). https://doi.org/10.1080/02678373.2017.1304463.
9. Kumar, S. *et al.* Time warp: The gap between developers' ideal vs actual workweeks in an AI-driven era (2025). https://doi.org/10.48550/arXiv.2502.15287.
10. Trinkenreich, B., Santos, F. & Stol, K.-J. Predicting attrition among software professionals: Antecedents and consequences of burnout and engagement. *ACM Transactions on Software Engineering and Methodology* **33**, 1–45 (2024). https://doi.org/10.1145/3691629.
11. Bjork, R. A., Dunlosky, J. & Kornell, N. Self-regulated learning: Beliefs, techniques, and illusions. *Annual Review of Psychology* **64**, 417–444 (2013). https://doi.org/10.1146/annurev-psych-113011-143823.
12. Soderstrom, N. C. & Bjork, R. A. Learning versus performance: An integrative review. *Perspectives on Psychological Science* **10**, 176–199 (2015). https://doi.org/10.1177/1745691615569000.
13. Darnon, C., Harackiewicz, J. M., Butera, F., Mugny, G. & Quiamzade, A. Performance-approach and performance avoidance goals: When uncertainty makes a difference. *Personality and Social Psychology Bulletin* **33**, 813–827 (2007). https://doi.org/10.1177/0146167207301022.
14. Wigfield, A. & Eccles, J. S. Chapter 4—The development of competence beliefs, expectancies for success, and achievement values from childhood through adolescence. In *Development of Achievement Motivation* (eds Wigfield, A. & Eccles, J. S.) 91–120 (Academic Press, San Diego, 2002). https://doi.org/10.1016/B978-012750053-9/50006-1.
15. Valentine, J. C., DuBois, D. L. & Cooper, H. The relation between self-beliefs and academic achievement: A meta-analytic review. *Educational Psychologist* **39**, 111–133 (2004). https://doi.org/10.1207/s15326985ep3902_3.
16. Muradoglu, M., Arnold, S. H., Leslie, S.-J. & Cimpian, A. 'What does it take to succeed here?': The belief that success requires brilliance is an obstacle to diversity. *Current Directions in Psychological Science* **32**, 379–386 (2023). https://doi.org/10.1177/09637214231173361.

17. Chater, N. & Loewenstein, G. The i-frame and the s-frame: How focusing on individual-level solutions has led behavioral public policy astray. *Behavioral and Brain Sciences* **46**, e147 (2023). https://doi.org/10.1017/S0140525X22002023.
18. Lesener, T., Gusy, B., Jochmann, A. & Wolter, C. The drivers of work engagement: A meta-analytic review of longitudinal evidence. *Work & Stress* **34**, 259–278 (2020). https://doi.org/10.1017/S0140525X22002023.
19. Hicks, C. M., Lee, C. & Foster-Marks, K. The new developer: AI skill threat, identity change & developer thriving in the transition to AI-assisted software development (2024). https://doi.org/10.31234/osf.io/2gej5.
20. Cohen, G. L. *Belonging: The Science of Creating Connection and Bridging Divides* (W. W. Norton & Company, New York, 2022).
21. Frazier, M. L., Fainshmidt, S., Klinger, R. L., Pezeshkan, A. & Vracheva, V. Psychological safety: A meta-analytic review and extension. *Personnel Psychology* **70**, 113–165 (2017). https://doi.org/10.1111/peps.12183.
22. Park, D., Tsukayama, E., Yu, A. & Duckworth, A. L. The development of grit and growth mindset during adolescence. *Journal of Experimental Child Psychology* **198**, 104889 (2020). https://doi.org/10.1016/j.jecp.2020.104889.
23. Vial, A. C., Muradoglu, M., Newman, G. E. & Cimpian, A. An emphasis on brilliance fosters masculinity-contest cultures. *Psychological Science* **33**, 595–612 (2022). https://doi.org/10.1177/09567976211044133.
24. Cheryan, S., Lombard, E. J., Hailu, F., Pham, L. N. H. & Weltzien, K. Global patterns of gender disparities in STEM and explanations for their persistence. *Nature Reviews Psychology* 1–14 (2024). https://doi.org/10.1038/s44159-024-00380-3.
25. Hadden, I. R. *et al.* Why the belief in meritocracy is so pervasive. *Trends in Cognitive Sciences* **29**, 101–104 (2025). https://doi.org/10.1016/j.tics.2024.12.008.
26. Mueller, C. M. & Dweck, C. S. Praise for intelligence can undermine children's motivation and performance. *Journal of Personality and Social Psychology* **75**, 33–52 (1998). https://doi.org/10.1037/0022-3514.75.1.33.
27. Walton, G. M., Logel, C., Peach, J. M., Spencer, S. J. & Zanna, M. P. Two brief interventions to mitigate a 'chilly climate' transform women's experience, relationships, and achievement in engineering. *Journal of Educational Psychology* **107**, 468–485 (2015). https://doi.org/10.1037/a0037461.
28. Hicks, C. M. & Hevesi, A. A cumulative culture theory for developer problem-solving (2024). https://doi.org/10.31234/osf.io/tfjyw.
29. Van Bavel, J. J., Hackel, L. M. & Xiao, Y. J. The group mind: The pervasive influence of social identity on cognition. In *New Frontiers in Social Neuroscience* (eds Decety, J. & Christen, Y.) 41–56 (Springer International Publishing, Cham, 2014). https://doi.org/10.1007/978-3-319-02904-7_4.
30. Cialdini, R. B. & Goldstein, N. J. Social influence: Compliance and conformity. *Annual Review of Psychology* **55**, 591–621 (2004). https://doi.org/10.1146/annurev.psych.55.090902.142015.
31. Brescoll, V. L., Dawson, E. & Uhlmann, E. L. Hard won and easily lost: The fragile status of leaders in gender-stereotype-incongruent occupations. *Psychological Science* **21**, 1640–1642 (2010). https://doi.org/10.1177/0956797610384744.

32. Meyer, M., Cimpian, A. & Leslie, S.-J. Women are underrepresented in fields where success is believed to require brilliance. *Frontiers in Psychology* **6** (2015). https://doi.org/10.3389/fpsyg.2015.00235.
33. Stavrova, O. & Ehlebracht, D. The cynical genius illusion: Exploring and debunking lay beliefs about cynicism and competence. *Personality and Social Psychology Bulletin* **45**, 254–269 (2019). https://doi.org/10.1177/0146167218783195.
34. Cheryan, S. *et al.* Double isolation: Identity expression threat predicts greater gender disparities in computer science. *Self and Identity* **19**, 412–434 (2020). https://doi.org/10.1080/15298868.2019.1609576.
35. Vorderwülbeke, E. & Graßl, I. Belonging beyond code: Queer software engineering and humanities student experiences (2025). https://doi.org/10.48550/arXiv.2503.04576.
36. Prana, G. A. A. *et al.* Including everyone, everywhere: Understanding opportunities and challenges of geographic gender-inclusion in OSS. *IEEE Transactions on Software Engineering* **48**, 3394–3409 (2022). https://doi.org/10.1109/TSE.2021.3092813.
37. Master, A., Meltzoff, A. N. & Cheryan, S. Gender stereotypes about interests start early and cause gender disparities in computer science and engineering. *Proceedings of the National Academy of Sciences* **118**, e2100030118 (2021). https://doi.org/10.1073/pnas.2100030118.
38. Corbett, C. & Hill, C. Solving the equation: The variables for women's success in engineering and computing. *American Association of University Women* (2015).
39. Margolis, J. & Fisher, A. *Unlocking the Clubhouse: Women in Computing* (MIT Press, Cambridge, 2002).
40. Mejias, M. *et al.* A framework for discussing black student threats to belonging in computer science. In *2024 Black Issues in Computing Education (BICE)* 15–20 (2024). https://doi.org/10.1109/BICE60192.2024.00011.
41. Murphy-Hill, E., Jaspan, C., Egelman, C. & Cheng, L. The pushback effects of race, ethnicity, gender, and age in code review. *Communications of the ACM* **65**, 52–57 (2022). https://doi.org/10.1145/3474097.
42. Brockner, J. & Sherman, D. K. Wise interventions in organizations. *Research in Organizational Behavior* **39**, 100125 (2019). https://doi.org/10.1016/j.riob.2020.100125.
43. Baldissarri, C. & Fourie, M. M. Dehumanizing organizations: Insidious effects of having one's human integrity denied at work. *Current Opinion in Behavioral Sciences* **49**, 101244 (2023). https://doi.org/10.1016/j.cobeha.2022.101244.
44. Ralph, P. & Tempero, E. Construct validity in software engineering research and software metrics. In *Proceedings of the 22nd International Conference on Evaluation and Assessment in Software Engineering 2018* 13–23 (Association for Computing Machinery, New York, NY, USA, 2018). https://doi.org/10.1145/3210459.3210461.
45. Sjøberg, D. I. K. & Bergersen, G. R. Construct validity in software engineering. *IEEE Transactions on Software Engineering* **49**, 1374–1396 (2023). https://doi.org/10.1109/TSE.2022.3176725.

46. Korbmacher, M. *et al.* The replication crisis has led to positive structural, procedural, and community changes. *Communications Psychology* **1**, 1–13 (2023). https://doi.org/10.1038/s44271-023-00003-2.
47. Makel, M. C., Plucker, J. A. & Hegarty, B. Replications in psychology research: How often do they really occur? *Perspectives on Psychological Science: A Journal of the Association for Psychological Science* **7**, 537–542 (2012). https://doi.org/10.1177/1745691612460688.
48. Auspurg, K. & Brüderl, J. Has the credibility of the social sciences been credibly destroyed? Reanalyzing the 'many analysts, one data set' project. *Socius* **7**, 23780231211024421 (2021). https://doi.org/10.1177/23780231211024421.
49. Lundberg, I., Johnson, R. & Stewart, B. M. What is your estimand? Defining the target quantity connects statistical evidence to theory. *American Sociological Review* **86**, 532–565 (2021). https://doi.org/10.1177/00031224211004187.
50. Elson, M., Hussey, I., Alsalti, T. & Arslan, R. C. Psychological measures aren't toothbrushes. *Communications Psychology* **1**, 1–4 (2023). https://doi.org/10.1038/s44271-023-00026-9.
51. Muthukrishna, M. *et al.* Beyond western, educated, industrial, rich, and democratic (WEIRD) psychology: Measuring and mapping scales of cultural and psychological distance. *Psychological Science* **31**, 678–701 (2020). https://doi.org/10.1177/0956797620916782.

CHAPTER 3 REFERENCES

1. Weir, A. A. S., Chappell, J. & Kacelnik, A. Shaping of hooks in new caledonian crows. *Science* **297**, 981–981 (2002). https://doi.org/10.1126/science.1073433.
2. Bird, C. D. & Emery, N. J. Insightful problem solving and creative tool modification by captive nontool-using rooks. *Proceedings of the National Academy of Sciences* **106**, 10370–10375 (2009). https://doi.org/10.1073/pnas.0901008106.
3. Beck, S. R., Apperly, I. A., Chappell, J., Guthrie, C. & Cutting, N. Making tools isn't child's play. *Cognition* **119**, 301–306 (2011). https://doi.org/10.1016/j.cognition.2011.01.003.
4. Rawlings, B. & Legare, C. H. Toddlers, tools, and tech: The cognitive ontogenesis of innovation. *Trends in Cognitive Sciences* **25**, 81–92 (2021). https://doi.org/10.1016/j.tics.2020.10.006.
5. Legare, C. H. Cumulative cultural learning: Development and diversity. *Proceedings of the National Academy of Sciences* **114**, 7877–7883 (2017). https://doi.org/10.1073/pnas.1620743114.
6. Hyde, J. S. & Mertz, J. E. Gender, culture, and mathematics performance. *Proceedings of the National Academy of Sciences* **106**, 8801–8807 (2009). https://doi.org/10.1073/pnas.0901265106.
7. Goddu, M. K. & Gopnik, A. The development of human causal learning and reasoning. *Nature Reviews Psychology* **3**, 319–339 (2024). https://doi.org/10.1038/s44159-024-00300-5.
8. Buchsbaum, D., Seiver, E., Bridgers, S. & Gopnik, A. Learning about causes from people and about people as causes: Probabilistic models and social causal reasoning. *Advances in Child Development and Behavior* **43**, 125–160 (JAI, 2012). https://doi.org/10.1016/B978-0-12-397919-3.00005-8.

9. Cheng, R., Wang, R., Zimmermann, T. & Ford, D. 'It would work for me too': How online communities shape software developers' trust in AI-powered code generation tools. *ACM Transactions on Interactive Intelligent Systems* **14**, 1–39 (2024). https://doi.org/10.1145/3651990.
10. Yale University. *A Timeline of Women at Yale.* (2025). https://celebrate-women.yale.edu/history/timeline-women-yale.
11. Sackman, H., Erikson, W. J. & Grant, E. E. Exploratory experimental studies comparing online and offline programming performance. *Communications of the ACM* **11**, 3–11 (1968). https://doi.org/10.1145/362851.362858.
12. Behroozi, M., Parnin, C. & Barik, T. Hiring is broken: What do developers say about technical interviews? In *2019 IEEE Symposium on Visual Languages and Human-Centric Computing (VL/HCC)* 1–9 (2019). https://doi.org/10.1109/VLHCC.2019.8818836.
13. Brooks, F. P. *The Mythical Man-Month—Essays on Software-Engineering* (Addison-Wesley, Boston, 1975). https://doi.org/10.1145/800027.808439.
14. Rattan, A. *et al.* Meta-lay theories of scientific potential drive underrepresented students' sense of belonging to science, technology, engineering, and mathematics (STEM). *Journal of Personality and Social Psychology* **115**, 54–75 (2018). https://doi.org/10.1037/pspi0000130.
15. Haslam, N., Bastian, B., Bain, P. & Kashima, Y. Psychological essentialism, implicit theories, and intergroup relations. *Group Processes & Intergroup Relations* **9**, 63–76 (2006). https://doi.org/10.1177/1368430206059861.
16. Master, A., Meltzoff, A. N. & Cheryan, S. Gender stereotypes about interests start early and cause gender disparities in computer science and engineering. *Proceedings of the National Academy of Sciences* **118**, e2100030118 (2021). https://doi.org/10.1073/pnas.2100030118.
17. Cheryan, S., Ziegler, S. A., Montoya, A. K. & Jiang, L. Why are some STEM fields more gender balanced than others? *Psychological Bulletin* **143**, 1–35 (2017). https://doi.org/10.1037/bul0000052.
18. Weinberg, G. M. *The Psychology of Computer Programming* (Leanpub, Victoria, 2014).
19. DeMarco, T. & Lister, T. Programmer performance and the effects of the workplace. In *Proceedings of the 8th International Conference on Software Engineering* 268–272 (IEEE Computer Society Press, Washington, DC, USA, 1985).
20. Wolfe, J. M. Perspectives on testing for programming aptitude. In *Proceedings of the 1971 26th Annual Conference on*—268–277 (ACM Press, Knoxville, 1971). https://doi.org/10.1145/800184.810494.
21. Stemler, S. E. & Sternberg, R. J. The assessment of aptitude. In *APA Handbook of Testing and Assessment in Psychology, Vol. 3: Testing and Assessment in School Psychology and Education* 281–296 (American Psychological Association, Washington, DC, US, 2013). https://doi.org/10.1037/14049-013.
22. Rutkowski, L., Rutkowski, D. & Thompson, G. What are we measuring in international assessments? Learning? Probably. Intelligence? Not likely. *Learning and Individual Differences* **110**, 102421 (2024). https://doi.org/10.1016/j.lindif.2024.102421.

23. Richardson, M., Abraham, C. & Bond, R. Psychological correlates of university students' academic performance: A systematic review and meta-analysis. *Psychological Bulletin* **138**, 353–387 (2012). https://doi.org/10.1037/a0026838.
24. Sternberg, R. J. Testing: For better and worse. *Phi Delta Kappan* **98**, 66–71 (2016). https://doi.org/10.1177/0031721716681780.
25. Sternberg, R. J. & Grigorenko, E. L. *Dynamic Testing: The Nature and Measurement of Learning Potential* (Cambridge University Press, Cambridge, 2002).
26. Suchy, Y., Mora, M. G., DesRuisseaux, L. A., Niermeyer, M. A. & Brothers, S. L. Pitfalls in research on ecological validity of novel executive function tests: A systematic review and a call to action. *Psychological Assessment* **36**, 243–261 (2024). https://doi.org/10.1037/pas0001297.
27. Miller-Cotto, D., Ribner, A., Ahmed, S., Ellis, A. & Czerwiński, S. Examining ethnic/racial measurement invariance in fourth-grade executive function: A registered report of data from the early childhood longitudinal study—Kindergarten. *Journal of Educational Psychology* **118**, 1–11 (2025). https://doi.org/10.1037/edu0000985.
28. Alcalá, L. The developing of executive function skills through culturally organized autonomy and helping. *Infant and Child Development* **32**, e2460 (2023). https://doi.org/10.1002/icd.2460.
29. Fendinger, N. J., Dietze, P. & Knowles, E. D. Beyond cognitive deficits: How social class shapes social cognition. *Trends in Cognitive Sciences* **27**, 528–538 (2023). https://doi.org/10.1016/j.tics.2023.03.004.
30. Walton, G. M. & Spencer, S. J. Latent ability: Grades and test scores systematically underestimate the intellectual ability of negatively stereotyped students. *Psychological Science* **20**, 1132–1139 (2009). https://doi.org/10.1111/j.1467-9280.2009.02417.x.
31. Flournoy, J. C., Lee, C. S., Wu, M. & Hicks, C. M. No silver bullets: Why understanding software cycle time is messy, not magic. *Empirical Software Engineering* **30**, 174 (2025). https://doi.org/10.1007/s10664-025-10735-w.
32. Hadden, I. R. *et al.* Why the belief in meritocracy is so pervasive. *Trends in Cognitive Sciences* **29**, 101–104 (2025). https://doi.org/10.1016/j.tics.2024.12.008.
33. Gilbert, D. T. & Malone, P. S. The correspondence bias. *Psychological Bulletin* **117**, 21–38 (1995). https://doi.org/10.1037/0033-2909.117.1.21.
34. Murphy-Hill, E. *et al.* What predicts software developers' productivity? *IEEE Transactions on Software Engineering* **47**, 582–594 (2021). https://doi.org/10.1109/TSE.2019.2900308.
35. Von Hippel, E. & Von Krogh, G. Free revealing and the private-collective model for innovation incentives. *R&D Management* **36**, 295–306 (2006). https://doi.org/10.1111/j.1467-9310.2006.00435.x.
36. Von Hippel, E. Open source software projects as "user innovation networks". In *Perspectives on Free and Open Source Software* (eds Feller, J., Fitzgerald, B., Hissam, S. A. & Lakhani, K. R.) 267–278 (The MIT Press, Cambridge, 2005). https://doi.org/10.7551/mitpress/5326.003.0021.

37. Shaw, M. Myths and mythconceptions: What does it mean to be a programming language, anyhow? *Proceedings of the ACM on Programming Languages* **4**, 1–44 (2022). https://doi.org/10.1145/3480947.
38. Miu, E., Gulley, N., Laland, K. N. & Rendell, L. Innovation and cumulative culture through tweaks and leaps in online programming contests. *Nature Communications* **9**, 2321 (2018). https://doi.org/10.1038/s41467-018-04494-0.
39. Petre, M. & Hoek, A. V. D. *Software Design Decoded: 66 Ways Experts Think* (MIT Press, Cambridge, 2016). https://doi.org/10.7551/mitpress/10612.001.0001.
40. Sternberg, R. J. Abilities are forms of developing expertise. *Educational Researcher* **27**, 11–20 (1998). https://doi.org/10.3102/0013189X027003011.
41. Sternberg, R. J. & Horvath, J. A. *Tacit Knowledge in Professional Practice: Researcher and Practitioner Perspectives* (Psychology Press, New York, 1999). https://doi.org/10.4324/9781410603098.
42. Elliot, A. J. & Dweck, C. S. *Handbook of Competence and Motivation, First Edition* (Guilford Publications, New York, 2013).
43. Hicks, C. M. & Hevesi, A. A cumulative culture theory for developer problem-solving (2024). https://doi.org/10.31234/osf.io/tfjyw.
44. Carpenter, S. K., Witherby, A. E. & Tauber, S. K. On students' (mis)judgments of learning and teaching effectiveness. *Journal of Applied Research in Memory and Cognition* **9**, 137–151 (2020). https://doi.org/10.1016/j.jarmac.2020.04.003.
45. Ertmer, P. A. & Newby, T. J. The expert learner: Strategic, self-regulated, and reflective. *Instructional Science* **24**, 1–24 (1996). https://doi.org/10.1007/BF00156001.
46. Ericsson, K. A. & Charness, N. Expert performance: Its structure and acquisition. *American Psychologist* **49**, 725–747 (1994). https://doi.org/10.1037/0003-066X.49.8.725.
47. Ericsson, Anders & Pool, Robert. *Peak* (HarperOne, San Francisco, 2017).
48. Tankelevitch, L. *et al.* The metacognitive demands and opportunities of generative AI. In *Proceedings of the 2024 CHI Conference on Human Factors in Computing Systems* 1–24 (Association for Computing Machinery, New York, NY, 2024). https://doi.org/10.1145/3613904.3642902.
49. Arciniegas-Mendez, M., Zagalsky, A., Storey, M.-A. & Hadwin, A. F. Using the model of regulation to understand software development collaboration practices and tool support. In *Proceedings of the 2017 ACM Conference on Computer Supported Cooperative Work and Social Computing* 1049–1065 (Association for Computing Machinery, New York, NY, 2017). https://doi.org/10.1145/2998181.2998360.
50. Bjork, R. A. & Bjork, E. L. Desirable difficulties in theory and practice. *Journal of Applied Research in Memory and Cognition* **9**, 475–479 (2020). https://doi.org/10.1016/j.jarmac.2020.09.003.
51. Bertsch, S., Pesta, B. J., Wiscott, R. & McDaniel, M. A. The generation effect: A meta-analytic review. *Memory & Cognition* **35**, 201–210 (2007). https://doi.org/10.3758/BF03193441.

52. Karpicke, J. D. & Grimaldi, P. J. Retrieval-based learning: A perspective for enhancing meaningful learning. *Educational Psychology Review* **24**, 401–418 (2012). https://doi.org/10.1007/s10648-012-9202-2.
53. Barbieri, C. A., Miller-Cotto, D., Clerjuste, S. N. & Chawla, K. A meta-analysis of the worked examples effect on mathematics performance. *Educational Psychology Review* **35**, 11 (2023). https://doi.org/10.1007/s10648-023-09745-1.
54. Kalyuga, S., Ayres, P., Chandler, P. & Sweller, J. The expertise reversal effect. *Educational Psychologist* **38**, 23–31 (2003). https://doi.org/10.1207/S15326985EP3801_4.
55. Giebl, S., Mena, S., Storm, B. C., Bjork, E. L. & Bjork, R. A. Answer first or Google first? Using the internet in ways that enhance, not impair, one's subsequent retention of needed information. *Psychology Learning & Teaching* **20**, 58–75 (2021). https://doi.org/10.1177/1475725720961593.
56. Pan, S. C. & Rivers, M. L. Metacognitive awareness of the pretesting effect improves with self-regulation support. *Memory & Cognition* **51**, 1461–1480 (2023). https://doi.org/10.3758/s13421-022-01392-1.
57. Petre, M. & Shaw, M. Contrasting to spark creativity in software development: Tactics used by high-performing teams. *IEEE Software* **42**, 67–74 (2025). https://doi.org/10.1109/MS.2025.3538670.
58. Bjork, E. L. & Bjork, R. A. Making things hard on yourself, but in a good way: Creating desirable difficulties to enhance learning. In *Psychology and the Real World: Essays Illustrating Fundamental Contributions to Society* 56–64 (Worth Publishers, New York, NY, US, 2011).
59. Prince, M. Does active learning work? A review of the research. *Journal of Engineering Education* **93**, 223–231 (2004). https://doi.org/10.1002/j.2168-9830.2004.tb00809.x.
60. Veenman, M. V. J., Van Hout-Wolters, B. H. A. M. & Afflerbach, P. Metacognition and learning: Conceptual and methodological considerations. *Metacognition and Learning* **1**, 3–14 (2006). https://doi.org/10.1007/s11409-006-6893-0.
61. Hattie, J. *Visible Learning: A Synthesis of Over 800 Meta-Analyses Relating to Achievement* (Routledge, London, 2008). https://doi.org/10.4324/9780203887332.
62. Hoffman, R. R. *et al. Accelerated Expertise: Training for High Proficiency in a Complex World* (Psychology Press, New York, 2013). https://doi.org/10.4324/9780203797327.
63. Aghajani, E. *et al.* Software documentation: The Practitioners' Perspective. In *Proceedings of the ACM/IEEE 42nd International Conference on Software Engineering* 590–601 (Association for Computing Machinery, New York, NY, USA, 2020). https://doi.org/10.1145/3377811.3380405.
64. Zhi, J. *et al.* Cost, Benefits and quality of software development documentation: A systematic mapping. *Journal of Systems and Software* **99**, 175–198 (2015). https://doi.org/10.1016/j.jss.2014.09.042.

65. Freeman, S. *et al.* Active learning increases student performance in science, engineering, and mathematics. *Proceedings of the National Academy of Sciences* **111**, 8410–8415 (2014). https://doi.org/10.1073/pnas.1319030111.
66. Abrahão, S., Grundy, J., Pezzè, M., Storey, M.-A. & Tamburri, D. A. Software engineering by and for humans in an AI era. *ACM Transactions on Software Engineering and Methodology* **34**, 1–46 (2025). https://doi.org/10.1145/3715111.

CHAPTER 4 REFERENCES

1. Guzdial, Mark. A minuscule percentage of students take high school computer science in the United States: Access isn't enough. *Communications of the ACM Blog* (2019).
2. Hicks, C. M., Liu, D. & Heyman, G. D. Young children's beliefs about self-disclosure of performance failure and success. *British Journal of Developmental Psychology* **33**, 123–135 (2015). https://doi.org/10.1111/bjdp.12077.
3. Heyman, G. D., Fu, G. & Lee, K. Reasoning about the disclosure of success and failure to friends among children in the United States and China. *Developmental Psychology* **44**, 908–918 (2008). https://doi.org/10.1037/a0013375.
4. Elliot, A. J. & Church, M. A. A hierarchical model of approach and avoidance achievement motivation. *Journal of Personality and Social Psychology* **72**, 218–232 (1997). https://doi.org/10.1037/0022-3514.72.1.218.
5. Senko, C. & Miles, K. M. Pursuing their own learning agenda: How mastery-oriented students jeopardize their class performance. *Contemporary Educational Psychology* **33**, 561–583 (2008). https://doi.org/10.1016/j.cedpsych.2007.12.001.
6. Guo, J. *et al.* Mastery-approach goals: A large-scale cross-cultural analysis of antecedents and consequences. *Journal of Personality and Social Psychology* **125**, 397–420 (2023). https://doi.org/10.1037/pspp0000436.
7. Baddoo, N., Hall, T. & Jagielska, D. Software developer motivation in a high maturity company: A case study. *Software Process: Improvement and Practice* **11**, 219–228 (2006). https://doi.org/10.1002/spip.265.
8. Godliauskas, P. & Šmite, D. The well-being of software engineers: A systematic literature review and a theory. *Empirical Software Engineering* **30**, 35 (2024). https://doi.org/10.1007/s10664-024-10543-8.
9. Senko, C. & Harackiewicz, J. M. Performance goals: The moderating roles of context and achievement orientation. *Journal of Experimental Social Psychology* **38**, 603–610 (2002). https://doi.org/10.1016/S0022-1031(02)00503-6.
10. Darnon, C., Harackiewicz, J. M., Butera, F., Mugny, G. & Quiamzade, A. Performance-approach and performance-avoidance goals: When uncertainty makes a difference. *Personality and Social Psychology Bulletin* **33**, 813–827 (2007). https://doi.org/10.1177/0146167207301022.
11. Murphy, M. C. & Dweck, C. S. A culture of genius: How an organization's lay theory shapes people's cognition, affect, and behavior. *Personality & Social Psychology Bulletin* **36**, 283–296 (2010). https://doi.org/10.1177/0146167209347380.
12. Canning, E. A. *et al.* Cultures of genius at work: Organizational mindsets predict cultural norms, trust, and commitment. *Personality & Social Psychology Bulletin* **46**, 626–642 (2020). https://doi.org/10.1177/0146167219872473.

13. Walton, G. M., Murphy, M. C. & Ryan, A. M. Stereotype threat in organizations: Implications for equity and performance. *Annual Review of Organizational Psychology and Organizational Behavior* **2**, 523–550 (2015). https://doi.org/10.1146/annurev-orgpsych-032414-111322.
14. Kamins, M. L. & Dweck, C. S. Person versus process praise and criticism: Implications for contingent self-worth and coping. *Developmental Psychology* **35**, 835–847 (1999). https://doi.org/10.1037/0012-1649.35.3.835.
15. Haimovitz, K. & Henderlong Corpus, J. Effects of person versus process praise on student motivation: Stability and change in emerging adulthood. *Educational Psychology* **31**, 595–609 (2011). https://doi.org/10.1080/01443410.2011.585950.
16. Chadwick, I. C. & Raver, J. L. Motivating organizations to learn: Goal orientation and its influence on organizational learning. *Journal of Management* **41**, 957–986 (2015). https://doi.org/10.1177/0149206312443558.
17. Fishbach, A. & Woolley, K. The structure of intrinsic motivation. *Annual Review of Organizational Psychology and Organizational Behavior* **9**, 339–363 (2022). https://doi.org/10.1146/annurev-orgpsych-012420-091122.
18. Oishi, S. & Westgate, E. C. A psychologically rich life: Beyond happiness and meaning. *Psychological Review* **129**, 790–811 (2022). https://doi.org/10.1037/rev0000317.
19. Manganelli, L., Thibault-Landry, A., Forest, J. & Carpentier, J. Self-determination theory can help you generate performance and well-being in the workplace: A review of the literature. *Advances in Developing Human Resources* **20**, 227–240 (2018). https://doi.org/10.1177/1523422318757210.
20. Yeager, D. S. & Dweck, C. S. Mindsets that promote resilience: When students believe that personal characteristics can be developed. *Educational Psychologist* **47**, 302–314 (2012). https://doi.org/10.1080/00461520.2012.722805.
21. Meyer, A. N., Barr, E. T., Bird, C. & Zimmermann, T. Today was a good day: The daily life of software developers. *IEEE Transactions on Software Engineering* **47**, 863–880 (2021). https://doi.org/10.1109/TSE.2019.2904957.
22. Meyer, A. N., Fritz, T., Murphy, G. C. & Zimmermann, T. Software developers' perceptions of productivity. In *Proceedings of the 22nd ACM SIGSOFT International Symposium on Foundations of Software Engineering* 19–29 (Association for Computing Machinery, New York, NY, USA, 2014). https://doi.org/10.1145/2635868.2635892.
23. Meyer, A. N., Murphy, G. C., Zimmermann, T. & Fritz, T. Enabling good work habits in software developers through reflective goal-setting. *IEEE Transactions on Software Engineering* **47**, 1872–1885 (2021). https://doi.org/10.1109/TSE.2019.2938525.
24. Hall, T., Baddoo, N., Beecham, S., Robinson, H. & Sharp, H. A systematic review of theory use in studies investigating the motivations of software engineers. *ACM Transactions on Software Engineering and Methodology* **18**, 1–29 (2009). https://doi.org/10.1145/1525880.1525883.
25. Robinson, K. A. *et al.* Motivation in transition: Development and roles of expectancy, task values, and costs in early college engineering. *Journal of Educational Psychology* **111**, 1081–1102 (2019). https://doi.org/10.1037/edu0000331.

26. Wigfield, A. Expectancy-value theory of achievement motivation: A developmental perspective. *Educational Psychology Review* **6**, 49–78 (1994). https://doi.org/10.1007/BF02209024.
27. Eccles, J. S. & Wigfield, A. From expectancy-value theory to situated expectancy-value theory: A developmental, social cognitive, and sociocultural perspective on motivation. *Contemporary Educational Psychology* **61**, 101859 (2020). https://doi.org/10.1016/j.cedpsych.2020.101859.
28. Lauermann, F., Tsai, Y.-M. & Eccles, J. S. Math-related career aspirations and choices within Eccles et al.'s expectancy-value theory of achievement-related behaviors. *Developmental Psychology* **53**, 1540–1559 (2017). https://doi.org/10.1037/dev0000367.
29. Bandura, A. Self-efficacy mechanism in human agency. *American Psychologist* **37**, 122–147 (1982). https://doi.org/10.1037/0003-066X.37.2.122.
30. Hoffman, B. & Schraw, G. The influence of self-efficacy and working memory capacity on problem-solving efficiency. *Learning and Individual Differences* **19**, 91–100 (2009). https://doi.org/10.1016/j.lindif.2008.08.001.
31. Bandura, A. Cultivate self-efficacy for personal and organizational effectiveness. In *Principles of Organizational Behavior* 113–135 (John Wiley & Sons, Ltd, Hoboken, 2023). https://doi.org/10.1002/9781394320769.ch6.
32. Hicks, C. M., Lee, C. S. & Ramsey, M. Developer thriving: Four sociocognitive factors that create resilient productivity on software teams. *IEEE Software* **41**, 68–77 (2024). https://doi.org/10.1109/MS.2024.3382957.
33. Sadowski, C. & Zimmermann, T. (eds). *Rethinking Productivity in Software Engineering* (Springer Nature, Berlin, 2019). https://doi.org/10.1007/978-1-4842-4221-6.
34. Drucker, P. F. Knowledge-worker productivity: The biggest challenge. *California Management Review* **41**, 79–94 (1999). https://doi.org/10.2307/41165987.
35. Bauer, C. A., Poddar, A., Brummelman, E. & Cimpian, A. The brilliance–belonging model: How cultural beliefs about intellectual ability undermine educational equity. *Educational Psychology Review* **37**, 64 (2025). https://doi.org/10.1007/s10648-025-10034-2.
36. Cimpian, A. & Leslie, S.-J. The brilliance trap. *Scientific American* **317**, 60–65 (2017). https://www.jstor.org/stable/27109296.
37. Leslie, S.-J., Cimpian, A., Meyer, M. & Freeland, E. Expectations of brilliance underlie gender distributions across academic disciplines. *Science (New York, N.Y.)* **347**, 262–265 (2015). https://doi.org/10.1126/science.1261375.
38. Jenifer, J. B., Jaxon, J., Levine, S. C. & Cimpian, A. 'You need to be super smart to do well in math!' Young children's field-specific ability beliefs. *Developmental Science* **27**, e13429 (2024). https://doi.org/10.1111/desc.13429.
39. Muradoglu, M. *et al.* Why a culture of brilliance is bad for physics. *Nature Reviews Physics* **6**, 75–77 (2024). https://doi.org/10.1038/s42254-023-00685-x.
40. Muradoglu, M. *et al.* The structure and motivational significance of early beliefs about ability. *Developmental Psychology* **62**, 583–596 (2025). https://doi.org/10.1037/dev0001910.
41. Murphy-Hill, E., Jaspan, C., Egelman, C. & Cheng, L. The pushback effects of race, ethnicity, gender, and age in code review. *Communications of the ACM* **65**, 52–57 (2022). https://doi.org/10.1145/3474097.

42. Hicks, C. M., Lee, C. S. & Foster-Marks, K. The new developer: AI skill threat, identity change & developer thriving in the transition to AI-assisted software development (2025). https://doi.org/10.31234/osf.io/2gej5_v2.
43. Walton, G. M. *et al.* Where and with whom does a brief social-belonging intervention promote progress in college? *Science* **380**, 499–505 (2023). https://doi.org/10.1126/science.ade4420.
44. Trinkenreich, B., Gerosa, M. A. & Steinmacher, I. Unraveling the drivers of sense of belonging in software delivery teams: Insights from a large-scale survey. In *Proceedings of the IEEE/ACM 46th International Conference on Software Engineering* 1–12 (Association for Computing Machinery, New York, NY, USA, 2024). https://doi.org/10.1145/3597503.3639119.
45. Trinkenreich, B., Gerosa, M. A., Sarma, A. & Steinmacher, I. Guidelines for cultivating a sense of belonging to reduce developer burnout. *IEEE Software* **42**, 84–91 (2025). https://doi.org/10.1109/MS.2024.3404361.
46. Boman, L., Andersson, J. & de Oliveira Neto, F. G. Breaking barriers: Investigating the sense of belonging among women and non-binary students in software engineering. In *Proceedings of the 46th International Conference on Software Engineering: Software Engineering Education and Training* 93–103 (Association for Computing Machinery, New York, NY, USA, 2024). https://doi.org/10.1145/3639474.3640072.

CHAPTER 5 REFERENCES

1. Butler, J. L., Zimmermann, T. & Bird, C. Objectives and key results in software teams: Challenges, opportunities and impact on development. In *Proceedings of the 46th International Conference on Software Engineering: Software Engineering in Practice* 358–368 (Association for Computing Machinery, New York, NY, USA, 2024). https://doi.org/10.1145/3639477.3639747.
2. Fisher, C. M., Pillemer, J. & Amabile, T. M. Deep help in complex project work: Guiding and path-clearing across difficult terrain. *Academy of Management Journal* **61**, 1524–1553 (2018). https://doi.org/10.5465/amj.2016.0207.
3. Oedzes, J. J., Van der Vegt, G. S., Rink, F. A. & Walter, F. On the origins of informal hierarchy: The interactive role of formal leadership and task complexity. *Journal of Organizational Behavior* **40**, 311–324 (2019). https://doi.org/10.1002/job.2330.
4. Reinero, D. A., Dikker, S. & Van Bavel, J. J. Inter-brain synchrony in teams predicts collective performance. *Social Cognitive and Affective Neuroscience* **16**, 43–57 (2021). https://doi.org/10.1093/scan/nsaa135.
5. Wuchty, S., Jones, B. F. & Uzzi, B. The increasing dominance of teams in production of knowledge. *Science* **316**, 1036–1039 (2007). https://doi.org/10.1126/science.1136099.
6. Kozlowski, S. W. J. & Ilgen, D. R. Enhancing the effectiveness of work groups and teams. *Psychological Science in the Public Interest* **7**, 77–124 (2006). https://doi.org/10.1111/j.1529-1006.2006.00030.x.

7. Van Bavel, J. J., Hackel, L. M. & Xiao, Y. J. The group mind: The pervasive influence of social identity on cognition. In *New Frontiers in Social Neuroscience* (eds Decety, J. & Christen, Y.) 41–56 (Springer International Publishing, Cham, 2014). https://doi.org/10.1007/978-3-319-02904-7_4.
8. Hogg, M. A., Sherman, D. K., Dierselhuis, J., Maitner, A. T. & Moffitt, G. Uncertainty, entitativity, and group identification. *Journal of Experimental Social Psychology* **43**, 135–142 (2007). https://doi.org/10.1016/j.jesp.2005.12.008.
9. Otten, S. The minimal group paradigm and its maximal impact in research on social categorization. *Current Opinion in Psychology* **11**, 85–89 (2016). https://doi.org/10.1016/j.copsyc.2016.06.010.
10. Balliet, D., Wu, J. & De Dreu, C. K. W. Ingroup favoritism in cooperation: A meta-analysis. *Psychological Bulletin* **140**, 1556–1581 (2014). https://doi.org/10.1037/a0037737.
11. Coman, A. & Hirst, W. Social identity and socially shared retrieval-induced forgetting: The effects of group membership. *Journal of Experimental Psychology: General* **144**, 717–722 (2015). https://doi.org/10.1037/xge0000077.
12. Schultner, D. T., Lindström, B. R., Cikara, M. & Amodio, D. M. Transmission of social bias through observational learning. *Science Advances* **10**, eadk2030 (2024). https://doi.org/10.1126/sciadv.adk2030.
13. Dunham, Y. Mere membership. *Trends in Cognitive Sciences* **22**, 780–793 (2018). https://doi.org/10.1016/j.tics.2018.06.004.
14. Yamagishi, T. & Kiyonari, T. The group as the container of generalized reciprocity. *Social Psychology Quarterly* **63**, 116–132 (2000). https://doi.org/10.2307/2695887.
15. Cikara, M., Botvinick, M. M. & Fiske, S. T. Us versus them: Social identity shapes neural responses to intergroup competition and harm. *Psychological Science* **22**, 306–313 (2011). https://doi.org/10.1177/0956797610397667.
16. Cikara, M., Van Bavel, J. J., Ingbretsen, Z. A. & Lau, T. Decoding 'us' and 'them': Neural representations of generalized group concepts. *Journal of Experimental Psychology: General* **146**, 621–631 (2017). https://doi.org/10.1037/xge0000287.
17. Wildschut, T. & Insko, C. A. Power effects on interindividual and intergroup competition. *British Journal of Social Psychology* **64**, e12831 (2025). https://doi.org/10.1111/bjso.12831.
18. Dou, R. & Cian, H. Constructing STEM identity: An expanded structural model for STEM identity research. *Journal of Research in Science Teaching* **59**, 458–490 (2022). https://doi.org/10.1002/tea.21734.
19. Hicks, C. M., Lee, C. S. & Ramsey, M. Developer thriving: Four sociocognitive factors that create resilient productivity on software teams. *IEEE Software* **41**, 68–77 (2024). https://doi.org/10.1109/MS.2024.3382957.
20. Hicks, C. M., Lee, C. S. & Foster-Marks, K. The new developer: AI skill threat, identity change & developer thriving in the transition to AI-assisted software development (2025). https://doi.org/10.31234/osf.io/2gej5_v2.

21. Walton, G. M. & Cohen, G. L. A brief social-belonging intervention improves academic and health outcomes of minority students. *Science (New York, N.Y.)* **331**, 1447–1451 (2011). https://doi.org/10.1126/science.1198364.
22. Walton, G. M. *et al.* Where and with whom does a brief social-belonging intervention promote progress in college? *Science (New York, N.Y.)* **380**, 499–505 (2023). https://doi.org/10.1126/science.ade4420.
23. Gelman, S. A. Psychological essentialism in children. *Trends in Cognitive Sciences* **8**, 404–409 (2004). https://doi.org/10.1016/j.tics.2004.07.001.
24. Rattan, A., Good, C. & Dweck, C. S. 'It's ok—Not everyone can be good at math': Instructors with an entity theory comfort (and demotivate) students. *Journal of Experimental Social Psychology* **48**, 731–737 (2012). https://doi.org/10.1016/j.jesp.2011.12.012.
25. Emerson, K. T. U. & Murphy, M. C. A company I can trust? Organizational lay theories moderate stereotype threat for women. *Personality and Social Psychology Bulletin* **41**, 295–307 (2015). https://doi.org/10.1177/0146167214564969.
26. Lee, H. Y. & Yeager, D. S. Adolescents with an entity theory of personality are more vigilant to social status and use relational aggression to maintain social status. *Social Development* **29**, 273–289 (2020). https://doi.org/10.1111/sode.12393.
27. Trinkenreich, B., Gerosa, M. A., Sarma, A. & Steinmacher, I. Guidelines for cultivating a sense of belonging to reduce developer burnout. *IEEE Software* **42**, 84–91 (2025). https://doi.org/10.1109/MS.2024.3404361.
28. Hall, W. M., Schmader, T. & Croft, E. Engineering exchanges: Daily social identity threat predicts burnout among female engineers. *Social Psychological and Personality Science* **6**, 528–534 (2015). https://doi.org/10.1177/1948550615572637.
29. Cohen, G. L. & Steele, C. M. A barrier of mistrust: How negative stereotypes affect cross-race mentoring. In *Improving Academic Achievement: Impact of Psychological Factors on Education* (ed. J. Aronson) 303–327 (Academic Press, San Diego, 2002). https://doi.org/10.1016/B978-012064455-1/50018-X.
30. Sherif, M. *Intergroup Conflict and Cooperation: The Robbers Cave Experiment*, vol. 10 (University Book Exchange, Norman, OK, 1961).
31. Fisher, C. M. *The Collective Edge* (Penguin Random House, New York, 2025).
32. Brewer, M. B. Superordinate goals versus superordinate identity as bases of intergroup cooperation. In *Social Identity Processes: Trends in Theory and Research* 118–132 (SAGE Publications Ltd, Thousand Oaks, 2000). https://doi.org/10.4135/9781446218617.n8.
33. Bavel, J. J. V. *et al.* Using social and behavioural science to support COVID-19 pandemic response. *Nature Human Behaviour* **4**, 460–471 (2020). https://doi.org/10.1038/s41562-020-0884-z.
34. Dawes, C. T., Fowler, J. H., Johnson, T., McElreath, R. & Smirnov, O. Egalitarian motives in humans. *Nature* **446**, 794–796 (2007). https://doi.org/10.1038/nature05651.

35. Mummendey, A., Otten, S., Berger, U. & Kessler, T. Positive-negative asymmetry in social discrimination: Valence of evaluation and salience of categorization. *Personality and Social Psychology Bulletin* **26**, 1258–1270 (2000). https://doi.org/10.1177/0146167200262007.
36. Wageman, R., Fisher, C. M. & Hackman, J. R. Leading teams when the time is right: Finding the best moments to act. *Organizational Dynamics* **38**, 192–203 (2009). https://doi.org/10.1016/j.orgdyn.2009.04.004.
37. Hogg, M. A. & Reid, S. A. Social identity, self-categorization, and the communication of group norms. *Communication Theory* **16**, 7–30 (2006). https://doi.org/10.1111/j.1468-2885.2006.00003.x.
38. Marques, J. M. & Paez, D. The 'black sheep effect': Social categorization, rejection of ingroup deviates, and perception of group variability. *European Review of Social Psychology* **5**, 37–68 (1994). https://doi.org/10.1080/14792779543000011.
39. Pinto, I. R., Marques, J. M., Levine, J. M. & Abrams, D. Membership status and subjective group dynamics: Who triggers the black sheep effect? *Journal of Personality and Social Psychology* **99**, 107–119 (2010). https://doi.org/10.1037/a0018187.
40. van Kleef, G. A., Wanders, F., Stamkou, E. & Homan, A. C. The social dynamics of breaking the rules: Antecedents and consequences of norm-violating behavior. *Current Opinion in Psychology* **6**, 25–31 (2015). https://doi.org/10.1016/j.copsyc.2015.03.013.
41. Begel, A. & Simon, B. Novice software developers, all over again. In *Proceedings of the Fourth International Workshop on Computing Education Research* 3–14 (Association for Computing Machinery, New York, NY, USA, 2008). https://doi.org/10.1145/1404520.1404522.
42. Steinmacher, I. *et al.* Being a Mentor in open source projects. *Journal of Internet Services and Applications* **12**, 7 (2021). https://doi.org/10.1186/s13174-021-00140-z.
43. Sparkman, G., Geiger, N. & Weber, E. U. Americans experience a false social reality by underestimating popular climate policy support by nearly half. *Nature Communications* **13**, 4779 (2022). https://doi.org/10.1038/s41467-022-32412-y.
44. Miller, D. T. A century of pluralistic ignorance: What we have learned about its origins, forms, and consequences. *Frontiers in Social Psychology* **1** (2023). https://doi.org/10.3389/frsps.2023.1260896.
45. Abrahão, S., Grundy, J., Pezzè, M., Storey, M.-A. & Tamburri, D. A. Software engineering by and for humans in an AI era. *ACM Transactions on Software Engineering and Methodology* **34**, 1–46 (2025). https://doi.org/10.1145/3715111.
46. Hackman, J. R. *Leading Teams: Setting the Stage for Great Performances* (Harvard Business Press, Cambridge, 2002).
47. Packer, D. J. & Chasteen, A. L. Loyal deviance: Testing the normative conflict model of dissent in social groups. *Personality and Social Psychology Bulletin* **36**, 5–18 (2010). https://doi.org/10.1177/0146167209350628.
48. Packer, D. J. & Miners, C. T. H. Tough love: The normative conflict model and a goal system approach to dissent decisions. *Social and Personality Psychology Compass* **8**, 354–373 (2014). https://doi.org/10.1111/spc3.12114.

49. Packer, D. J. Avoiding groupthink: Whereas weakly identified members remain silent, strongly identified members dissent about collective problems. *Psychological Science* **20**, 546–548 (2009). https://doi.org/10.1111/j.1467-9280.2009.02333.x.
50. De Dreu, C. K. W. & West, M. A. Minority dissent and team innovation: The importance of participation in decision making. *Journal of Applied Psychology* **86**, 1191–1201 (2001). https://doi.org/10.1037/0021-9010.86.6.1191.
51. Sparkman, G. & Walton, G. M. Dynamic norms promote sustainable behavior, even if it is counternormative. *Psychological Science* **28**, 1663–1674 (2017). https://doi.org/10.1177/0956797617719950.
52. van Kleef, G. A., Homan, A. C., Finkenauer, C., Blaker, N. M. & Heerdink, M. W. Prosocial norm violations fuel power affordance. *Journal of Experimental Social Psychology* **48**, 937–942 (2012). https://doi.org/10.1016/j.jesp.2012.02.022.
53. Rattan, A., Kroeper, K., Arnett, R., Brown, X. & Murphy, M. Not such a complainer anymore: Confrontation that signals a growth mindset can attenuate backlash. *Journal of Personality and Social Psychology* **124**, 344–361 (2023). https://doi.org/10.1037/pspi0000399.
54. HBO Max Help [@HBOMaxHelp]. We mistakenly sent out an empty test email to a portion of our HBO Max mailing list this evening. We apologize for the inconvenience, and as the jokes pile in, yes, it was the intern. No, really. And we're helping them through it. 💜. *Twitter* (2021).
55. Foreman, A. Twitter comforts the intern behind that mass HBO Max email. *Mashable* (2021).
56. Fu, H., Lin, Y., Shao, Y. & Zhang, Z. Using self-directed humor to regulate emotion: Effects comparison of self-enhancing humor and self-defeating humor. *Journal of Happiness Studies* **25**, 47 (2024). https://doi.org/10.1007/s10902-024-00748-5.
57. Stutts, L. Increasing self-compassion: Review of the literature and recommendations. *Journal of Undergraduate Neuroscience Education* **20**, A115–A119 (2022). https://doi.org/10.59390/WSZK3327.
58. Governor, J. HugOps is the best ops. On empathy and site reliability engineering. *Redmonk Blog* (2017).
59. Fischer, P. *et al.* The bystander-effect: A meta-analytic review on bystander intervention in dangerous and non-dangerous emergencies. *Psychological Bulletin* **137**, 517–537 (2011). https://doi.org/10.1037/a0023304.
60. Drury, J. Collective resilience in mass emergencies and disasters: A social identity model. In *The Social Cure* (Psychology Press, Abingdon, 2012).
61. Helsloot, I. & Ruitenberg, A. Citizen response to disasters: A survey of literature and some practical implications. *Journal of Contingencies and Crisis Management* **12**, 98–111 (2004). https://doi.org/10.1111/j.0966-0879.2004.00440.x.
62. Cocking, C. The role of 'zero-responders' during 7/7: Implications for the emergency services. *International Journal of Emergency Services* **2**, 79–93 (2013). https://doi.org/10.1108/IJES-08-2012-0035.

63. Alexander, D. A. & Klein, S. First responders after disasters: A review of stress reactions, at-risk, vulnerability, and resilience factors. *Prehospital and Disaster Medicine* **24**, 87–94 (2009). https://doi.org/10.1017/S1049023X00006610.
64. Drury, J. *et al.* Facilitating collective psychosocial resilience in the public in emergencies: Twelve recommendations based on the social identity approach. *Frontiers in Public Health* **7** (2019). https://doi.org/10.3389/fpubh.2019.00141.
65. Tarrant, M., Dazeley, S. & Cottom, T. Social categorization and empathy for outgroup members. *British Journal of Social Psychology* **48**, 427–446 (2009). https://doi.org/10.1348/014466608X373589.
66. Jami, P. Y., Walker, D. I. & Mansouri, B. Interaction of empathy and culture: A review. *Current Psychology* **43**, 2965–2980 (2024). https://doi.org/10.1007/s12144-023-04422-6.
67. Cikara, M. Chapter two - causes and consequences of coalitional cognition. In *Advances in Experimental Social Psychology* (ed. Gawronski, B.), vol. **64**, 65–128 (Academic Press, San Diego, 2021). https://doi.org/10.1016/bs.aesp.2021.04.002.
68. Fuochi, G., Veneziani, C. A. & Voci, A. Exploring the social side of self-compassion: Relations with empathy and outgroup attitudes. *European Journal of Social Psychology* **48**, 769–783 (2018). https://doi.org/10.1002/ejsp.2378.
69. Sherman, D. K. Self-affirmation: Understanding the effects. *Social and Personality Psychology Compass* **7**, 834–845 (2013). https://doi.org/10.1111/spc3.12072.
70. Schneider, C. R. & Weber, E. U. Motivating prosocial behavior by leveraging positive self-regard through values affirmation. *Journal of Applied Social Psychology* **52**, 106–114 (2022). https://doi.org/10.1111/jasp.12841.
71. Lee, C. S. & Hicks, C. M. Understanding and effectively mitigating code review anxiety. *Empirical Software Engineering* **29**, 161 (2024). https://doi.org/10.1007/s10664-024-10550-9.
72. Brady, J. M., Hammer, L. B. & Westman, M. Supervisor resilience promotes employee well-being: The role of resource crossover. *Journal of Vocational Behavior* **156**, 104076 (2025). https://doi.org/10.1016/j.jvb.2024.104076.
73. D'Innocenzo, L., Mathieu, J. E. & Kukenberger, M. R. A meta-analysis of different forms of shared leadership–team performance relations. *Journal of Management* **42**, 1964–1991 (2016). https://doi.org/10.1177/0149206314525205.

CHAPTER 6 REFERENCES

1. Weatherholtz, K. *et al.* Use of Khan Academy Official SAT Practice and SAT Achievement: An Observational Study. Technical Report (Khan Academy, 2020).
2. Rowland, C. A. & Hall, R. D. Organizational justice and performance: Is appraisal fair? *EuroMed Journal of Business* **7**, 280–293 (2012). https://doi.org/10.1108/14502191211265334.

3. Ko, A. J. Why we should not measure productivity. In *Rethinking Productivity in Software Engineering* (eds Sadowski, C. & Zimmermann, T.) 21–26 (Apress, Berkeley, CA, 2019). https://doi.org/10.1007/978-1-4842-4221-6_3.
4. Cohen, G. L., Purdie-Vaughns, V. & Garcia, J. An identity threat perspective on intervention. In *Stereotype Threat: Theory, Process, and Application* 280–296 (Oxford University Press, New York, NY, US, 2012). https://doi.org/10.1093/acprof:oso/9780199732449.003.0018.
5. Duhigg, C. What Google learned from its quest to build the perfect team. *The New York Times Magazine* (2016).
6. Edmondson, A. C. & Lei, Z. Psychological safety: The history, renaissance, and future of an interpersonal construct. *Annual Review of Organizational Psychology and Organizational Behavior* **1**, 23–43 (2014). https://doi.org/10.1146/annurev-orgpsych-031413-091305.
7. Dyne, L. V., Ang, S. & Botero, I. C. Conceptualizing employee silence and employee voice as multidimensional constructs. *Journal of Management Studies* **40**, 1359–1392 (2003). https://doi.org/10.1111/1467-6486.00384.
8. Zhang, K., Zhao, B. & Yin, K. The double-edged sword of error sharing in organizations: From a self-disclosure perspective. *Journal of Management Studies* **61**, 3108–3147 (2024). https://doi.org/10.1111/joms.13003.
9. van Mourik, O., Grohnert, T. & Gold, A. Mitigating work conditions that can inhibit learning from errors: Benefits of error management climate perceptions. *Frontiers in Psychology* **14** (2023). https://doi.org/10.3389/fpsyg.2023.1033470.
10. Smith, H. J. & Keil, M. The reluctance to report bad news on troubled software projects: A theoretical model. *Information Systems Journal* **13**, 69–95 (2003). https://doi.org/10.1046/j.1365-2575.2003.00139.x.
11. Park, C. & Keil, M. Organizational silence and whistle-blowing on IT projects: An integrated model. *Decision Sciences* **40**, 901–918 (2009) https://doi.org/10.1111/j.1540-5915.2009.00255.x.
12. Eskreis-Winkler, L., Woolley, K., Kim, M. & Polimeni, E. The failure gap. *Journal of Personality and Social Psychology* (2025). https://doi.org/10.1037/pspa0000468.
13. Edmondson, A. C. & Bransby, D. P. Psychological safety comes of age: Observed themes in an established literature. *Annual Review of Organizational Psychology and Organizational Behavior* **10**, 55–78 (2023). https://doi.org/10.1146/annurev-orgpsych-120920-055217.
14. Fisher, C. M. *The Collective Edge* (Penguin Random House, New York, NY, USA 2025).
15. Elsayed, A. M., Zhao, B., Goda, A. E. & Elsetouhi, A. M. The role of error risk taking and perceived organizational innovation climate in the relationship between perceived psychological safety and innovative work behavior: A moderated mediation model. *Frontiers in Psychology* **14** (2023). https://doi.org/10.3389/fpsyg.2023.1042911.
16. Storey, M.-A., Houck, B. & Zimmermann, T. How developers and managers define and trade productivity for quality. In *Proceedings of the 15th International Conference on Cooperative and Human Aspects of Software Engineering* 26–35 (Association for Computing Machinery, New York, NY, USA, 2022). https://doi.org/10.1145/3528579.3529177.

17. Bouwers, E., Visser, J. & Van Deursen, A. Getting what you measure. *Communications of the ACM* **55**, 54–59 (2012). https://doi.org/10.1145/2209249.2209266.
18. Bouwers, E., van Deursen, A. & Visser, J. Software metrics: Pitfalls and best practices. In *2013 35th International Conference on Software Engineering (ICSE)* 1491–1492 (2013). https://doi.org/10.1109/ICSE.2013.6606755.
19. Wallace, L. G. & Sheetz, S. D. The adoption of software measures: A technology acceptance model (TAM) perspective. *Information & Management* **51**, 249–259 (2014). https://doi.org/10.1016/j.im.2013.12.003.
20. Hicks, C. M., Lee, C. S. & Ramsey, M. Developer thriving: Four sociocognitive factors that create resilient productivity on software teams. *IEEE Software* **41**, 68–77 (2024). https://doi.org/10.1109/MS.2024.3382957.
21. Goodhart, C. A. E. Problems of monetary management: The UK experience. In *Monetary Theory and Practice: The UK Experience* (ed. Goodhart, C. A. E.) 91–121 (Macmillan Education UK, London, 1984). https://doi.org/10.1007/978-1-349-17295-5_4.
22. Rodamar, J. There ought to be a law! Campbell versus Goodhart. *Significance* **15**, 9–9 (2018). https://doi.org/10.1111/j.1740-9713.2018.01205.x.
23. Baron, R. M. & Kenny, D. A. The moderator–mediator variable distinction in social psychological research: Conceptual, strategic, and statistical considerations. *Journal of Personality and Social Psychology* **51**, 1173–1182 (1986). https://doi.org/10.1037/0022-3514.51.6.1173.
24. Hicks, C. Change agents: How experienced engineering managers use triage, advocacy and implementation to drive transformation cycles (2024). https://doi.org/10.31234/osf.io/kpxw5.
25. Lee, C. S., Ramsey, M. & Hicks, C. M. Is our organization actually measuring productivity? How contrasting organizational and individual measures of engineering success is an opportunity to drive engineering transformation (2023). https://doi.org/10.48550/arXiv.2305.11030.
26. Walton, G. M. The new science of wise psychological interventions. *Current Directions in Psychological Science* **23**, 73–82 (2014). https://doi.org/10.1177/0963721413512856.
27. Chen, O., Kalyuga, S. & Sweller, J. The worked example effect, the generation effect, and element interactivity. *Journal of Educational Psychology* **107**, 689–704 (2015). https://doi.org/10.1037/edu0000018.
28. Belland, B. R., Kim, C. & Hannafin, M. J. A framework for designing scaffolds that improve motivation and cognition. *Educational Psychologist* **48**, 243–270 (2013). https://doi.org/10.1080/00461520.2013.838920.
29. Krumrei-Mancuso, E. J. *et al.* Toward an understanding of collective intellectual humility. *Trends in Cognitive Sciences* **29**, 15–27 (2025). https://doi.org/10.1016/j.tics.2024.09.006.
30. Owens, B. P. & Hekman, D. R. How does leader humility influence team performance? Exploring the mechanisms of contagion and collective promotion focus. *Academy of Management Journal* **59**, 1088–1111 (2016). https://doi.org/10.5465/amj.2013.0660.
31. Cornish, F. *et al.* Participatory action research. *Nature Reviews Methods Primers* **3**, 34 (2023). https://doi.org/10.1038/s43586-023-00214-1.

32. Mischel, W. & Ebbesen, E. B. Attention in delay of gratification. *Journal of Personality and Social Psychology* **16**, 329–337 (1970). https://doi.org/10.1037/h0029815.
33. Mischel, W., Shoda, Y. & Rodriguez, M. L. Delay of gratification in children. *Science* **244**, 933–938 (1989). https://doi.org/10.1126/science.2658056.
34. Kidd, C., Palmeri, H. & Aslin, R. N. Rational snacking: Young children's decision-making on the marshmallow task is moderated by beliefs about environmental reliability. *Cognition* **126**, 109–114 (2013). https://doi.org/10.1016/j.cognition.2012.08.004.
35. Sperber, J. F., Vandell, D. L., Duncan, G. J. & Watts, T. W. Delay of gratification and adult outcomes: The Marshmallow test does not reliably predict adult functioning. *Child Development* **95**, 2015–2029 (2024). https://doi.org/10.1111/cdev.14129.
36. Frank, M. C., Braginsky, M., Cachia, J., Coles, N. A. & Hardwicke, T. E. *Experimentology: An Open Science Approach to Experimental Psychology Methods* (MIT Press, Cambridge, 2025). https://doi.org/10.7551/mitpress/14810.001.0001.
37. Vazire, S., Schiavone, S. R. & Bottesini, J. G. Credibility beyond replicability: Improving the four validities in psychological science. *Current Directions in Psychological Science* **31**, 162–168 (2022). https://doi.org/10.1177/09637214211067779.
38. Landy, J. F. *et al.* Crowdsourcing hypothesis tests: Making transparent how design choices shape research results. *Psychological Bulletin* **146**, 451–479 (2020). https://doi.org/10.1037/bul0000220.
39. Petre, M. & Shaw, M. Contrasting to spark creativity in software development: Tactics used by high-performing teams. *IEEE Software* **42**, 67–74 (2025). https://doi.org/10.1109/MS.2025.3538670.
40. Berthet, V. The impact of cognitive biases on professionals' decision-making: A review of four occupational areas. *Frontiers in Psychology* **12** (2022). https://doi.org/10.3389/fpsyg.2021.802439.
41. Bryan, C. J., Tipton, E. & Yeager, D. S. Behavioural science is unlikely to change the world without a heterogeneity revolution. *Nature Human Behaviour* **5**, 980–989 (2021). https://doi.org/10.1038/s41562-021-01143-3.
42. IJzerman, H. *et al.* Use caution when applying behavioural science to policy. *Nature Human Behaviour* **4**, 1092–1094 (2020). https://doi.org/10.1038/s41562-020-00990-w.
43. Corneille, O. & Gawronski, B. Self-reports are better measurement instruments than implicit measures. *Nature Reviews Psychology* **3**, 835–846 (2024). https://doi.org/10.1038/s44159-024-00376-z.
44. Petre, M. How expert engineering teams use disciplines of innovation. *Design Studies* **25**, 477–493 (2004). https://doi.org/10.1016/j.destud.2004.05.003.
45. Walton, G. M. *et al.* Where and with whom does a brief social-belonging intervention promote progress in college? *Science* **380**, 499–505 (2023). https://doi.org/10.1126/science.ade4420.
46. Meyer, A. N., Barr, E. T., Bird, C. & Zimmermann, T. Today was a good day: The daily life of software developers. *IEEE Transactions on Software Engineering* **47**, 863–880 (2021). https://doi.org/10.1109/TSE.2019.2904957.

47. Moore, J. W. What is the sense of agency and why does it matter? *Frontiers in Psychology* **7** (2016). https://doi.org/10.3389/fpsyg.2016.01272.
48. Obi, I. *et al.* Identifying factors contributing to 'bad days' for software developers: A mixed-methods study. In *2025 IEEE/ACM 47th International Conference on Software Engineering: Software Engineering in Practice (ICSE-SEIP)* 1–11 (2025). https://doi.org/10.1109/ICSE-SEIP66354.2025.00006.

CHAPTER 7 REFERENCES

1. Brown, D. J., Arnold, R., Fletcher, D. & Standage, M. Human thriving. *European Psychologist* **22**, 167–179 (2017). https://doi.org/10.1027/1016-9040/a000294.
2. Feeney, B. C. & Collins, N. L. A new look at social support: A theoretical perspective on thriving through relationships. *Personality and Social Psychology Review* **19**, 113–147 (2015). https://doi.org/10.1177/1088868314544222.
3. Lerner, R. M., von Eye, A., Lerner, J. V., Lewin-Bizan, S. & Bowers, E. P. Special issue introduction: The meaning and measurement of thriving: A view of the issues. *Journal of Youth and Adolescence* **39**, 707–719 (2010). https://doi.org/10.1007/s10964-010-9531-8.
4. Epel, E. S., McEwen, B. S. & Ickovics, J. R. Embodying psychological thriving: Physical thriving in response to stress. *Journal of Social Issues* **54**, 301–322 (1998). https://doi.org/10.1111/j.1540-4560.1998.tb01220.x.
5. Lewin, K. *Group Decision and Social Change* 284 (American Psychological Association, Washington, DC, US, 1999). https://doi.org/10.1037/10319-010.
6. Lewin, G. W. Frontiers in group dynamics (1947). In *Resolving Social Conflicts and Field Theory in Social Science* 301–336 (American Psychological Association, Washington, DC, US, 1997). https://doi.org/10.1037/10269-023.
7. Cohen, G. L., Purdie-Vaughns, V. & Garcia, J. An identity threat perspective on intervention. In *Stereotype threat: Theory, process, and application* 280–296 (Oxford University Press, New York, NY, US, 2012). https://doi.org/10.1093/acprof:oso/9780199732449.003.0018.
8. Eberhardt, J. L., Goff, P. A., Purdie, V. J. & Davies, P. G. Seeing black: Race, crime, and visual processing. *Journal of Personality and Social Psychology* **87**, 876–893 (2004). https://doi.org/10.1037/0022-3514.87.6.876.
9. Markus, H. R. & Kitayama, S. Cultures and selves: A cycle of mutual constitution. *Perspectives on Psychological Science* **5**, 420–430 (2010). https://doi.org/10.1177/1745691610375557.
10. Fiske, A. P., Kitayama, S., Markus, H. R. & Nisbett, R. E. The cultural matrix of social psychology. In *The Handbook of Social Psychology*, vols. 1–2, 4th ed, 915–981 (McGraw-Hill, New York, NY, US, 1998).
11. Hamedani, M. Y. G. & Markus, H. R. Understanding culture clashes and catalyzing change: A culture cycle approach. *Frontiers in Psychology* **10** (2019). https://doi.org/10.3389/fpsyg.2019.00700.
12. Markus, H. R. & Kitayama, S. Cultures and selves. *Perspectives on Psychological Science* (2010). https://doi.org/10.1177/1745691610375557.

13. Vial, A. C., Muradoglu, M., Newman, G. E. & Cimpian, A. An emphasis on brilliance fosters masculinity-contest cultures. *Psychological Science* **33**, 595–612 (2022). https://doi.org/10.1177/09567976211044133.
14. Rattan, A., Savani, K., Naidu, N. V. R. & Dweck, C. S. Can everyone become highly intelligent? Cultural differences in and societal consequences of beliefs about the universal potential for intelligence. *Journal of Personality and Social Psychology* **103**, 787–803 (2012). https://doi.org/10.1037/a0029263.
15. Chater, N. & Loewenstein, G. The i-frame and the s-frame: How focusing on individual-level solutions has led behavioral public policy astray. *Behavioral and Brain Sciences* **46**, e147 (2023). https://doi.org/10.1017/S0140525X22002023.
16. Roozenbeek, J., Young, D. J. & Madsen, J. K. The wilful rejection of psychological and behavioural interventions. *Current Opinion in Psychology* **66**, 102138 (2025). https://doi.org/10.1016/j.copsyc.2025.102138.
17. Pagoto, S. L. & Lemon, S. C. Efficacy vs effectiveness. *JAMA Internal Medicine* **173**, 1262–1263 (2013). https://doi.org/10.1001/jamainternmed.2013.6521.
18. List, J. A. Optimally generate policy-based evidence before scaling. *Nature* **626**, 491–499 (2024). https://doi.org/10.1038/s41586-023-06972-y.
19. List, J. A. Field experiments: Here today gone tomorrow? *The American Economist* **69**, 214–234 (2024). https://doi.org/10.1177/05694345241261340.
20. Seo, E. *et al.* Trait attributions and threat appraisals explain why an entity theory of personality predicts greater internalizing symptoms during adolescence. *Development and Psychopathology* **34**, 1104–1114 (2022). https://doi.org/10.1017/S0954579420001832.
21. Walton, G. M. *et al.* Where and with whom does a brief social-belonging intervention promote progress in college? *Science* **380**, 499–505 (2023). https://doi.org/10.1126/science.ade4420.
22. Yeager, D. S. *et al.* A national experiment reveals where a growth mindset improves achievement. *Nature* **573**, 364–369 (2019). https://doi.org/10.1038/s41586-019-1466-y.
23. Yeager, D. *10 to 25: The Science of Motivating Young People: A Groundbreaking Approach to Leading the Next Generation—And Making Your Own Life Easier* (Simon and Schuster, New York, 2024).
24. Walton, Gregory. *Ordinary Magic* (Harmony, New York, NY, US, 2025).
25. Yeager, D. S. *et al.* A synergistic mindsets intervention protects adolescents from stress. *Nature* **607**, 512–520 (2022). https://doi.org/10.1038/s41586-022-04907-7.
26. Broda, M. *et al.* Reducing inequality in academic success for incoming college students: A randomized trial of growth mindset and belonging interventions. *Journal of Research on Educational Effectiveness* **11**, 317–338 (2018). https://doi.org/10.1080/19345747.2018.1429037.
27. Walton, G. M. & Yeager, D. S. Seed and soil: Psychological affordances in contexts help to explain where wise interventions succeed or fail. *Current Directions in Psychological Science* **29**, 219–226 (2020). https://doi.org/10.1177/0963721420904453.

28. Bauer, C. A., Poddar, A., Brummelman, E. & Cimpian, A. The brilliance–belonging model: How cultural beliefs about intellectual ability undermine educational equity. *Educational Psychology Review* **37**, 64 (2025). https://doi.org/10.1007/s10648-025-10034-2.
29. Tankard, M. E. & Paluck, E. L. Norm perception as a vehicle for social change. *Social Issues and Policy Review* **10**, 181–211 (2016). https://doi.org/10.1111/sipr.12022.
30. Cohen, G. L. & Sherman, D. K. The psychology of change: Self-affirmation and social psychological intervention. *Annual Review of Psychology* **65**, 333–371 (2014). https://doi.org/10.1146/annurev-psych-010213-115137.
31. Shafir, E. *The Behavioral Foundations of Public Policy* (Princeton University Press, Princeton, 2013). https://doi.org/10.1515/9781400845347.
32. Geoffrey, L. Cohen. *Belonging* (W. W. Norton & Company, New York, 2022).
33. Carroll, J. M. *et al.* Mindset context: Schools, classrooms, and the unequal translation of expectations into math achievement. *Monographs of the Society for Research in Child Development* **88**, 7–109 (2023). https://doi.org/10.1111/mono.12471.
34. Hicks, C. Psychological affordances can provide a missing explanatory layer for why interventions to improve developer experience take hold or fail (2024). https://doi.org/10.31234/osf.io/qz43x.
35. Miller, C. *et al.* "Maybe we need some more examples:" Individual and team drivers of developer GenAI tool use (2025). https://doi.org/10.48550/arXiv.2507.21280.
36. Lee, Carol & Dreizin, Yanya. Testing the effect of peer-driven social pressure on leave no trace behaviors in rock climbers. *International Journal of Wilderness* **28** (2022).
37. Hayes-Skelton, S. A. & Lee, C. S. Decentering in mindfulness and cognitive restructuring for social anxiety: An experimental study of a potential common mechanism. *Behavior Modification* **44**, 817–840 (2020). https://doi.org/10.1177/0145445519850744.
38. Lee, C. S. & Hicks, C. M. Understanding and effectively mitigating code review anxiety. *Empirical Software Engineering* **29**, 161 (2024). https://doi.org/10.1007/s10664-024-10550-9.
39. Lee, Carol & Foster-Marks, Kristen. *Code Review Anxiety Workbook.* https://developer-success-lab.gitbook.io/code-review-anxiety-workbook-1 (2024).
40. Lee, H. R., Santana, L. M., McPartlan, P. & Eccles, J. S. Components of engagement in saying-is-believing exercises. *Current Psychology* **42**, 14903–14918 (2023). https://doi.org/10.1007/s12144-022-02782-z.
41. Ferrari, M. *et al.* Self-compassion interventions and psychosocial outcomes: A meta-analysis of RCTs. *Mindfulness* **10**, 1455–1473 (2019). https://doi.org/10.1007/s12671-019-01134-6.
42. Neff, K. D. Self-compassion: Theory, method, research, and intervention. *Annual Review of Psychology* **74**, 193–218 (2023). https://doi.org/10.1146/annurev-psych-032420-031047.

43. Cohen, G. L. *Belonging: The Science of Creating Connection and Bridging Divides* (W. W. Norton & Company, New York, 2022).
44. Lee, C. S., Hicks, C. M. & Foster-Marks, K. L. 'My code is shit': Negative automatic thoughts and outcomes of a behavioral experiment for code review anxiety (2024). https://doi.org/10.31234/osf.io/hz3et.
45. Lombard, E. J. & Cheryan, S. Does my work matter? Reduced sense of mattering as a source of gender disparities. *Social and Personality Psychology Compass* **18**, e12907 (2024). https://doi.org/10.1111/spc3.12907.
46. Maier, S. F. & Seligman, M. E. Learned helplessness: Theory and evidence. *Journal of Experimental Psychology: General* **105**, 3–46 (1976). https://doi.org/10.1037/0096-3445.105.1.3.
47. Bandura, A. Toward a psychology of human agency. *Perspectives on Psychological Science* **1**, 164–180 (2006). https://doi.org/10.1111/j.1745-6916.2006.00011.x.
48. Sherman, D. K. & Cohen, G. L. The psychology of self-defense: Self-affirmation theory. In *Advances in Experimental Social Psychology*, vol. **38**, 183–242 (Academic Press, San Diego, 2006). https://doi.org/10.1016/S0065-2601(06)38004-5.
49. Baumsteiger, R. What the world needs now: An intervention for promoting prosocial behavior. *Basic and Applied Social Psychology* **41**, 215–229 (2019). https://doi.org/10.1080/01973533.2019.1639507.
50. Laguna, M., Mazur, Z., Kędra, M. & Ostrowski, K. Interventions stimulating prosocial helping behavior: A systematic review. *Journal of Applied Social Psychology* **50**, 676–696 (2020). https://doi.org/10.1111/jasp.12704.
51. van Goethem, A., van Hoof, A., Orobio de Castro, B., Van Aken, M. & Hart, D. The role of reflection in the effects of community service on adolescent development: A meta-analysis. *Child Development* **85**, 2114–2130 (2014). https://doi.org/10.1111/cdev.12274.
52. Dasgupta, N. Ingroup experts and peers as social vaccines who inoculate the self-concept: The stereotype inoculation model. *Psychological Inquiry* **22**, 231–246 (2011). https://doi.org/10.1080/1047840X.2011.607313.
53. Critcher, C. R. & Dunning, D. Self-affirmations provide a broader perspective on self-threat. *Personality and Social Psychology Bulletin* **41**, 3–18 (2015). https://doi.org/10.1177/0146167214554956.
54. Badea, C. & Sherman, D. K. Self-affirmation and prejudice reduction: When and why? *Current Directions in Psychological Science* **28**, 40–46 (2019). https://doi.org/10.1177/0963721418807705.
55. Schumann, K. & Walton, G. M. Rehumanizing the self after victimization: The roles of forgiveness versus revenge. *Journal of Personality and Social Psychology* **122**, 469–492 (2022). https://doi.org/10.1037/pspi0000367.
56. Howard, M. C. Applying the approach/avoidance framework to understand the relationships between social courage, workplace outcomes, and well-being outcomes. *The Journal of Positive Psychology* **14**, 734–748 (2019). https://doi.org/10.1080/17439760.2018.1545043.

57. Howard, M. C. & Holmes, P. E. Social courage fosters both voice and silence in the workplace: A study on multidimensional voice and silence with boundary conditions. *Journal of Organizational Effectiveness: People and Performance* 7, 53–73 (2020). https://doi.org/10.1108/JOEPP-04-2019-0034.
58. Kaltiainen, J., Virtanen, A. & Hakanen, J. J. Social courage promotes organizational identification via crafting social resources at work: A repeated-measures study. *Human Relations* **77**, 53–80 (2024). https://doi.org/10.1177/00187267221125374.
59. Fuligni, A. J. The need to contribute during adolescence. *Perspectives on Psychological Science* **14**, 331–343 (2019). https://doi.org/10.1177/1745691618805437.
60. Fuligni, A. J., Trimble, A. & Smola, X. A. The significance of feeling needed and useful to family and friends for psychological well-being during adolescence. *Journal of Adolescence* **97**, 292–300 (2025). https://doi.org/10.1002/jad.12403.
61. Ryff, C. D. & Singer, B. Interpersonal flourishing: A positive health agenda for the new millennium. *Personality and Social Psychology Review* **4**, 30–44 (2000). https://doi.org/10.1207/S15327957PSPR0401_4.
62. Tennie, C., Call, J. & Tomasello, M. Ratcheting up the ratchet: On the evolution of cumulative culture. *Philosophical Transactions of the Royal Society B: Biological Sciences* (2009). https://doi.org/10.1098/rstb.2009.0052.
63. Hicks, C. M. & Hevesi, A. A cumulative culture theory for developer problem-solving (2024). https://doi.org/10.31234/osf.io/tfjyw.

Index

F

G

H

I

K

L

M

N

O

P

R

S

For Product Safety Concerns and Information please contact our EU representative GPSR@taylorandfrancis.com
Taylor & Francis Verlag GmbH, Kaufingerstraße 24, 80331 München, Germany

www.ingramcontent.com/pod-product-compliance
Lightning Source LLC
LaVergne TN
LVHW010602110826
845149LV00003B/739

* 9 7 8 1 0 3 2 9 6 3 3 8 9 *